Knit One, Make One
in Classic Knitted Cotton

Lace edged handkerchiefs (section 14, p.77).

Knit One, Make One

in Classic Knitted Cotton

Furze Hewitt

Kangaroo Press

To Jane, Gillian, Douglas and their families.

Reprinted 1990 and 1991
First published in 1990 by Kangaroo Press Pty Ltd
3 Whitehall Road (P.O. Box 75) Kenthurst NSW 2156
Typeset by G.T. Setters Pty Limited
Printed in Singapore by Fong & Sons Printers Pte Ltd

ISBN 0 86417 334 2

Contents

Handtowels: Oblique, Domino, Hendra Vale and Clover designs (section 11, p.63).

Foreword

If you enjoy knitting lace, you can now discover the satisfaction of creating accessories for your home. This book illustrates the full potential of knitted textiles and the delicate beauty of white cotton knitting. The collection includes easy to follow patterns for soft furnishings and gift ideas of all kinds, to suit traditional, and modern decors. Knitting novices will find items that they can tackle with ease, whilst knitting experts will be able to exercise their abilities with the larger, more complex pieces.

How you use the designs depends on you. You may wish to furnish your home in a personal way, or simply desire to create an heirloom.

I hope you will find this book a continuous source of inspiration, and pleasure.

Happy knitting!

Acknowledgments

My grateful thanks to my family.

A special thank you to Robert Roach, photographer, for his skill and dedication.

To Gillian Colquhoun for once again typing the patterns, ably assisted by Anneta Yap.

To Josephine Hoggan for her delightful drawings.

To Edna Lomas, and Kathy Grin for their help with the knitting.

To John Cummin of Queanbeyan Books and Prints, for his constant search for old knitting patterns.

To Jane Cottee for her help with the proof reading.

To Carol Davey for supplying many of the interesting items used in the illustrations.

To Roslyn Panetta for her technical drawings.

My appreciation to the following for their help in various ways: James and Patsy Ranger, Elizabeth Nugent, James Botham, Joan Clayton, Maria Basilisco, Diane Donahue, Ann Dalton, Maria Dalton, Patricia Wain, Carol Coates, Jos Csibi, Sue Allan, Ellen Watt, Ros Vidgen, Gertrude Kuehl, Anna Sliwinski, Florence Wilkie, Don McCleod, Robert Beard, Aileen Sellen, Rina Tagliapietra, Lucy Duff, Michael Roath, Glyn Hopson, June Witt, Jo Waring, and to everyone who made this book possible.

Basket lid: Plait design (section 7. p.47).

Introduction

Lace knitting is a creative craft. It is easy to learn, and needs the minimum of equipment: two basic stitches—knit and purl, a set of needles, and a ball of cotton. The patterns in this book have been collected from many sources, some of which dated back to the mid 19th century, and have been used to create interesting items for the home. Experiment with the patterns; interchange types of thread, and needles. A pattern knitted with 100 cotton on extremely fine needles, takes on a different appearance if worked with 4 ply cotton, and a thicker needle. By changing the application of the designs, you will add your personal touch, and provide your family with an heirloom of your creation.

Lace knitting can be as delicate, and intricate, as any form of traditional lace. The laciness is created by deliberately made holes, formed by increasing and decreasing in the pattern. The lace can be used to enhance any decor. It is easy to care for and all patterns in this book are within the scope of the average knitter.

Cotton can be worked during the summer months, when other yarns have been set aside. White cotton knitting is enjoying a return to popularity, as a gentle, satisfying craft. Apart from the delight in producing exquisite lace, you will relax to the gentle rhythm of classic cotton knitting.

In this book you will find familiar laces used in unusual ways. Knitting from the traditional patterns you can experiment with your own ideas for displaying your work.

The filigree plate (section 19, p.95) looks charming hanging on a wall, or sitting on a plate stand.

The miniature aromatic cushions in section one (photo p.17) make excellent pin (or brooch) cushions. The larger cushion (pattern 'Rosedale', from section 1, illustrated on p.74) would be ideal as a wedding ring holder. The little cushions, without inserts, make delightful gift containers.

Pomander balls from section 1 make ideal Christmas tree decorations, or pile them in a colourful bowl—as gifts for your friends. The tiny balls knitted on fine needles can also be used as pin cushions.

Consider the applications of the designs in this book. You will find many are useful in conserving raw materials, especially paper.

Bread cloths (section 9, p.57) and basket lids (section 7, p.47) utilise materials that would have been discarded. The use of these utility cloths in Victorian homes was a necessity: kitchen were without plastic film, or foil, to protect the food from dust and insects. Similar cloths were used in the dairy and larder.

Basket lids would have had several roles. They were used in the kitchen, taken to the harvest fields, and covered the large baskets of white linen waiting for the laundress.

You will see another use on p.35: in this photo the lid covers a picnic basket!

The face washer designs (section 12, p.68) also help in conserving paper. They are durable, easy to care for, pleasant to use, and need no ironing. The washers can be used as barbecue or picnic napkins: using clean terracotta pots, wrap each napkin around a set of cutlery, and place in pot. Those illustrated on p.91 were topped with a colourful wooden flower. You could use this idea for a children's party, too.

There are endless ideas waiting for you to create. Consider these suggestions: basket lids as tray cloths; curtains as table covers; doilies framed as window hangings or works of art; table cloths as shawls to wear or to toss on a couch; stiffened bowls (section 1) become small doilies, or table mats, as shown on p.18.

All the designs in this book are worthy of your expertise as a knitter. If you are new to the craft, you will discover that the lace that looks so intricate is really very simple. All lace knitting is based on the familiar plain (knit) and purl actions, the origins of which are lost in antiquity.

It is up to you to discover how you will use this book; I hope you will enjoy the charm of white cotton knitting, and do as the title suggests!

The Victorian Era

Knitting is a craft suitable to all ranks, its instructions can be carried out by all capacities. Therefore, let us hope, that while the work may grace the Boudoir of the Peeress, it shall also penetrate into the Cottage of the Peasant, that while it can become a source of useful recreation to the rich, it may also prove a reliable aid to the industrious effort of the poor.

From a 19th century needlework book

Many exquisite examples of knitted lace were produced in the Victorian era.

This craft was enjoyed all over Europe, but in Britain it was of particular importance. Tariffs were imposed on the importation of lace into Britain, so the knitting of white cotton lace became a worthy substitute.

The Victorian era saw rapid economic expansion. Knitting cotton became freely available, and early magazines advertised quality cotton yarns at a penny a ball.

Women's magazines became popular in the mid-19th century and provided, for the first time, knitting patterns. Each issue contained new stitches and designs, and intricate combinations of purl and plain emerged.

The craze for white knitting swept the country. Yards of fine lace were produced to trim household and personal linen. At its finest, the lace was made on extremely fine needles with thread 100 or 120. This fine work was referred to as 'gossamer' and 'fairy knitting'.

Other articles, like bedspreads, were made from a heavier yarn, worked on a size 16 needle. These magnificent bedspreads needed approximately eight pounds of cotton, plus months of work.

Unfortunately, by the mid-20th century the vogue for white knitting had ebbed. Consequently, much of the early work has disappeared.

With the emerging interest in lace knitting many of the antique pieces will be treated with respect, and preserved for future generations to care for.

Abbreviations and Terms

Abbreviations are used in knitting instructions to save space, and to make the pattern easier to follow. It is important to read, and understand, the abbreviations before beginning to knit a pattern.

In this book most of the patterns use standard British abbreviations.

Some Helpful Abbreviations

k	knit
p	purl
st	stitch
sts	stitches
b	back
f	front
sl	slip
wyib	with yarn in back
wyif	with yarn in front
tog	together
*m1	make one stitch by winding yarn round needle
turn	work is turned before end of row
dpn	double pointed needle
motif	design unit
st st	stocking stitch—knit right side, purl wrong side
garter st	knit all rows
mb	make bobble
beg	beginning
psso	pass slipped stitch over
p2sso	pass 2 slipped stitches over
p-wise	purlwise
k-wise	knitwise
tbl	through back of loop
ybk	yarn back
yfwd	yarn forward
yon	yarn over needle
yrn	yarn around needle
R.H.	right hand
L.H.	left hand
tw st	twist stitch
inc	increase
dc	double crochet
ch	chain

*In old knitting publications the increase in laceknitting was referred to in several different ways ie. o — over. m1 — make one, and cast up.

In ordinary knitting the made sts consist of the following:

y fwd	between two knit stitches.
yon	between a purl and knit action.
yrn	between two purl actions

In this book the above actions are referred to as m1 — make one, as they were commonly written in old lace patterns.

Comparative Terms

British	American
cast off	bind off
tension	gauge
alternate rows	every other row
miss	skip
work straight	work even
stocking stitch	stockinette stitch
shape cap	shape top

Purchasing Your Cotton

Quantity will depend on the size of the article being knitted. It is wise to purchase your cotton from the same dye lot, as you can get an optical variation in white cotton. Buy an extra ball; any left over can be used to trim, or to make smaller articles. Use a well known brand of thread. It is false economy to use inferior quality yarn. Choose a yarn with a fine firm finish. Cheaper threads often have a slight furry feel. This causes the holes in the lace to become partly obscured, and you lose the crisp texture of your work.

Purchasing and caring For Your Needles

Sets of fine needles are available for lace knitting. These are sold in sets of five. The very small sets of glove needles can sometimes be found, amongst the jars of plastic needles, in opportunity shops. A set of these tiny needles make a perfect gift for a lace knitter.

The old needles need care. This is essential when using them to knit white cotton. Do not store old steel needles in plastic film as the film can cause moisture to build up which will rust the metal. When storing old needles, use a coating of beeswax and wrap them in acid free tissue or soft cloth. Should your needles become sticky whilst knitting, rub the needle through your hair. The sets of needles now on the market can be returned to their packet for safe keeping, and size identification. Take care of the points.

You need undamaged, straight needles with smooth points, to produce perfect work.

If you bend your needles while knitting, relax. You are probably holding your work too tightly! The size of your needle will depend on the material you have chosen for your work. Most of the articles in this book were knitted on 2 mm, or size 14, needles.

Notes On Knitting

Vital information can easily be missed, if introductory details are ignored. Read the instructions before commencing knitting.

The use of notebook and pencil to record the row, or round, being worked, is essential in lace knitting, do not use ball point pens as the marks are difficult to remove. If a stitch is dropped, try to catch the stitch with a safety pin, then undo the knitting, row by row, until the dropped stitch has been reached. It is easier to re-knit the lace than to attempt to retrieve a tiny stitch. Do not forget to record the number of rows unpicked, so that you can resume your knitting in the correct place.

Avoid joins in the middle of your lace. Try to join on the straight edge of your work. Use the piece of thread you have left after joining to stitch the seam.

Turning your work. Slip the first stitch on the return row. This prevents a hole, and makes a neater turn.

Right side of work is the first row of pattern, unless otherwise stated.

Asterisks. Take care to repeat *—* the number of times stated.

Parenthesis. The instructions inside the brackets must be worked the number of times stated immediately after the brackets.

Allow ample fullness when attaching lace, especially around corners.

Knitters accustomed to working with wool, will often find a change in tension working with cotton and finer needles. Work a sample, and if necessary adjust your needle size.

Using *bleach* on mercerised cotton thread reduces the sheen, and could spoil the appearance of your knitting.

Use only cotton thread when sewing your cotton knitting. Mend your cotton lace before it gets beyond repair. Carefully pick up the exposed loops and secure with matching yarn. Work a darn, in chain stitch, over the hole. Try to use the same tension as the knitted fabric.

Caring For Your Work

Always wrap your white cotton knitting in a soft cloth before putting it away. Spread the cloth over your lap whilst knitting. The constant pulling of a thread over a rough fabric garment can damage the yarn. Hands play an important role in producing all crafts, so they need special care. Keep them smooth with a good hand cream, in hot sticky weather a little talcum powder helps to keep them dry.

Wash Your Knitting Frequently. Dirt and grit can cause deterioration of the fibres. Articles can be safely washed in a machine. Remember that cotton absorbs moisture so large articles will need support when drying so that they do not sag. Remove as much moisture as possible before hanging over a sheet stretched across two lines. Small articles can be dried flat.

Avoid exposing white washing to strong sunlight, which can yellow the threads.

Cotton knitting responds to a light pressing. Use a towel underneath the knitting to prevent the design being flattened. Ribbed knitting should not be pressed. Some articles benefit from a light spray of starch after blocking. Allow to dry naturally. *Baskets, bowls,* and *plates* need to be heavily starched to retain their shape. Immerse the article in a *raw* starch mixture of 30 gm starch to approx. 200 ml of warm water. Squeeze out excess moisture from the knitting. Place over bowl or container of the shape desired. Gently mould into position, and leave to dry naturally. Do not remove until completely dry.

Fabric stiffening solutions are available from most craft shops.

Casting on

1   2   3   4

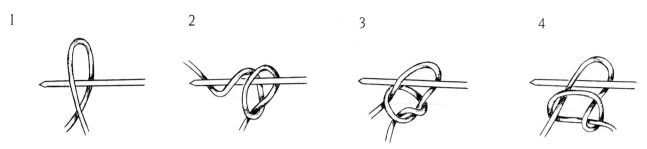

Thumb method

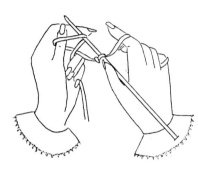 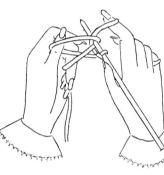 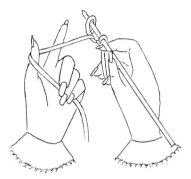

How to knit   How to purl

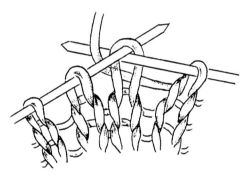

Invisible cast on method

Invisible cast on method
1. Using contrasting thread, cast on the number of stitches required, work two rows in stocking stitch.
2. With main thread, continue work until length required.
3. When work is completed, remove contrasting thread. Either graft or sew together open stitches from both ends of work.

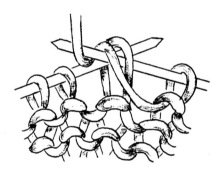

Increasing in lace knitting

There are three methods of increasing the number of stitches on a row, or in a round. One way is to knit twice into a stitch (Fig. 1). This increase can be worked k-wise or p-wise. Read your pattern carefully and work as directed.

A second method is to pick up a loop between two sts, and knit into that loop (Fig. 2). This prevents a hole in the knitting.

The third method, make one (or m1), produces the holes in lace knitting. The way it is worked depends on whether the extra stitch is to be made between two knit stitches, a knit and a purl, or two purl stitches. Between knit sts the yarn is brought forward, and over the needle as you knit the next stitch, thus forming a new stitch.

Fig. 3
(a) Make one between two knit stitches.
(b) Make one between two purl stitches.
(c) Make one between a knit and a purl stitch.
Once again, read your pattern carefully.

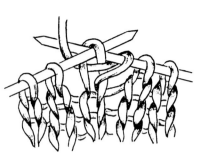

Fig. 1

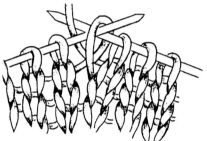

Fig.2

Fig.3

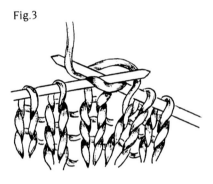

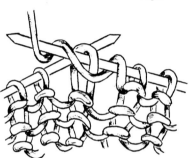

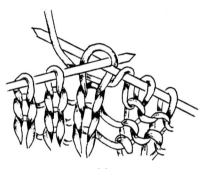

(a)　　　　　　　　　　(b)　　　　　　　　　　(c)

14

Decreasing in lace knitting

Again there are several methods. One method is to knit or purl two stitches together (Fig. 4a and b). A second method is to pass the next but one stitch previously worked over the latter (Fig. 4c and d).

Fig. 4

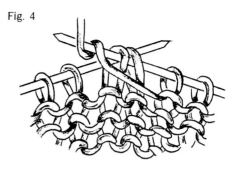

(a)

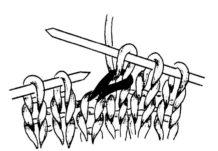

(b)

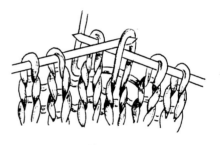

(c)

Knitted picot cast off

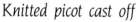

Knit 1st st. *Sl 1 st from R.H. needle on to L.H. needle. Insert needle into this st, cast on 2 sts, then cast off 5 sts. Repeat from * until all sts have been cast off. These methods of casting off can be seen in the miniature motifs colour plate at the bottom of page 18.

Knitting off your stitches if you can't crochet

K1, *k2 tog, m1, k2 tog, turn. P1, *(k1, p1) twice, k1 * in next st.
P1, sl 1 purlwise, turn. Cast off 7 sts (1 st left on R.H. needle)*.
Repeat from *—* to last 5 sts. K3 tog, m1, k2 tog, turn, p1 (k1, p1) twice, k1, in next st, p1, sl 1. purlwise, turn. Cast off remaining sts.
For a larger loop on your edging, make 9 sts instead of 5 sts described above.

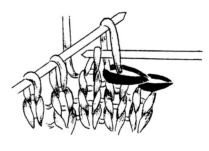

(d)

A knitter's corner featuring curtains (section 16, p.83), cushions (section 2, p.26) and tablecloth (section 22, p.100).

Aromatic Delights (section 1, p.19).

Right: Table centre: Pansy and knitted bowls/doilies (section 8, p.56).
Leaf and mallow (section 1, pp.21–2).
Below left: Close up of Leaf design (section 1, p.21).
Bottom: Cushions (section 2, p.26).

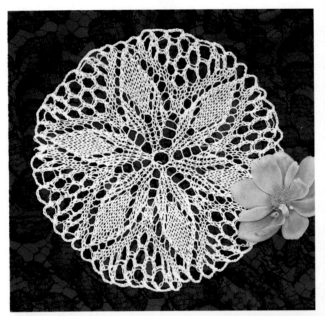

1. Aromatic Delights

A collection of Aromatic Delights:

Lavender Cornucopia was designed to utilise the whole bunch of lavender, and to retain the fragrance of the stalks as well as the flowers.

A Delightful Lavender Showers Umbrella. This holds tiny sprigs of lavender spikes. Hang it in your wardrobe or from a dainty coat hanger. Trim with tassels or ribbons.

The Knitted Baskets are from a 19th century work book, and are useful to hold pot pourri or a posy of dried flowers.

Pomanders With a Difference. Knitted on fine needles, they appear to be studded with tiny chalk-white beads. Decorate with tiny flowers and matching ribbons.

Two Knitted Bowls to hold dried petals or flower heads; or use without starching as small doilies.

The Aromatic Cushions are miniatures with a variety of uses. Complete your knitted articles with a *pot pourri* of your own flowers. Here is a recipe you might enjoy. . .

Collect your favourite flowers and leaves, on a dry day. Spread in a dry, well-ventilated place, stir occasionally.

Leave for about a week, until the material is crisp to touch.

You will need approx. half a cup of powdered orris root to about ten handfuls of dried flowers. Mix well, add lavender or rose oil sparingly.

The addition of cinnamon bark, cloves and bay leaves gives a warm spicy aroma OR the combination of lemon verbena, melissa, lime or orange blossoms gives a light fresh fragrance.

Materials

Lavender Cornucopia 1 ball 20 cotton (50 gm)
set of 4 needles 2.75 mm
Lavender Showers 1 ball 4 ply cotton (50 gm)
set of 4 needles 3.25 mm
Plastic hook or pipe cleaner
Knitted Baskets 1 ball 4 ply cotton (50 gm)
set of 4 needles 2 mm
Pomanders Each requires:
1 ball 20 cotton (20 gm)
pair of needles 1.25 mm
polyester fibre fill and *pot pourri*
embroidery thread for the tiny
flowers or purchase floral motifs
to stitch into position
approx. half metre of narrow
ribbon to match flowers
Knitted Bowls 1 bowl requires 1 ball 20 cotton
set of 2 mm (14) needles
Aromatic Cushions 1 ball 20 cotton (50 gm)
1 pair of needles 1.75 mm
Cushions are made following basic cushion instructions.

Basic Cushion: Cut a piece of backing fabric the size of the cushion front + approx. 8 cm (3") on the length side. Cut this in half and hem the two edges. Overlap these edges until you have a square the same size as your cushion front. With right sides facing, stitch the front and back together, then carefully turn the cushion right side out. Press lightly, then place cushion insert in opening. Alternatively: insert a zip or touch and close fastening, at the overlap.

Lavender Cornucopia

Cast on 72 sts.
Row 1: *K1, (k2 tog) 3 times, (m1, k1) 5 times, m1 (k2 tog) 3 times. Repeat from * to end of row.
Row 2: Knit.
Row 3: Knit.
Row 4: Purl.
Repeat 1–4 until 96 rows have been worked.
Divide sts on 3 needles. K 2 rounds.
Round 3: K tog every 4th and 5th st to end of round.
Round 4: Knit.
Round 5: Knit.
Round 6: K tog. every 3rd and 4th st to end of round.
Round 7: Knit.
Round 8: Knit.
Round 9: K tog. every 2nd and 3rd st to end of round.
Round 10: Knit.
Round 11: Knit.
Round 12: K2 tog to end of round.
Round 13: Knit.
Leave a length of cotton and draw through remaining sts; fasten off. Sew side seam and press.
Make 2 cords and 2 tassels.
Tassels are made by winding cotton 30 times around matchbox. Cord can be crochet chain approx. 30 cm (12").

Lavender Showers

Cast on 8 sts; 3 sts on each of 2 needles, 2 sts on 3rd needle. Knit with 4th needle.
Round 1: Knit.
Round 2: *M1, k1, repeat from * to end of round (16 sts). Knit 3 rounds.
Round 6: As round 2 (32 sts). Knit 3 rounds.
Round 10: K1, *m1, k2, repeat from * to last st, m1, k1 (48 sts).
Round 11: K1, *k1, p1, in m1 of previous round. K2, repeat from * to last 2 sts, k1, p1, into m1 of previous round. K1 (64 sts).
Round 12: *K2 tog, m1, sl 1, k1, psso, repeat from * to end of round (48 sts).
Repeat rounds 11 and 12 4 times.
Round 21: K1, *k1, p1, k1 in m1 of previous round. K2, repeat from * to last 2 sts, k1, p1, k1 in m1 of previous round. K1 (80 sts).
Knit 3 rounds.
Round 25: *M1, k5, repeat from * to end of round (96 sts).
Round 26 and alternate rounds: Knit.
Round 27: *K1, m1, sl 1, k1, psso, k1, k2 tog, m1. Repeat from * to end of round.
Round 29: *M1, k2 tog, m1, sl 1, k2 tog, psso, m1, k1. Repeat from * to end of round.

Round 31: *Sl 1, k1, psso, m1. Repeat from * to end of round.
Round 33: *M1, k2 tog. Repeat from * to end of round.
Round 34: Knit.
Round 35: K1, *sl st from R.H. needle on to L.H. needle. Insert needle into this st. Cast on 2 sts. Cast off 5 sts. Repeat from * until all sts have been cast off.
To make up:
Press with warm iron. Place pipe cleaner or plastic hook through centre ring. Attach top of umbrella at intervals to pipe cleaner or hook. Insert full lavender spikes into umbrella. Decorate with tassels, or ribbon ties.

Knitted Basket 1: WOODRUFF

Cast on 13 sts.
Row 1: Sl 1, k1, (m1, k2 tog) 3 times, (m2, k2 tog) twice, k1.
Row 2: K3, p1, k2, p1, k1, (m1, k2 tog) 3 times, k1.
Row 3: Sl 1, k1, (m1, k2 tog) 3 times, k2, (m2, k2 tog) twice, k1.
Row 4: K3, p1, k2, p1, k3, (m1, k2 tog) 3 times, k1.
Row 5: Sl 1, k1, (m1, k2 tog) 3 times, k4, (m2, k2 tog) twice, k1.
Row 6: K3, p1, k2, p1, k5, (m1, k2 tog) 3 times, k1.
Row 7: Sl 1, k1, (m1, k2 tog) 3 times, k6, (m2, k2 tog) twice, k1.
Row 8: Cast off 8 sts. K5, (m1, k2 tog) 3 times, k1.
Repeat rows 1–8 11 times.
** Press, sew edge together. On each of 3 needles pick up 33 sts, from the straight edge of knitting. Knit 2 rounds. Then * k1, k2 tog, k to last 3 sts, k2 tog. K1. Repeat from * to end of round. Knit one round; and one decreasing round, until 4 sts remain on each needle. Draw cotton through sts. Fasten off securely.**

Braid for Handle

Cast on 3 sts.
M1, k2 tog, k1.
Work every row thus. Continue until handle is the length your require. Cast off. The baskets illustrated were stiffened with a cold water starch, using approx. 1 level tbl. spoon of starch to 1 cup of warm water. Dampen knitting and immerse it in starch solution. Squeeze out excess moisture and form into required shape. Allow to dry naturally. The handle may require extra starch. You can purchase glue or special fabric stiffener. The starch method was the one that came with the basket pattern, from the 19th century.

Basket 2: BEDSTRAW

Cast on 17 sts.
Row 1: K2, m1, k2 tog, k1, m1, k2 tog, k1, sl 1, k1, psso, m1, k3, m2, k2 tog, m2, k2.
Row 2: K3, p1, k2, p1, k3, p5, k5.
Row 3: K2, m1, k2 tog, k1, m1, k2 tog, k1, sl 1, k1, psso, m1, k10.
Row 4: K2, m2, k2 tog, k1, k2 tog, m2, k2 tog, k2, p3, k6.
Row 5: K2, m1, k2 tog, k2, m1, k3 tog, m1, k4, p1, k4, p1, k2.
Row 6: K12, p3, k6.
Row 7: K2, m1, (k2 tog) twice, m1, k3, m1, k2 tog, k2, m2, sl 1, k3 tog, psso, m2, (K2 tog) twice.
Row 8: K3, p1, k2, p1, k3, p5, k5.
Row 9: As row 3.
Row 10: Cast off 3 sts, k6, p2, m1, p2 tog, p1, k5.
Repeat rows 1–10, 11 times.
To make base of basket work from ** to ** in pattern of basket 1.

Basket 2 Handle

Cast on 3 sts.
Row 1: M1, k2 tog, k1.
Row 2: K3.
Repeat these 2 rows until handle is length required.
To stiffen basket 2 follow starching directions for basket 1.
Both these baskets can be decorated as you wish.
They can be used for a variety of things: to hold *pot pourri*, dried flowers, or party favours.

Pomander Ball

Cast on 40 sts.
Row 1: K to last st. Turn.
Row 2: Sl 1, knit to last st. Turn.
Row 3 and 4: K to last 2 sts. Turn.
Row 5 and 6: K to last 3 sts. Turn.
Continue working this way until 10 sts remain at end and beginning of row. K to end of row.
Repeat until 8 sections are completed.
The completed ball can be stuffed with a soft fibre to which you have added a spoonful of lavender, or *pot pourri*. Sew seam as neatly as possible. The ball can be left plain: it has the appearance of tiny beads, which is most attractive. Tiny flowers or ribbons can be used as decoration and the use of contrasting colours adds charm. The ball would also make a delightful Christmas snow ball, decorated with red or green ribbon and topped with a sprig of holly. For a snow ball the addition of a few cloves and cinnamon bark into the stuffing adds a festive fragrance.

For the balls illustrated I used DMC 20 cotton, and 2 mm (size 14) needles. By using different size cotton and needles you could make a variety of sizes. The segments could also be made in different colours to match your decor.

Bowl 1: LEAF

Cast on 12 sts; 4 sts on each of 3 needles.
Round 1 and 2: K tbl.
Round 3: *M2, k2 tbl. Repeat from * to end of round (24 sts).
Round 4 and alternate rounds: K tbl, working p1, k1 into m2 of previous round.
Round 5: K1 tbl to right. * M2, k4 tbl. Repeat from * to end of round (36 sts).
Round 7: K1 tbl to right. *M2, k6 tbl. Repeat from * to end of round (48 sts).
Round 9: K1 tbl to right. * M1, k4, tbl. Repeat from * to end of round (60 sts).
Round 10: K tbl, k into m1 of previous round.
Round 11: *M1, k1, m1, k4 tbl. Repeat from * to end of round (84 sts).
Round 12: *K3, k4 tbl. Repeat from * to end of round.
Round 13: *M1, k3, m1, k2 tog tbl, k2 tbl, m1, k3, m1, k2 tbl, k2 tog tbl. Repeat from * to end of round (96 sts).
Round 14: *K5, k3 tbl. Repeat from * to end of round.
Round 15: *M1, k2 tog, k1, sl 1, k1, psso, m1, k2 tog tbl, k1 tbl, m1, k5, m1, k1 tbl, k2 tog tbl. Repeat from * to end of round.
Round 16: *K5, k2 tbl, k7, k2 tbl. Repeat from * to end of round.
Round 17: *M1, k2, k twice in next st, k2, m1, k2 tog, tbl, m1, k7, m1, k2 tog tbl. Repeat from * to end of round (114 sts).
Round 18: *K8, k1 tbl, k9, k1 tbl. Repeat from * to end of round.
Round 19: *M1, k2, k2 tog, m2, sl 1, k1, psso, k2, m1, sl 1, k1, psso, k7, k2 tog. Repeat from * to end of round.
Round 20 and alternate rounds: Knit, working p1, k1, into each m2 of previous round.
Round 21: *M1, k3, m2, sl 1, k1, psso, k2 tog, m2, k3, m1, sl 1, k1, psso, k5, k2 tog. Repeat from * to end of round (126 sts).
Round 23: *M1, k3, m2, (sl 1, k1, psso, k2 tog, m2) twice, k3, m1, sl 1, k1, psso, k3, k2 tog. Repeat from * to end of round (138 sts).
Round 25: *M1, k3, m2, (sl 1, k1, psso, k2 tog, m2) 3 times, k3, m1, sl 1, k1, psso, k1, k2 tog. Repeat from * to end of round. (150 sts)
Round 27: *M1, k3, m2, (sl 1, k1, psso, k2 tog, m2) 4 times, k3, m1, sl 1, k2 tog, psso. Repeat from * to end of round. (162 sts)
Round 28: K1 to right, knit, working p1, k1, into each m2 of previous round.

Edging: Using crochet hook, insert hook into 1st 4 sts, pull cotton through 9ch *(1dc into next 4 sts, 9ch) 3 times. 1dc into next 3 sts, 9 ch (1 dc into next 4 sts, 9 ch) 3 times. Repeat from * omitting 1 dc at end of last repeat. 1 sl st into 1st st. Fasten off.

Press lightly, stiffen with cold starch solution, place over shallow bowl to dry. Useful for dried petals, sweets, or party nibbles.

Bowl 2: MALLOW

Cast on 8 sts; 3 sts on each of 2 needles and 2 sts on 3rd needle.

Round 1: K.

Round 2: *M1, k1 tbl. Repeat from * to end of round (16 sts).

Round 3: *M1, k1, m1, k1 tbl. Repeat from * to end of round (32 sts).

Round 4: *M1, k3, m1, k1 tbl. Repeat from * to end of round (48 sts).

Round 5: *M1, sl 1, k1, psso, sl 1, k2 tog, psso, m1, k1 tbl. Repeat from * to end of round (40 sts)

Round 6: *M1, sl 1, k1 psso, m1, k2 tog, m1, k1 tbl. Repeat from * to end of round (48 sts)

Round 7 to 11: *M1, sl 1, k1, psso, m1, sl 1, k2 tog, psso, m1, k1 tbl. Repeat from * to end of round.

Round 12: *Sl 1, k1, psso, k1, k2 tog, m1, k1 tbl, m1. Repeat from * to end of round.

Round 13: *Sl 1, k2 tog, psso, m1, k3, m1. Repeat from * to end of round.

Round 14: *K1 tbl, m1, k5, m1. Repeat from * to end of round (64 sts).

Round 15: *K1 tbl, m1, k7, m1. Repeat from * to end of round (80 sts).

Round 16: *K1 tbl, m1, k9, m1. Repeat from * to end of round (96 sts).

Round 17: K.

Round 18: *K5, k2 tog, m1, k5. Repeat from * to end of round.

Round 19: *K4, k2 tog, m1, k1, m1, sl 1, k1, psso, k3. Repeat from * to end of round.

Round 20: *K3, k2 tog, m1, k3, m1, sl 1, k1, psso, k2. Repeat from * to end of round.

Round 21: *K2 k2 tog, m1, k5, m1, sl 1, k1, psso, k1. Repeat from * to end of round.

Round 22: *k1, k2 tog, m1, k7, m1, sl 1, k1, psso. Repeat from * to end of round

Round 23: Before commencing round, k2 sts from L.H. needle on to R.H. needle. *M1, k9, m1, sl 1, k2 tog, psso. Repeat from * to end of round.

Round 24: *M1, k11, m1, k1 tbl. Repeat from * to end of round (112 sts).

Round 25: *M1, k13, m1, k1 tbl. Repeat from * to end of round (128 sts).

Round 26: K.

Round 27: *M1, k4, m2, k7, m2, k4, m1, k1 tbl. Repeat from * to end of round.

Round 28 and following alternate rounds: Knit. Working k1, p1, into each m2 of previous round (176 sts).

Round 29: *M1, sl 1, k1, psso, k1, k3 tog, m2, sl 1, k2 tog, psso, k3, k3 tog, m2, sl 1, k2 tog, psso, k1, k2 tog, m1, k1 tbl. Repeat from * to end of round (144 sts).

Round 31: *M1, sl 1, k1, psso, k3 tog, m2, sl 1, k2 tog, psso, k1, k3 tog, m2, sl 1, k2 tog, psso, k2, tog, m1, k1 tbl. Repeat from * to end of round (112 sts).

Round 33: Before commencing round, k1 st from L.H. needle on to R.H. needle. *K3 tog, m1, sl 1, k2 tog, psso, k2 tog. M1, sl 1, k2 tog, psso, (m1, k1) 3 times, m1. Repeat from * to end of round (104 sts).

Round 34 and following alternate rounds: Knit.

Round 35: *K6, (m1, k1) 7 times, m1. Repeat from * to end of round (168 sts).

Round 37: *K6, m1, k15, m1. Repeat from * to end of round (184 sts).

Round 39: *K6, m1, k17, m1. Repeat from * to end of round (200 sts).

Round 40: Knit.

Using crochet hook, insert hook into 1st 6 sts, *12 ch (1 dc into next 3 sts, 12 ch) 5 times, 1 dc into next 4 sts, 12 ch, 1 dc into next 6 sts. Repeat from * omitting 1 dc at end of last repeat. 1 sl st into 1st dc. Fasten off. Wash and starch the knitting. Place over shallow bowl to dry naturally.

Aromatic Cushion 1: ROSEDALE

Cast on 3 sts.

Row 1: (M1, k1) 3 times.

Row 2: M1, p6.

Row 3: M1, p1, k2, m1, k1, m1, k2, p1.

Row 4: M1, k1, p7, k2.

Row 5: M1, p2, k3, m1, k1, m1, k3, p2.

Row 6: M1, k2, p9, k3.

Row 7: M1, p3, k4, m1, k1, m1, k4, p3.

Row 8: M1, k3, p11, k4.

Row 9: M1, p4, k5, m1, k1, m1, k5, p4.

Row 10: M1, k4, p13, k5.

Row 11: M1, p5, k6, m1, k1, m1, k6, p5.

Row 12: M1, k5, p15, k6.

Row 13: M1, p6, sl 1, k1, psso, k11, k2 tog, p6.

Row 14: M1, k6, p13, k7.

Row 15: M1, p7, sl 1, k1, psso, k9, k2 tog, p7.

Row 16: M1, k7, p11, k8.

Row 17: M1, p8, sl 1, k1, psso, k7, k2 tog, p8.

Row 18: M1, k8, p9, k9.

Row 19: M1, p9, sl 1, k1, psso, k5, k2 tog, p9.

Row 20: M1, k9, p7, k10.

Row 21: M1, p10, sl 1, k1, psso, k3, k2 tog, p10.

Row 22: M1, k10, p5, k11.

Row 23: M1, p11, sl 1, k1, psso, k1, k2 tog, p11.

Row 24: M1, k11, p3, k12.

Row 25: M1, p12, sl 1, k2 tog, psso, p12.
Row 26: M1, k26.
Row 27: M1, k27.
Row 28: M1, p28.
Row 29: M1, k29.
Row 30: M1, p30.
Row 31: M1, p31.
Row 32: M1, k32.
Row 33: M1, p33.
Row 34: M1, k34.
Row 35: M1, p35.
Row 36: M1, p36.
Row 37: M1, k37.
Row 38: M1, p38.
Row 39: M1, k2, (m1, sl 1, k1, psso) 18 times, k1.
Row 40: M1, p40.
Row 41: M1, k2, (m1, sl 1, k1, psso) 19 times, k1.
Row 42: M1, p42.
Row 43: M1, k2, (m1, sl 1, k1, psso) 20 times, k1.
Row 44: M1, p44.
Row 45: M1, k45.
Row 46: M1, p46.
Row 47: M1, k47.
Row 48: M1, k48.
Row 49: M1, p49.
Row 50: M1, k50.
Row 51: M1, p51.
Row 52: M1, k52.
Row 53: M1, k53.
Row 54: M1, p54.
Row 55: M1, k55.
Row 56: M1, p56.
Row 57: M1, (p2, k1, m1, k1, m1, k1, p5) 5 times, p2 (k1, m1) twice, k1, p2.
Row 58: M1, (k2, p5, k5) 5 times, k2, p5, k3.
Row 59: M1, (p3, k2, m1, k1, m1, k2, p4) 5 times, p3, k2, m1, k1, m1, k2, p3.
Row 60: M1, (k3, p7, k4) 6 times.
Row 61: M1, (p4, k3, m1, k1, m1, k3, p3) 6 times, p1.
Row 62: M1, (k4, p9, k3) 6 times, k2.
Row 63: M1, (p5, k4, m1, k1, m1, k4, p2) 6 times, p3.
Row 64: M1, (k5, p11, k2) 6 times, k4.
Row 65: M1, (p6, k5, m1, k1, m1, k5, p1) 6 times, p5.
Row 66: M1, (k6, p13, k1) 6 times, k6.
Row 67: M1, (p7, k6, m1, k1, m1, k6) 6 times, p7.
Row 68: M1, k7, (p15, k7) 6 times, k1.
Row 69: M1, p8, (sl 1, k1, psso, k11, k2 tog, p7) 6 times, p1.
Row 70: M1, k8, (p13, k7) 6 times, k2.
Row 71: M1, p9, (sl 1, k1, psso, k9, k2 tog, p7) 6 times. P2.
Row 72: M1, k9, (p11, k7) 6 times, k3.
Row 73: M1, p10, (sl 1, k1, psso, k7, k2 tog, p7) 6 times, p3.
Row 74: M1, k10, (p9, k7) 6 times, k4.
Row 75: M1, p11, (sl 1, k1, psso, k5, k2 tog, p7) 6 times, p4.
Row 76: M1, k11, (p7, k7) 6 times, k5.
Row 77: M1, p12, (sl 1, k1, psso, k3, k2 tog, p7) 6 times, p5.
Row 78: M1, k12, (p5, k7) 6 times, k6.
Row 79: M1, p13, (sl 1, k1, psso, k1, k2 tog, p7) 6 times, p6.
Row 80: M1, k13, (p3, k7) 6 times, k7.

Row 81: M1, p14, (sl 1, k2 tog, psso, p7) 6 times, p7.
Row 82: M1, p70.
Row 83: M1, k2, (m1, sl 1, k1, psso) 34 times, k1.
Row 84: M1, p72.
Row 85: M1, k2, (m1, sl 1, k1, psso) 35 times, k1.
Row 86: M1, p74.
Row 87: M1, k2, (m1, sl 1, k1, psso) 36 times, k1.
Row 88: M1, p76.
Row 89: K77.
Cast off.
Make 4 triangles. Join together to form square.

Edging:

Cast on 16 sts.
Row 1: Sl 1, k2, m2, p2 tog, k10, p1.
Row 2: M1, k2 tog, k1, m1, k8, m2, p2 tog, k3.
Row 3: Sl 1, k2, m2, p2 tog, k11, p1.
Row 4: M1, k2 tog, k1, m1, k2 tog, m1, k7, m2, p2 tog, k3.
Row 5: Sl 1, k2, m2, p2 tog, k12, p1.
Row 6: M1, k2 tog, k1, (m1, k2 tog) twice, m1, k6, m2, p2 tog, k3.
Row 7: Sl 1, k2, m2, p2 tog, k13, p1.
Row 8: M1, k2 tog, k1, (m1, k2 tog) 3 times, m1, k5, m2, p2 tog, k3.
Row 9: Sl 1, k2, m2, p2 tog, k14, p1.
Row 10: M1, k2 tog, k1, (m1, k2 tog) 4 times, m1, k4, m2, p2 tog, k3.
Row 11: Sl 1, k2, m2, p2 tog, k15, p1.
Row 12: M1, k2 tog, k1, (m1, k2 tog) 5 times, m1, k3, m2, p2 tog, k3.
Row 13: Sl 1, k2, m2, p2 tog, k16, p1.
Row 14: M1, (k2 tog) twice, (m1, k2 tog) 5 times, k3, m2, p2 tog, k3.
Row 15: Sl 1, k2, m2, p2 tog, k15, p1.
Row 16: M1, (k2 tog) twice, (m1, k2 tog) 4 times, k4, m2, p2 tog, k3.
Row 17: Sl 1, k2, m2, p2 tog, k14, p1.
Row 18: M1, (k2 tog) twice, (m1, k2 tog) 3 times, k5, m2, p2 tog, k3.
Row 19: Sl 1, k2, m2, p2 tog, k13, p1.
Row 20: M1, (k2 tog) twice, (m1, k2 tog) twice, k6, m2, p2 tog, k3.
Row 21: Sl 1, k2, m2, p2 tog, k12, p1.
Row 22: M1, (k2 tog) twice, m1, k2 tog, k7, m2, p2 tog, k3.
Row 23: Sl 1, k2, m2, p2 tog, k11, p1.
Row 24: M1, (k2 tog) twice, k8, m2, p2 tog, k3.
Repeat rows 1–24 until length desired—the cushion illustrated has 35 repeats. Make cushion the same size as the knitted square. Attach knitted edging to knitted square, allowing a gentle fullness at corners. Slip-stitch cushion to top. Your choice of closure can be used. The one illustrated has a centre back overlap—not only is this a simple method, but the aromatic insert can be easily removed for renewal. I used a tiny bow in each corner of the cushion. These small pillows or cushions can be used as a ring cushion or as a brooch cushion. The fragrant

insert is approx. 20 cm (8") square. Stuff with soft fibre, plus half a cup of your favourite *pot pourri* or plain lavender. For excellent *pot pourri* recipes see Bibliography.

Aromatic Cushion 2: VERBENA

Cast on 3 sts.
Row 1: (K1, p1) in 1st st, sl 1, m1, (p1, k1) in last st.
Row 2: (K1, p1) in 1st st, k1, p1, k1, (p1, k1) in last st (7 sts).
Row 3: Sl 1, k1, p3, k1, (p1, k1) in last st.
Row 4: Sl 1, k3, m1, k1, m1, k2, (p1, k1) in last st.
Row 5: Sl 1, k1, sl 1, m1, p5, sl 1, k1, (p1, k1) in last st.
Row 6: Sl 1, k5, m1, k1, m1, k4, (p1, k1) in last st.
Row 7: Sl 1, k1, sl 1, k1, p7, k1, sl 1, k1, (p1, k1) in last st.
Row 8: Sl 1, k7, m1, k1, m1, k6, (p1, k1) in last st.
Row 9: Sl 1, (k1, sl 1) twice, p9, (sl 1, k1) twice, (p1, k1) in last st.
Row 10: Sl 1, k9, m1, k1, m1, k8, (p1, k1) in last st.
Row 11: Sl 1, (k1, sl 1) twice, k1, p11, (k1, sl 1) twice, k1, (p1, k1) in last st.
Row 12: Sl 1, k11, m1, k1, m1, k10, (p1, k1) in last st.
Row 13: Sl 1, (k1, sl 1) 3 times, p13, (sl 1, k1) 3 times, (p1, k1) in last st.
Row 14: Sl 1, k13, m1, k1, m1, k12, (p1, k1) in last st.
Row 15: Sl 1, (k1, sl 1) 3 times, k1, p15, (k1, sl 1) 3 times, k1, (p1, k1) in last st.
Row 16: Sl 1, k8, sl 1, k1, psso, k11, k2 tog, k7, (p1, k1) in last st.
Row 17: Sl 1, (k1, sl 1) 4 times, p13, (sl 1, k1) 4 times, (p1, k1) in last st.
Row 18: Sl 1, k9, sl 1, k1, psso, k9, k2 tog, k8, (p1, k1) in last st.
Row 19: (Sl 1, k1) 5 times, p11, (k1, sl 1) 4 times, k1, (p1, k1) in last st.
Row 20: Sl 1, k10, sl 1, k1, psso, k7, k2 tog, k9, (p1, k1) in last st.
Row 21: Sl 1, (k1, sl 1) 5 times, p9, (sl 1, k1) 5 times, (p1, k1) in last st.
Row 22: Sl 1, k11, sl 1, k1, psso, k5, k2 tog, k10, (p1, k1) in last st.
Row 23: (Sl 1, k1) 6 times, p7, (k1, sl 1) 5 times, k1, (p1, k1) in last st.
Row 24: Sl 1, k12, sl 1, k1, psso, k3, k2 tog, k11, (p1, k1) in last st.
Row 25: Sl 1, (k1, sl 1) 6 times, p5, (sl 1, k1) 6 times, (p1, k1) in last st.
Row 26: Sl 1, k13, sl 1, k1, psso, k1, k2 tog, k12, (p1, k1) in last st.
Row 27: (Sl 1, k1) 7 times. P3, (k1, sl 1) 6 times. K1, (p1, k1) in last st.
Row 28: Sl 1, k14, sl 1, k2 tog, psso, k13, (p1, k1) in last st.
Row 29 *to* 48: Continue sl 1st st of every row and inc. in last st keeping (sl 1, k1) pattern correct as in previous rows.
Row 49: Sl 1, purl to last st, (p1, k1) inc.
Row 50: As row 49.

Row 51: Sl 1, k to last st, (p1, k1) inc.
Row 52: As row 49.
Row 53: As row 51 (56 sts).
Row 54: Sl 1, k1, m1, k2, k2 tog, * (sl 1, k1, psso, k3, m1, k1, m1, k3, k2 tog) 4 times *, sl 1, k1, psso, k2, m1, k1, (p1, k1) in last st.
Row 55: As row 49.
Row 56: Sl 1, k1, m1, k3, k2 tog. Repeat from *—* of row 54, sl 1, k1, psso, k3, m1, k1, (p1, k1) in last st.
Row 57: As row 49.
Row 58: Sl 1, (k1, m1) twice, k3, k2 tog. Repeat from *—* of row 54, sl 1, k1, psso, k3, (m1, k1) twice, k1, (no inc in last st).
Row 59: P to end (no inc in last st).
Row 60: Sl 1, k2, m1, k1, m1, k3, k2 tog. Repeat from *—* of row 54, sl 1, k1, psso, k3, m1, k1, m1, k3.
Row 61: As row 59.
Row 62: Sl 1, k3, m1, k1, m1, k3, k2 tog. Repeat from *—* of row 54, sl 1, k1, psso, k3, m1, k1, m1, k4.
Row 63: As row 59.
Row 64: Sl 1, k4, m1, k1, m1, k3, k2 tog. Repeat from *—* of row 54. Sl 1, k1, psso, k3, m1, k1, m1, k5.
Row 65 *and* 66: P.
Row 67: K.
Row 68: P.
Cast off.
Repeat rows 1–68 3 times; join to form square. Make cushion as cushion 1, omitting knitted edging, and using self-fabric frill.

Aromatic Cushion 3: DIANTHUS

Cast on 1 st; k1, p1, k1, into this st.
Row 1: (M1, k1) 3 times.
Row 2: M1, k1, p3, k2.
Row 3: M1, k3, m1, k1, m1, k3.
Row 4: M1, k2, p5, k3.
Row 5: M1, k5, m1, k1, m1, k5.
Row 6: M1, k3, p7, k4.
Row 7: M1, k7, m1, k1, m1, k7.
Row 8: M1, k4, p9, k5.
Row 9: M1, k9, m1, k1, m1, k9.
Row 10: M1, k5, p11, k6.
Row 11: M1, k11, m1, k1, m1, k11.
Row 12: M1, k6, p13, k7.
Row 13: M1, k13, m1, k1, m1, k13.
Row 14: M1, k7, p15, k8.
Row 15: M1, k8, k2 tog, k11, sl 1, k1, psso, k8.
Row 16: M1, k8, p13, k9.
Row 17: M1, k9, k2 tog, k9, sl 1, k1, psso, k9.
Row 18: M1, k9, p11, k10.
Row 19: M1, k10, k2 tog, k7, sl 1, k1, psso, k10.
Row 20: M1, k10, p9, k11.
Row 21: M1, k11, k2 tog, k5, sl 1, k1, psso, k11.
Row 22: M1, k11, p7, k12.

Row 23: M1, k12, k2 tog, k3, sl 1, k1, psso, k12.
Row 24: M1, k12, p5, k13.
Row 25: M1, k13, k2 tog, k1, sl 1, k1, psso, k13.
Row 26: M1, k13, p3, k14.
Row 27: M1, k14, sl 1, k2 tog, psso, k14.
Row 28: M1, p30.
Row 29: M1, k2 tog, k1, *(m1, k1) twice, sl 1, k1, psso, k1, k2 tog, k1 *. Repeat *—* twice, m1, k1, m1, k2 tog, k1.
Row 30: M1, p32.
Row 31: M1, k2 tog, k1, *m1, k3, m1, k1, sl 1, k2 tog, psso, k1*. Repeat *—* twice, m1, k3, m1, k2 tog, k1.
Row 32: M1, p34.
Row 33: M1, k4, k2 tog, k1, m1, k1, *m1, k1, sl 1, k1, psso, k1, k2 tog, k1, m1, k1 *. Repeat *—* twice, m1, k2 tog, k1.
Row 34: M1, p36.
Row 35: M1, k2, * m1, k1, sl 1, k2 tog, psso, k1, m1, k3 *. Repeat *—* 3 times, m1, k2 tog, k1.
Row 36: M1, p38.
Row 37: M1, k4, k2 tog, k1, *(m1, k1) twice, sl 1, k1, psso, k1, k2 tog, k1 *. Repeat *—* twice, (m1, k1) twice, sl 1, k1, psso, k4.
Row 38: M1, p40.
Row 39: M1, k4, k2 tog, k1, * m1, k3, m1, k1, sl 1, k2 tog, psso, k1 *. Repeat *—* twice, m1, k3, m1, k1, sl 1, k2 tog, psso, k3.

Row 40: M1, p41.
Row 41: M1, p42.
Row 42: M1, k43.
Row 43: M1, p44.
Cast off. Repeat rows 1–43 3 times. Sew 4 sections together to form square. The following edging complements the tiny square.

Edging:

Cast on 7 sts.
Row 1: Sl 1, k2, (m2, k2 tog) twice.
Row 2: Sl 1, k1, p1, k2, p1, k3.
Row 3: Sl 1, k4, (m2, k2 tog) twice.
Row 4: Sl 1, k1, p1, k2, p1, k5.
Row 5: Sl 1, k6, (m2, k2 tog) twice.
Row 6: Sl 1, k1, p1, k2, p1, k7.
Row 7: Sl 1, k12.
Row 8: Cast off 6 sts, k6.
Repeat rows 1–8 (the cushion illustrated had the pattern repeated 48 times). Follow cushion-making directions given for Cushion 1. You will need an insert approx. 10 cm (4'') square.

2. Six Cushions

Six Victorian-style boudoir cushions recapture the romantic look of the Victorian era—these cushions would enhance any decor. Pile them on cane furniture or use them to soften the country look.

In spite of the fragile appearance, knitted lace is easily cared for and the covers are suitable for laundering.

Materials

Cushions:

1 Fantasy	1 ball no 20 cotton (20 gm)
	1 set of 4 needles 2 mm
2 Cathedral Windows	2 balls no 20 cotton (20 gm)
	1 set of 4 needles 2 mm
3 Autumn Leaves	1 ball no 20 cotton (20 gm)
	set of 4 needles (2 mm)
4 Tulips of Amsterdam	1 ball no 20 cotton
	set of 4 needles 2 mm
5 Spinning Wheel	1 ball no 20 cotton (20 gm)
	set of 4 needles 2 mm
6 Mantilla	2 balls no 20 cotton (20 gm)
	2 needles 2 mm

Cushion 1: FANTASY

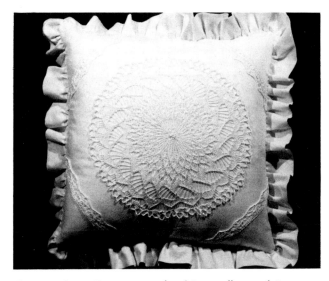

Cast on 8 sts (3 sts on each of 2 needles and 2 sts on 3rd needle, work with 4th needle). Knit one round.

Round 1: K1 tbl into each st.
Round 2: Into each st, k1, p1, k1.
Round 3: As round 1.
Round 4: *K1 tbl, into next st work k1, p1, k1 tbl. Repeat from * to end of round.
Round 5 *to* 10: As round 1.
Round 11: *Into next st work k1, p1, k1, k1 tbl. Repeat from * to end of round.
Round 12: *k1 tbl, into next st work k1, p1, k1 (k1 tbl) twice. Repeat from * to end of round.
Round 13: *K1 tbl, k1, into next st work k1, p1, k1, k1 (k1 tbl) twice. Repeat from * to end of round.
Round 14: *Sl 1, k1, psso, k3, k2 tog, into next st work k1, p1, k1. Repeat from * to end of round.
Round 15: *Sl 1, k1, psso, k1, k2 tog, k1 tbl, into next st work k1, p1, k1, k1 tbl. Repeat from * to end of round.
Round 16: *Sl 1, k2 tog, psso, k1 tbl, k1, into next st work k1, p1, k1, k1 tbl. Repeat from * to end of round.
Round 17: *Into next st work k1, p1, k1, sl 1, k1, psso, k3, k2 tog. Repeat from * to end of round.
Round 18: *K1 tbl, into next st work k1, p1, k1, k1 tbl, sl 1, k1, psso, k1, k2 tog. Repeat from * to end of round.
Round 19: *K1 tbl, k1, into next st work k1, p1, k1, k1, k1 tbl, sl 1, k2 tog, psso. Repeat from * to end of round.
Round 20 *to* 22: As round 14–16.
Round 23: *M1, k1 tbl, m1, sl 1, k1, psso, k3, k2 tog. Repeat from * to end of round.
Round 24: *M1, k3, m1, sl 1, k1, psso, k1, k2 tog. Repeat from * to end of round.
Round 25: *M1, k5, m1, sl 1, k2 tog, psso. Repeat from * to end of round.
Round 26: *M1, k7, m1, k1 tbl. Repeat from * to end of round.
Round 27 *to* 29: K.
Round 30: Before commencing this round, k4 sts from L.H. needle on to R.H. needle, * sl 1, k2 tog, psso, k7, m2. Repeat from * to end of round. N.B. In next and following rounds work p1, k1, into m2 of previous round.
Round 31 *to* 35: Work from * on 30th round.
Round 36 *to* 38: K.
Round 39: *K1, k2 tog, m1, k7. Repeat from * to end of round.
Round 40: Before commencing this round k2 sts from L.H. needle on to R.H. needle. * M1, into next st work (k1, p1) twice and k1, m1, sl 1, k1, psso, k5, k2 tog. Repeat from * to end of round.
Round 41: *M1, k7, m1, sl 1, k1, psso, k3, k2 tog. Repeat from * to end of round.

Round 42: *M1, k9, m1, sl 1, k1, psso, k1, k2 tog. Repeat from * to end of round.
Round 43: *M1, k9, m1, sl 1, k2 tog, psso. Repeat from * to end of round.
Round 44: K.
K1 st off L.H. needle on to R.H. needle with crochet hook. Work * 1 dc into next 4 sts, slip off. 8 ch, 1 dc into next 3 sts, slip off, 8 ch. Repeat from * ending with 1 sl st into 1st dc. Fasten off.
Damp and pin out work; spray lightly with starch.

Cushion 2:
CATHEDRAL WINDOWS

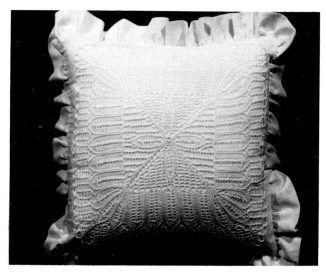

Cast on 12 sts; 3 sts on each of 2 needles, and 6 sts on 3rd needle.
Round 1: Knit.
Round 2: Knit.
Round 3: *K1 tbl, m1, k2, tbl. Repeat from * to end of round (16 sts).
Round 4: *K1 tbl, k1, k2 tbl. Repeat from * to end of round.
Round 5: *M1, k1 tbl. Repeat from * to end of round (32 sts).
Round 6: *K1, (k1 tbl, p1) twice, k1 tbl, k1, k1 tbl. Repeat from * to end of round.
Round 7: * (M1, k1 tbl) twice, p1, m1, k1 tbl, m1, p1, k1 tbl (m1, k1 tbl) twice. Repeat from * to end of round (56 sts).
Round 8 and following alternate rounds: Work sts as set.
Round 9: *M1, k1 tbl, m1, k2 tog, m1, k1 tbl, p2, m1, k1 tbl, m1, p2, k1 tbl, m1, sl 1, k1, psso, (m1, k1 tbl) twice. Repeat from * to end of round (80 sts).
Round 11: *M1, k2 tog, m2, sl 1, k2 tog, psso, m1, k1 tbl, p2, m1, sl 1, k2 tog, psso, m1, p2, k1 tbl, m1, sl 1, k2 tog, psso, m2, sl 1, k1, psso, m1, k1 tbl. Repeat from * to end of round (88 sts).
Round 12 and following alternate rounds: As 8th round, working k1, p1, into m2 of previous round.
Round 13: *M1, k1 tbl, m1, k2 tog, m2, sl 1, k2 tog, psso,

m1, k1 tbl, p2, m1, sl 1, k2 tog, psso, m1, p2, k1 tbl, m1, sl 1, k2 tog, psso, m2, sl 1, k1, psso, (m1, k1 tbl) twice. Repeat from * to end of round (104 sts).
Round 15: *M1, k2 tog, (m2, sl 1, k2 tog, psso) twice, m1, k1 tbl, p2, m1, sl 1, k2 tog, psso, m1, p2, k1 tbl, m1, (sl 1, k2 tog, psso, m2) twice, sl 1, k1, psso, m1, k1 tbl. Repeat from * to end of round (112 sts).
Round 17: *M1, k1 tbl, m1, k2 tog, (m2, sl 1, k2 tog, psso) twice, m1, k1 tbl, p2, m1, sl 1, k2 tog, psso, m1, p2, k1 tbl, m1, (sl 1, k2 tog, psso, m2) twice, sl 1, k1, psso, (m1, k1 tbl) twice. Repeat from * to end of round (128 sts).
Round 19: *M1, k2 tog, (m2, sl 1, k2 tog, psso) 3 times, m1, k1 tbl, p2, k3, p2, k1 tbl, m1, (sl 1, k2 tog, psso, m2) 3 times, sl 1, k1, psso, m1, k1 tbl. Repeat from * to end of round (136 sts).
Round 21: *M1, k1 tbl, m1, k2 tog, (m2, sl 1, k2 tog, psso) 3 times, m1, k1 tbl, p2, sl 1, k2 tog, psso, p2, k1 tbl, m1, (sl 1, k2 tog, psso, m2) 3 times, sl 1, k1, psso, (m1, k1 tbl) twice. Repeat from * to end of round (144 sts).
Round 23: *M1, k2 tog, (m2, sl 1, k2 tog, psso) 3 times, m2, sl 1, k1, psso, (m1, k1 tbl) twice, p1, p3 tog, p1, (k1 tbl, m1) twice, k2 tog, m2, (sl 1, k2 tog, psso, m2) 3 times, sl 1, k1, psso, m1, k1 tbl. Repeat from * to end of round (160 sts).
Round 25: *M1, k1 tbl, m1, k2 tog, (m2, sl 1, k2 tog, psso) 4 times, m2, sl 1, k1, psso, m1, k1 tbl, p3 tog, k1 tbl, m1, k2 tog, m2, (sl 1, k2 tog, psso, m2) 4 times, sl 1, k1, psso, (m1, k1 tbl) twice. Repeat from * to end of round (176 sts).
Round 27: *M1, k2 tog, (m2, sl 1, k2 tog, psso) 6 times, m1, sl 1, k2 tog, psso, m1, (sl 1, k2 tog, psso, m2) 6 times, sl 1, k1, psso, m1, k1 tbl. Repeat from * to end of round (176 sts).
Round 29: *M1, k1 tbl, m1, k2 tog, (m2, sl 1 k2 tog, psso) 6 times, m1, k1 tbl, m1, (sl 1, k2 tog, psso, m2) 6 times, sl 1, k1, psso, (m1, k1, tbl) twice. Repeat from * to end of round (192 sts).
Round 31 and 32: Knit (192 sts).
Round 33: K 1 st from L.H. needle to R.H. needle. *(K tbl, p2, m1, sl 1, k2 tog, psso, m1, p2, k1 tbl) 5 times, (k1, k1 tbl, into next st) 3 times. Repeat from * to end of round (204 sts).
Round 35: *(K1 tbl, p2, m1, sl 1, k2 tog, psso, m1, p2, k1 tbl) 5 times, (k1 tbl, m1, k1 tbl) 3 times. Repeat from * to end of round (216 sts).
Round 37: *(K1 tbl, p2, m1, sl 1, k2 tog, psso, m1, p2, k1 tbl) 5 times, (k1 tbl, m1, k1, m1, k1 tbl) 3 times. Repeat from * to end of round (240 sts).
Round 39: *(K1 tbl, p2, m1, sl 1, k2 tog, psso, m1, p2, k1 tbl) 5 times, (k1 tbl, p1, m1, k1 tbl, m1, p1, k1 tbl) 3 times. Repeat from * to end of round (264 sts).
Round 41: *K1 tbl, p2, m1, sl 1, k2 tog, psso, m1, p2, k1 tbl) 5 times, (k1 tbl, p2, m1, k1 tbl, m1, p2, k1 tbl) 3 times. Repeat from * to end of round (288 sts).
Round 43: *K1 tbl, p2, m1, sl 1, k2 tog, psso, m1, p2, k1 tbl. Repeat from * to end of round (288 sts).
Round 45, 47, 49 and 51: As round 43.
Round 53: *K1 tbl, p2, k3, p2, k1 tbl. Repeat from * to end of round (288 sts).

Round 55: *M1, k1 tbl, p2, sl 1, k2 tog, psso, p2, k1 tbl. Repeat from * to end of round (256 sts).
Round 57: *M1, work k1, k1 tbl, into next st, m1, k1 tbl, p1, p3 tog, p1, k1 tbl. Repeat from * to end of round (288 sts).
Round 59: *M1, k2 tog, m2, sl 1, k1, psso, m1, k1 tbl, p3 tog, k1 tbl. Repeat from * to end of round.
Round 61: *M2, sl 1, k2 tog, psso. Repeat from * to end of round (288 sts).
Round 63: K 1 st from L.H. needle to R.H. needle. *(M2, sl 1, k2 tog, psso) 20 times, m2, k1 tbl, (m1, k1 tbl) twice, (m2, sl 1, k2 tog, psso) 3 times. Repeat from * to end of round (304 sts).
Round 65: K 1 st, from L.H. needle to R.H. needle. *(M2, sl 1, k2 tog, psso) 20 times, m2, sl 1, k1, psso, (m1, k1 tbl) 3 times, m1, k2 tog (m2, sl 1, k2 tog, psso) 3 times. Repeat from * to end of round (320 sts).
Round 67: K 1 st from L.H. needle to R.H. needle. *(M2, sl 1, k2 tog, psso) 21 times, m2, sl 1, k1, psso, m1, k1 tbl, m1, k2 tog, (m2, sl 1, k2 tog, psso) 4 times. Repeat from * to end of round (328 sts).
Round 69: K 1 st from L.H. needle to R.H. needle. *(M2, sl 1, k2 tog, psso) 21 times, m2, sl 1, k1, psso, (m1, k1 tbl) 3 times, m1, k2 tog, (m2, sl 1, k2 tog, psso) 4 times. Repeat from * to end of round (344 sts).
Round 70: K1 tbl, k1, p1, in m2 of previous round.
Using crochet hook * 1 dc into next 4 sts. Slip off. Make 8 ch. *. Repeat from *—* ending with 1 sl st into 1st dc. Fasten off.
Dampen work. Pin out and spray with starch.

To make cushion:
Cut 1 36 cm square—front of cushion
Cut 1 36 cm × 40 cm—back of cushion.
Insert zipper in centre back. Place knitting in centre of front, attach with fine sewing. Cut 9 cm wide strip approx. 2 m long; sew into circle; gather to form frill; insert between front and back of cushion. Press lightly and insert cushion pad.

Cushion 3: AUTUMN LEAVES

Cast on 8 sts; 3 sts on 2 needles and 2 sts on 3rd needle.
Round 1: Knit.
Round 2: *M1, k1 tbl, Repeat from * to end of round.
Round 3 *and* 4: Purl.
Round 5: As round 2.
Round 6: Knit.
Round 7: *M1, sl 1, k1, psso, m1, k2. Repeat from * to end of round.
Round 8: *K3, m1, k1, k1 tbl. Repeat from * to end of round.
Round 9: *M1, sl 1, k1, psso, k1, m1, k2, k1 tbl. Repeat from * to end of round.
Round 10: *K4, m1, k2, k1 tbl. Repeat from * to end of round.
Round 11: *M1, sl 1, k1, psso, k2, m1, k3, k1 tbl. Repeat from * to end of round.
Round 12: *K5, m1, k3, k1 tbl. Repeat from * to end of round.
Round 13: *M1, sl 1, k1, psso, k3, m1, k4, k1 tbl. Repeat from * to end of round.
Round 14: *K6, m1, k4, k1 tbl. Repeat from * to end of round.
Round 15: *M1, sl 1, k2 tog, psso, k3, m1, k4, k2 tog. Repeat from * to end of round.
Round 16: As round 14.
Round 17: *M1, sl 1, k1, psso, k10. Repeat from * to end of round.
Round 18: Knit.
Round 19: *M1, k1 tbl, m1, k11. Repeat from * to end of round.
Round 20: *M1, k2 tog, m1, k1, m1, sl 1, k1, psso, k7, k2 tog. Repeat from * to end of round.
Round 21: *K2, m1, k12. Repeat from * to end of round.
Round 22: *M1, (k3, m1) twice, sl 1, k1, psso, k5, k2 tog. Repeat from * to end of round.
Round 23: *K4, m1, k12. Repeat from * to end of round.

Round 24: *M1, (k5, m1) twice, sl 1, k1, psso, k3, k2 tog. Repeat from * to end of round.
Round 25: *K6, m1, k12. Repeat from * to end of round.
Round 26: *M1, sl 1, k1, psso, k5, m1, k5, k2 tog, m1, sl 1, k1, psso, k1, k2 tog. Repeat from * to end of round.
Round 27: *K7, m1, k11. Repeat from * to end of round.
Round 28: *M1, sl 1, k1, psso, k6, m1, k6, k2 tog, m1, sl 1, k2 tog, psso. Repeat from * to end of round.
Round 29: *K8, m1, k10. Repeat from * to end of round.
Round 30: *M1, sl 1, k1, psso, k7, m1, k7, k2 tog, m1, k1 tbl. Repeat from * to end of round.
Round 31: *K9, m1, k11. Repeat from * to end of round.
Round 32: *M1, sl 1, k1, psso, k8, m1, k8, k2 tog, m1, k1 tbl. Repeat from * to end of round.
Round 33: Knit.
Round 34: *M1, sl 1, k1, psso, k17, k2 tog, m1, k1 tbl. Repeat from * to end of round.
Round 35: Knit.
Round 36: K1 st from L.H. needle on to R.H. needle: *k19, m1, k3, m1. Repeat from * to end of round.
Round 37: Knit.
Round 38: *Sl 1, k1, psso, k15, k2 tog, m1, k5, m1. Repeat from * to end of round.
Round 39: Knit.
Round 40: *Sl 1, k1, psso, k13, k2 tog, m1, k7, m1. Repeat from * to end of round.
Round 41: Knit.
Round 42: *Sl 1, k1, psso, k11, k2 tog, m1, k9, m1. Repeat from * to end of round.
Round 43: Knit.
Round 44: *Sl 1, k1, psso, k9, k2 tog, m1, k11, m1. Repeat from * to end of round.
Round 45: Knit.
Round 46: *Sl 1, k1, psso, k7, k2 tog, (m1, k1 tbl, k1) m1, k1, m1, (k1, k1 tbl, m1) 3 times. Repeat from * to end of round.
Round 47: *K12, (m1, k3) 6 times. Repeat from * to end of round.
Round 48: *Sl 1, k1, psso, k5, k2 tog, (m1, k2 tog tbl, k2) 3 times, m1, sl 1, k2 tog, psso, m1, (k2, k2 tog, m1) 3 times. Repeat from * to end of round.
Round 49: *K7, (k2, k2 tog, m1) 3 times, k3 (m1, k2 tog tbl, k2) 3 times. Repeat from * to end of round.
Round 50: *Sl 1, k1, psso, k3, k2 tog, (m1, k2 tog tbl, k2) 3 times, m1, sl 1, k2 tog, psso, m1, (k2, k2 tog, m1) 3 times. Repeat from * to end of round.
Round 51: *K5, (k2, k2 tog, m1) 3 times, k3, (m1, k2 tog tbl, k2) 3 times. Repeat from * to end of round.
Round 52: *Sl 1, k1, psso, k1, k2 tog, (m2, k2 tog tbl, k2) 3 times, m2, sl 1, k2 tog, psso, m2, (k2, k2 tog, m2), 3 times. Repeat from * to end of round.
Round 53: N.B. Knit only once into m2 of previous round. The same applies for following rounds. *K3, (k2, k2 tog, m2) 3 times, k3, (m2, k2 tog tbl, k2) 3 times. Repeat from * to end of round.
Round 54: *Sl 1, k2 tog, psso, (m2, k2 tog tbl, k2) 3 times, m2, sl 1, k2 tog, psso, m2, (k2, k2 tog, m2) 3 times. Repeat from * to end of round.

Round 55: *K1, (k2, k2 tog, m2) 3 times, k3 (m2, k2 tog tbl, k2) 3 times. Repeat from * to end of round.
Round 56: *K1 tbl, (m2, k2 tog tbl, k2) 3 times, m2, sl 1, k2 tog, psso, m2, (k2, k2 tog, m2) 3 times. Repeat from * to end of round.
Round 57: Knit.
Knit 2 sts from L.H. needle onto R.H. needle.
Cast off with crochet hook as follows:
*1 dc into next 4 sts ch 10—twice.
1 dc into next 3 sts ch 10—3 times.
1 dc into next 4 sts ch 10—twice.
1 dc into next 3 sts ch 10—*. Repeat from *—* until all sts have been cast off, ending with sl st into first dc.
Next row dc 12 sts into every 10 ch loop.
Fasten off.

Cushion 4:
TULIPS FROM AMSTERDAM

Cast on 10 sts; 3 sts on each of 2 needles, 4 sts on 3rd needle. Mark beginning of round. Knit 10 sts tbl.
Round 1: *K twice into next st. Repeat from * to end of round (20 sts).
Round 2: K tbl to end of round.
Round 3: *K1 tbl, m2, k1 tbl. Repeat from * to end of round (40 sts).
Round 4: *K1 tbl, k1, p1, into m2 of previous round, k1 tbl. Repeat from * to end of round.
Round 5: *M2, sl 1, k1, psso, k2 tog. Repeat from * to end of round.
Round 6: Knit, k1, & p1, into m2 of previous round.
Round 7: K 1 st on L.H. needle onto R.H. needle (mark beginning of round). *K2 tog, m2, sl 1, k1, psso. Repeat from * to end of round.
Round 8: *K1 tbl, (k1, p1) 4 times, k1 into m2 of previous round, k1 tbl. Repeat from * to end of round (110 sts).
Round 9 to 16: *(K1 tbl, p1) 5 times, k1 tbl. Repeat from * to end of round.

Round 17: *M2, (k1 tbl, p1) 5 times, k1 tbl. Repeat from * to end of round (130 sts).

Round 18: *K1, p1 into m2 of previous round, (k1 tbl, p1) 5 times, k1 tbl. Repeat from * to end of round.

Round 19: *M1, k2 tbl, m1, sl 1, k1, psso, (k1 tbl, p1) 3 times, k1 tbl, k2 tog. Repeat from * to end of round.

Round 20: K working tbl and p sts as before.

Round 21: *M1, k2 tog, m2, sl 1, k1, psso, m1, sl 1, k1, psso (p1, k1 tbl) twice, p1, k2 tog. Repeat from * to end of round.

Round 22: As round 20 working k1, p1, into m2 of previous round.

Round 23: *M1, k1 tbl, m2, k1 tbl, m2, k1 tbl, m2, k1 tbl, m1, sl 3 purlwise. K4, psso. Repeat from * to end of round (180 sts).

Round 24 and following alternate rounds: K tbl, working k1 into m1, and k1, p1 into m2 of previous round.

Round 25: *M1, k2 tog, k1 tbl, m2, k tbl, sl 1, k1, psso, m2, k2 tog, k1 tbl, m2, k1 tbl, sl 1, k1, psso, m1 (tw2) twice. Repeat from * to end of round (220 sts).

Round 27: *M1, k2 tog, k2 tbl, m2, k2 tbl, sl 1, k1, psso, m2, k2 tog, k2 tbl, m2, k2 tbl, sl 1, k1, psso, m1, sl 1, k3 tog, psso. Repeat from * to end of round (230 sts).

Round 29: *Sl 2, k1, psso, k2 tbl, m2, k2 tbl, sl 1, k1, psso, m1, k1 tbl, m2, k1 tbl, m1, sl 1, k1, psso, k2 tbl, m2, k2 tbl, sl 2, k1, psso, k1 tbl. Repeat from * to end of round (250 sts).

Round 30 and alternate rounds: As round 22.

Round 31: *Sl 1, k1, psso, k2 tbl, p1, k2 tbl, k2 tog, m1, k1 tbl, m2, sl 1, k1, psso, k2 tog, m2, k1 tbl, m1, sl 1, k1, psso, k2 tbl, p1, k2 tbl, k2 tog, k1 tbl. Repeat from * to end of round.

Round 33: *Sl 1, k1, psso, k1 tbl, p1, k1 tbl, k2 tog, m1, k1 tbl (m2, sl 1, k1, psso, k2 tog) twice, m2, k1 tbl, m1, sl 1, k1, psso, k1 tbl, p1, k1 tbl, sl 2, k1, psso. Repeat from * to end of round (240 sts).

Round 35: *Sl 1, k1, psso, p1, k2 tog, m1, k1 tbl, (m2, sl 1, k1, psso, k2 tog) 3 times, m2, k1 tbl, m1, sl 1, k1, psso, p1, k2 tog. Repeat from * to end of round.

Round 37: *Sl 1, k2 tog, psso, m1, k1 tbl, (m2, sl 1, k1, psso, k2 tog) 4 times, m2, k1 tbl, m1, sl 1, k2 tog, psso. Repeat from * to end of round (240 sts).

Round 38: K. Working k1, p1, into each m2 of previous round.

Round 39: K 1st st on L.H. needle onto R.H. needle. *M1, k1 tbl, (m2, sl 1, k1, psso, k2 tog) 5 times, m2, k1 tbl, m1, k2 tog. * Repeat from * to end of round.

Round 40: As round 38.

Motif Edging:

Round 1: Using crochet hook work * 1 dc into next 4 sts, 6 ch. Repeat from * ending with 1 sl st into 1st dc.

Round 2: * Into next loop work 3 dc 3 ch 1 dc into 3rd from hook and 3 dc — a picot made. 1 sl st into next dc. Repeat from * ending with 1 sl st into 1st dc. Fasten off. Damp and pin out.

Edging:

Cast on 13 sts.

Row 1 and every alternate row: K2, p to last 2 sts, k2.

Row 2: Sl 1, k3, m1, k5, m1, k2 tog, m1, k2.

Row 4: Sl 1, k4, sl 1, k2 tog, psso, k2, (m1, k2 tog) twice k1.

Row 6: Sl 1, k3, sl 1, k1, psso, k2, (m1, k2 tog) twice, k1.

Row 8: Sl 1, k2, sl 1, k1, psso, k2, (m1, k2 tog) twice, k1.

Row 10: Sl 1, k1, sl 1, k1, psso, k2, (m1, k2 tog) twice, k1.

Row 12: K1, sl 1, k1, psso, k2, m1, k1, m1, k2 tog, m1, k2.

Row 14: Sl 1, (k3, m1) twice, k2 tog, m1, k2.

Repeat rows 1–14 until length desired.

Make cushion thus:

Cut 1 — 36 × 36 cm for front

1 — 36 × 40 cm for back

Cut strip approx. 2 m long for frill. Place doily in centre front of cushion. Sew with tiny stitches. Pin and sew edging around cushion square.

Insert zipper in back. Sew the long strip into circle, fold and press. Gather and sew frill between front and back of cushion. Insert pad.

Cushion 5: SPINNING WHEEL

Cast on 8 sts; 3 sts on each of 2 needles, 2 sts on 3rd needle. Knit one round.

Round 1: *K1, m2. Repeat to end of round (24 sts).

Round 2 and alternate rounds unless otherwise stated: K. Working k1, p1 into m2 of previous round.

Round 3: *K2, m2, k1. Repeat from * to end of round (40 sts).

Round 5: *K1, k2 tog, m2, sl 1, k1, psso. Repeat from * to end of round.

Round 7: *K3, m2, k2. Repeat from * to end of round (56 sts).

Round 9: *K2, k2 tog, m2, sl 1, k1, psso, k1. Repeat from * to end of round.

Round 11: *K4, m2, k3. Repeat from * to end of round (72 sts).

Round 13: *K3, k2 tog, m2, sl 1, k1, psso, k2. Repeat from * to end of round.

Round 15: *K5, m2, k4. Repeat from * to end of round.

Round 17: K 1st st from L.H. needle on to R.H. needle. *M1, k3, k2 tog, m2, sl 1, k1, psso, k2, k2 tog. Repeat from * to end of round.

Round 19: *M1, k1 tbl, m1, sl 1, k1, psso, k3, m2, k3, k2 tog. Repeat from * to end of round (104 sts).

Round 21: * (M1, k1) 3 times, m1, sl 1, k1, psso, k1, k2 tog, m2, sl 1, k1, psso, k1, k2 tog. Repeat from * to end of round (120 sts).

Round 23: *M1, k1, m1, sl 1, k1, psso, k1, k2 tog, m1, k1, m1, sl 1, k1, psso, k2, m2, k2, k2 tog. Repeat from * to end of round (136 sts).

Round 25: *M1, k1, m1, sl 1, k1, psso, m1, sl 1, k2 tog, psso, m1, k2 tog, m1, k1, m1, sl 1, k2 tog, psso, m1, k2, m1, sl 1, k2 tog, psso. Repeat from * to end of round.

Round 26 and alternate rounds: Knit.

Round 27: K 1st st on L.H. needle from R.H. needle. * Sl 1, k1, psso, m1, sl 1, k1, psso, k1, (k2 tog, m1) 3 times, k4, m1, sl 1, k1, psso, m1. Repeat from * to end of round.

Round 29: *Sl 1, k1, psso, m1, sl 1, k2 tog, psso, (m1, k2 tog) twice, m1, k6, m1, sl 1, k1, psso, m1. Repeat from * to end of round.

Round 31: *Sl 1, k1, psso, k1, (k2 tog, m1) twice, k8, m1, sl 1, k1, psso, m1. Repeat from * to end of round.

Round 33: *Sl 1, k2 tog, psso, m1, k2 tog, m1, k10, m1, sl 1, k1, psso, m1. Repeat from * to end of round.

Round 35: *K1, k2 tog, m1, k4, k2 tog, m2, sl 1, k1, psso, k4, m1, sl 1, k1, psso. Repeat from * to end of round.

Round 36 and alternate rounds: As round 2.

Round 37: K 1st 2 sts on L.H. needle from R.H. needle. *M1, k4, k2 tog, (m2) twice, sl 1, k1, psso, k4, m1, sl 1, k2 tog, psso. Repeat from * to end of round.

Round 39: *K4, k2 tog, k1 tbl, p1, k1 tbl, m2, k1 tbl, p1, k1 tbl, sl 1, k1, psso, k3, k2 tog, m1. Repeat from * to end of round.

Round 40 and alternate rounds: As round 2 working k tbl, p into k1 tbl, and p sts on previous round.

Round 41: *K3, k2 tog, k1 tbl, p1, k1 tbl, (m2) twice, k1 tbl, p1, k1 tbl, sl 1, k1, psso, k4. Repeat from * to end of round (168 sts).

Round 43: *K2, k2 tog, (k1 tbl, p1, k1 tbl) twice, m2, (k1 tbl, p1, k1 tbl) twice, sl 1, k1, psso, k3. Repeat from * to end of round.

Round 45: *K1, k2 tog, (k1 tbl, p1, k1 tbl) twice, (m2) twice, (k1 tbl, p1, k1 tbl) twice, sl 1, k1, psso, k2. Repeat from * to end of round (184 sts).

Round 47: *K2 tog, (k1 tbl, p1, k1 tbl) 3 times, m2, (k1 tbl, p1, k1 tbl) 3 times, m2, (k1 tbl, p1, k1 tbl) 3 times, sl 1, k1, psso, k1. Repeat from * to end of round.

Round 49: K 1st st on L.H. needle from R.H. needle. * (K1 tbl, p1, k1 tbl) 3 times, (m2) twice, (k1 tbl, p1, k1 tbl) 3 times, sl 1, k2 tog, psso. Repeat from * to end of round.

Round 51: *(K1 tbl, p1, k1 tbl) 4 times, m1, (k1 tbl, p1, k1 tbl) 4 times, m1, k1 tbl, m1. Repeat from * to end of round (224 sts).

Round 53: * (K1 tbl, p1, k1 tbl) 4 times, m2, (k1 tbl, p1, k1 tbl) 4 times, m1, sl 1, k2 tog, psso, m1. Repeat from * to end of round (240 sts).

Round 55, 57 and 59: *(K1 tbl, p1, k1 tbl) 9 times, m1, sl 1, k2 tog, psso, m1. Repeat from * to end of round.

Round 60: Work sts as set (240 sts).

Using crochet hook work * 1 dc into next 3 sts, slip off. 10 ch *. Repeat from * ending with 1 sl st into 1st dc. Next round 12 dc into each 10 ch loop.

Cast off.

Cushion 6: MANTILLA

Cast on 138 sts.

Knit one edge st at beginning and end of each row.

Rows 1, 5, 9: *K3, k2 tog, k4, m1, p2, (k2, m1, sl 1, k1, psso) 3 times, p2, m1, k4, sl 1, k1, psso, k3 * to end of row.

Rows 2, 6, 10: *P2, p2 tog tbl, p4, m1, p1, k2 (p2, m1, p2 tog) 3 times, k2, p1, m1, p4, p2 tog, p2 * to end of row.

Rows 3, 7, 11: *K1, k2 tog, k4, m1, k2, p2, (k2, m1, sl 1, k1, psso) 3 times, p2, k2, m1, k4, sl 1, k1, psso, k1 * to end of row.

Rows 4, 8, 12: *P2 tog tbl, p4, m1, p3, k2, (p2, m1, k2 tog) 3 times, k2, p3, m1, p4, p2 tog * to end of row.

Rows 13, 17, 21: *M1, sl 1, k1, psso, k2, m1, sl 1, k1, psso, p2, m1, k4, sl 1, k1, psso, k6, k2 tog, k4, m1, p2, k2, m1, sl 1, k1, psso, k2 * to end of row.

Rows 14, 18, 22: *M1, p2 tog, p2, m1, p2 tog, k2, p1, m1, p4, p2 tog, p4, p2 tog tbl, p4, m1, p1, k2, p2, m1, p2 tog, p2 * to end of row.

Rows 15, 19, 23: *M1, sl 1, k1, psso, k2, m1, sl 1, k1, psso, p2, k2, m1, k4, sl 1, k1, psso, k2, k2 tog, k4, m1, k2, p2, k2, m1, sl 1, k1, psso, k2 * to end of row.

Rows 16, 20, 24: *M1, p2 tog, p2, m1, p2 tog, k2, p3, m1, p4, p2 tog, p2 tog tbl, p4, m1, p3, k2, p2, m1, p2 tog, p2 * to end of row.

Repeat rows 1–24 6 times.

Cast off.
Pick up 138 sts evenly on side of work.
Row 1: *Knit.
Row 2: Purl.
Row 3: K3, * cast off 2sts k2 * to end of row.
Row 4: P3, * cast on 2 sts p2 * to end of row.
Row 5: Knit.
Row 6: Purl.
Continue in mantilla pattern for 24 rows.
Cast off *.
Pick up 138 sts on other side. Repeat *—*.

Make mantilla cushion thus:
Cut piece of lawn 5 cm longer than knitted fabric. Another piece 2 cm longer. Insert zipper. Sew knitting on to lawn with fine sts. Fold side of material 1 cm, then sew on to knitted fabric. Insert cushion pad. Thread ribbon through eyelets. Tighten to form bon-bon. Make a bow at each end.

3. A Collection of Doilies

These attractive patterns could be made into table mat sets.

Materials

Doilies 1–2 20 cotton. 2 mm needles—size 22 cm
Doily 3   20 cotton. 2 mm needles—size 37 cm
Doilies 4–5 40 cotton. 2.25 mm needles—approx 25 cm
Doily 6   40 cotton. 2.25 mm needles—approx. 27 cm square

Each doily requires 50 gm of the size cotton indicated.

Doily 1: INDRA

Cast on 8 sts; 3 sts on 2 needles, 2 sts on 3rd needle. Mark beginning of round.
Round 1: Knit.
Round 2: *K1, p1 in next st. Repeat from * to end of round (16 sts).
Round 3, 5, 7 and 8: Knit.
Round 4: As round 2 (32 sts).
Round 6: As round 2 (64 sts).
Round 9: K1 to right. *M1, k4. Repeat from * to end of round (80 sts).

Round 10 and following alternate rounds unless otherwise stated: Knit, work k1, p1, in each m1 (96 sts).
Round 11: K1 to right, *m1, sl 1, k1, psso, k2, k2 tog. Repeat from * to end of round (80 sts).
Round 13, 15 and 17: As round 11 (80 sts).
Round 18: *(K1, p1) 3 times in next m1, k4. Repeat from * to end of round (160 sts).
Round 19: K1 to right, *m1, k4 tbl, m1, sl 1, k1, psso, k2, k2 tog. Repeat from * to end of round (160 sts).
Rounds 21, 23, 25, 27, 29, 31 and 33: As round 11 (160 sts).
Round 35: K1 to right, *m1, sl 1, k1, psso, k1, m2, k1, k2 tog, m1, sl 1, k1, psso, k2, k2 tog. Repeat from * to end of round (192 sts).
Round 36: Knit, work k1, p1 in each m1, and (k1, p1) twice in each m2. Repeat to end of round (256 sts).
Round 37: K1 to right *m1, sl 1, k1, psso, k6 tbl, k2 tog, m1, sl 1, k1, psso, k2, k2 tog. Repeat from * to end of round (224 sts).
Round 39 and 41: K1 to right, *m1, sl 1, k1, psso, k6, k2 tog, m1, sl 1, k1, psso, k2, k2 tog. Repeat from * to end of round (224 sts.)
Round 40 and 42: As round 10 (256 sts).
Round 43: K1 to right, *m1, sl 1, k1, psso (k1, p1 in next st) 6 times, k2 tog, m1, (sl 1, k1, psso) twice, k2 tog. Repeat from * to end of round (304 sts).
Round 44: *K1, p1, in each m1, k18 sts, sl 1, k2 tog, psso. Repeat from * to end of round (304 sts).
Round 45: K1 to right *m1, k1 tbl, k4, m1, k6, m1, k4, k1 tbl, m1, sl 1, k2 tog, psso. Repeat from * to end of round (336 sts).
Round 46: As round 10 (400 sts).
Round 47: K1 to right, *m1, sl 1, k1, psso, k3, k2 tog, m1, sl 1, k1, psso, (k1, k2 tog) twice, m1, sl 1, k1, psso, k3, k2 tog, m1, sl 1, k2 tog, psso. Repeat from * to end of round (320 sts).
Round 48: *K1, p1 in next m1, sl 1, k1, psso, k1, k2 tog, (m4, sl 1, k1, psso, k1, k2 tog) twice, k1, p1 in next m1, k1. Repeat from * to end of round (352 sts).
Round 49: K1 to right, *(m1, sl 1, k1, psso, k1, k2 tog, m1, k2 tbl) twice, m1, sl 1, k1, psso, k1, k2 tog, m1, sl 1, k2 tog, psso. Repeat from * to end of round (320 sts).
Round 50: *K1, p1 in next m1, (sl 1, k2 tog, psso, k1, p1, in each m1, k6 sts) twice, sl 1, k2 tog, psso, k1, p1 in next m1, k1. Repeat from * to end of round (320 sts).
Cast off.

Doily 2: ZENA

Cast on 8 sts; 3 sts on each of 2 needles, and 2 sts on 3rd needle. Join in circle, mark beginning of round.

N.B. Where instructions read k1–k7 or k10 to right, knit the 1st 1–7 or 10 stitches from L.H. needle on to R.H. needle, pass the same number of stitches off remaining 2 needles on to end of previous needle.

Round 1: Knit.
Round 2: *K1, p1, in next st. Repeat from * to end of round (16 sts).
Round 3: Knit.
Round 4: As round 2 (32 sts).
Round 5: *M1, k4. Repeat from * to end of round (40 sts).
Round 6 and alternate rounds unless otherwise stated: Knit—k1, p1 into each m1 (48 sts).
Round 7, 9 and 11: K1 to right, *m1, sl 1, k1, psso, k2, k2 tog. Repeat from * to end of round (40 sts).
Round 8 and 10: As round 6 (48 sts).
Round 12: *(K1, p1) twice, k into m1, k4. Repeat from * to end of round (72 sts).
Round 13: K1 to right, *(m1, k1 tbl) 3 times, m1, sl 1, k1, psso, k2, k2 tog. Repeat from * to end of round (88 sts).
Round 14 to 22 (even numbers): As round 6 (120 sts).
Round 15, 17, 19 and 21: Knit to right, *(m1, sl 1, k2 tog, psso) 3 times, m1, sl 1, k1, psso, k2, k2 tog. Repeat from * to end of round (88 sts).
Round 23: K10 to right, *m1, k3, m2, k3, m1, (sl 1, k2 tog, psso) 3 times. Repeat from * to end of round (104 sts).
Round 24: Knit—k1, p1 in m1, (k1, p1) 3 times in each m2 (152 sts).
Round 25: K1 to right, *m1, k3, k2 tog, m1, k4 tbl, m1, sl 1, k1, psso, k3, m1, sl 1, k1, psso, k1, k2 tog. Repeat from * to end of round (152 sts).
Round 26, 28, 30, 32: As round 6 (184 sts).

Round 27: K7 to right, *m1, k6, m1, sl 1, k1, psso, k4, k2 tog, k1, sl 1, k1, psso, k4, k2 tog. Repeat from * to end of round (168 sts).
Round 29: K1 to right, *m1, k8, m1, sl 1, k1, psso, k3, k2 tog, k1, sl 1, k1, psso, k3, k2 tog. Repeat from * to end of round (168 sts).
Round 31: K1 to right, *m1, k10, m1, sl 1, k1, psso, k2, k2 tog, k1, sl 1, k1, psso, k2, k2 tog. Repeat from * to end of round (168 sts).
Round 33: K1 to right, *m1, sl 1, k1, psso, k4, m2, k4, k2 tog, m1, sl 1, k1, psso, k1, k2 tog, k1, sl 1, k1, psso, k1, k2 tog. Repeat from * to end of round (168 sts).
Round 34: As round 24 (216 sts).
Round 35: K1 to right, *m1, sl 1, k1, psso, k3, k2 tog, m1, k4 tbl, m1, sl 1, k1, psso, k3, k2 tog, m1, sl 1, k1, psso, k2 tog, k1, sl 1, k1, psso, k2 tog. Repeat from * to end of round (184 sts).
Round 36: As round 6 (216 sts).
Round 37: K1 to right, *m1, sl 1, k1, psso, k3, k2 tog, m1, k6 (m1, sl 1, k1, psso, k3, k2 tog) twice. Repeat from * to end of round (200 sts).
Round 38: As round 6 (232 sts).
Round 39: K1 to right, *m1, sl 1, k1, psso, k3, k2 tog, (m1, sl 1, k1, psso) 4 times, (m1, sl 1, k1, psso, k3, k2 tog) twice. Repeat from * to end of round (208 sts).
Round 40: As round 6 (264 sts).
Round 41 and 43: K1 to right, *m1, sl 1, k1, psso, k3, k2 tog, (m1, sl 1, k2 tog, psso) 4 times, (m1, sl 1, k1, k3, k2 tog) twice. Repeat from * to end of round (208 sts).
Round 42 and 44: As round 6 (264 sts).
Round 45: K1 to right, *m1, sl 1, k1, psso, sl 1, k2 tog, psso, k2 tog, (m1, sl 1, k2 tog, psso) 4 times, (m1, sl 1, k1, psso, sl 1, k2 tog, psso, k2 tog) twice. Repeat from * to end of round (160 sts).
Round 46: *M4, sl 1, k2 tog, psso, (m4, k1 tbl) 4 times, (m4, sl 1, k2 tog, psso) twice. Repeat from * to end of round (280 sts).
Cast off.

Above left: Shelf edgings (section 6, p.45).   *Above right*: Basket lid: Reed design (section 7, p.47).   *Above*: Preserve covers (section 5, p.43).

Table centre: Hyacinth design (section 8, p.52).

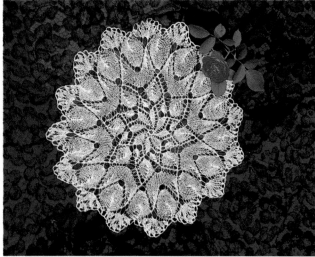

Table centre: Pansy design (section 8, p.52).

Table centre: Cosmos design (section 8, p.52).

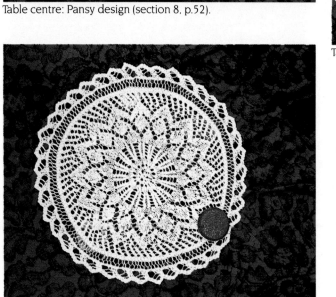

Filigree plate (section 19, p.94).

Doily 3: KRYSTYNA

Cast on 6 sts; 2 sts on each of 3 needles. Join into circle.
Round 1: *K1, m1. Repeat from * to end of round.
Round 2 and every following alternate round unless otherwise stated: K.
Round 3: *K1, m1. Repeat from * to end of round.
Round 5: *K1, m1, k3, m1. Repeat from * to end of round.
Round 7: *K1, m1, k5, m1. Repeat from * to end of round.
Round 9: *K1, m1, k7, m1. Repeat from * to end of round.
Round 11: *K1, m1, k9, m1. Repeat from * to end of round.
Round 13: *K1, m1, k11, m1. Repeat from * to end of round.
Round 15: *K1, m1, k13, m1. Repeat from * to end of round.
Round 17: *K1, m1, k15, m1. Repeat from * to end of round.
Round 19: *K1, m1, k7, k2 tog, m1, k8, m1. Repeat from * to end of round.
Round 21: *K1, m1, k7, k2 tog, m1, k1, m1, sl 1, k1, psso, k7, m1. Repeat from * to end of round.
Round 23: *K8, k2 tog, m1, k1, m2, k1, m2, k1, m1, sl 1, k1, psso, k7. Repeat from * to end of round.
Round 24 and every following alternate round unless otherwise stated: Knit, but work 2 sts (k1, p1) into the m2 of previous round.
Round 25: *K7, k2 tog, m1, sl 1, k1, psso, k1, m2, k3, m2, k1, k2 tog, m1, sl 1, k1, psso, k6. Repeat from * to end of round.
Round 27: *K6, k2 tog, m1, sl 1, k1, psso, k2, m2, k5, m2, k2, k2 tog, m1, sl 1, k1, psso, k5. Repeat from * to end of round.
Round 29: *K5, k2 tog, m1, sl 1, k1, psso, k3, m2, k7, m2, k3, k2 tog, m1, sl 1, k1, psso, k4. Repeat from * to end of round.
Round 31: *K4, k2 tog, m1, sl 1, k1, psso, k4, m2, k9, m2, k4, k2 tog, m1, sl 1, k1, psso, k3. Repeat from * to end of round.
Round 33: *K3, k2 tog, m1, sl 1, k1, psso, k5, m2, k11, m2, k5, k2 tog, m1, sl 1, k1, psso, k2. Repeat from * to end of round.

Round 35: *K2, k2 tog, m1, sl 1, k1, psso, k6, m2, k13, m2, k6, k2 tog, m1, sl 1, k1, psso, k1. Repeat from * to end of round.
Round 37: *K1, k2 tog, m1, sl 1, k1, psso, k7, m2, k15, m2, k7, k2 tog, m1, sl 1, k1, psso. Repeat from * to end of round.
Round 39: Before commencing this round sl 2 sts from L.H. needle to R.H. needle. *M1, sl 1, k1, psso, k6, k2 tog, m1, sl 1, k1, psso, k13, k2 tog, m1, sl 1, k1, psso, k6, k2 tog, m1, sl 1, k2 tog, psso. Repeat from * to end of round.
Round 41: *M1, sl 1, k1, psso, k5, k2 tog, m1, k1, m1, sl 1, k1, psso, k11, k2 tog, m1, k1, m1, sl 1, k1, psso, k5, k2 tog, m1, k1 tbl. Repeat from * to end of round.
Round 43: *M1, sl 1, k1, psso, k4, k2 tog, m1, k3, m1, sl 1, k1, psso, k9, k2 tog, m1, k3, m1, sl 1, k1, psso, k4, k2 tog, m1, k1 tbl. Repeat from * to end of round.
Round 45: *M1, sl 1, k1, psso, k3, k2 tog, m1, k5, m1, sl 1, k1, psso, k7, k2 tog, m1, k5, m1, sl 1, k1, psso, k3, k2 tog, m1, k1 tbl. Repeat from * to end of round.
Round 47: *M1, sl 1, k1, psso, k2, k2 tog, m1, k7, m1, sl 1, k1, psso, k5, k2 tog, m1, k7, m1, sl 1, k1, psso, k2, k2 tog, m1, k1 tbl. Repeat from * to end of round.
Round 49: *M1, sl 1, k1, psso, k1, (k2 tog, m1, k1, m1, sl 1, k1, psso, k3) 3 times, k2 tog, m1, k1, m1, sl 1, k1, psso, k1, k2 tog, m1, k1 tbl. Repeat from * to end of round.
Round 51: *M1, sl 1, k1, psso, (k2 tog, m1, k3, m1, sl 1, k1, psso, k1) 3 times, k2 tog, m1, k3, m1, sl 1, k1, psso, k2 tog, m1, k1 tbl. Repeat from * to end of round.
Round 53: *(M1, sl 1, k2 tog, psso, m1, k5) 4 times, m1, sl 1, k2 tog, psso, m1, k1 tbl. Repeat from * to end of round.
Round 55: *M1, sl 1, k1, psso (m1, k7, m1, k1 tbl) 3 times, m1, k7, m1, k2 tog, m1, k1 tbl. Repeat from * to end of round (264 sts).
Round 56 to 62: Knit.
Cast off loosely.

Edging

Cast on 6 sts.
Special Abbreviation: Inc 1 = k into front and back of 1st st.
Row 1: (Right side) Inc 1, (m1, k1) twice, m1, k2 tog tbl, k1 (9 sts).
Row 2 and alternate rows: Sl 1 knitwise, p to last 2 sts, p2 tog.
Row 3: Inc 1, m1, k2 tog, (m1, k1) twice, m1, k2 tog tbl, k1 (11 sts).
Row 5: Inc 1, m1, k2 tog, m1, sl 2, k1, psso, m1, k1, m1, k2 tog tbl, k1 (11 sts).
Row 7: Inc 1, m1, sl 2, k1, psso, m1, k3 tog, m1, k2 tog tbl, k1 (9 sts).
Row 9: Inc 1, m1, sl 2, k2 tog, psso, m1, k2 tog tbl, k1 (7 sts).
Row 10: As row 2 (6 sts).
Repeat rows 1–10 until length desired.
Press edging, slip stitch around centre of doily.

Doily 4: BRIGITTE

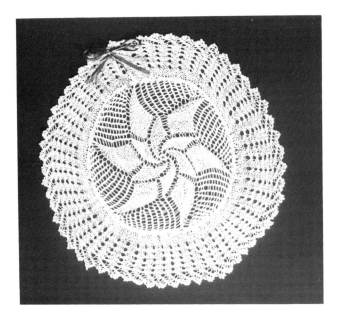

Cast on 6 sts; 2 sts on each of 3 needles. Mark beginning of round.

Round 1 and alternate rounds: Knit.
Round 2: *M1, k1. Repeat from * to end of round.
Round 4: *M1, k2. Repeat from * to end of round.
Round 6: *M1, k3. Repeat from * to end of round.
Round 8: *M1, k4. Repeat from * to end of round.
Round 10: *M1, k5. Repeat from * to end of round.
Round 12: *M1, k6. Repeat from * to end of round.
Round 14: *M1, k7. Repeat from * to end of round.
Round 16: *M1, k8. Repeat from * to end of round.
Round 18: *M1, k1, m1, sl 1, k1, psso, k6. Repeat from * to end of round.
Round 20: *M1, k3, m1, sl 1, k1, psso, k5. Repeat from * to end of round.
Round 22: *M1, k5, m1, sl 1, k1, psso, k4. Repeat from * to end of round.
Round 24: *M1, k7, m1, sl 1, k1, psso, k3. Repeat from * to end of round.
Round 26: *M1, k9, m1, sl 1, k1, psso, k2. Repeat from * to end of round.
Round 28: *M1, k11, m1, sl 1, k1, psso, k1. Repeat from * to end of round.
Round 30: *M1, k13, m1, sl 1, k1, psso. Repeat from * to end of round.
Round 32: Before commencing round, k1 st from L.H. needle on to R.H. needle, also pass the first st of remaining 2 needles on to previous needle, *sl 1, k1, psso, k11, m1, k1 tbl, m1, sl 1, k1, psso, m1. Repeat from * to end of round.
Round 34: *Sl 1, k1, psso, k10, m1, k1 tbl, (m1, sl 1, k1, psso) twice, m1. Repeat from * to end of round.
Round 36: *Sl 1, k1, psso, k9, m1, k1 tbl, (m1, sl 1, k1, psso) 3 times, m1. Repeat from * to end of round.

Round 38: *Sl 1, k1, psso, k8, m1, k1 tbl, (m1, sl 1, k1, psso) 4 times, m1. Repeat from * to end of round.
Round 40: *Sl 1, k1, psso, k7, m1, k1 tbl, (m1, sl 1, k1, psso) 5 times, m1. Repeat from * to end of round.
Round 42: *Sl 1, k1, psso, k6, m1, k1 tbl, (m1, sl 1, k1, psso) 6 times, m1. Repeat from * to end of round.
Round 44: *Sl 1, k1, psso, k5, m1, k1 tbl, (m1, sl 1, k1, psso) 7 times, m1. Repeat from * to end of round.
Round 46: *Sl 1, k1, psso, k4, m1, k1 tbl, (m1, sl 1, k1, psso) 8 times, m1. Repeat from * to end of round.
Round 48: *Sl 1, k1, psso, k3, m1, k1 tbl, (m1, sl 1, k1, psso) 9 times, m1. Repeat from * to end of round.
Round 50: *Sl 1, k1, psso, k2, m1, k1 tbl, (m1, sl 1, k1, psso) 10 times, m1. Repeat from * to end of round.
Round 52: *Sl 1, k1, psso, k1, m1, k1 tbl, (m1, sl 1, k1, psso) 11 times, m1. Repeat from * to end of round.
Round 54: *Sl 1, k1, psso, m1, k1 tbl, (m1, sl 1, k1, psso) 12 times, m1. Repeat from * to end of round.
Round 55: Knit.
Cast off loosely.

Border or Edging:
Cast on 18 sts.
Row 1: K2, (m1, k2 tog) 6 times, m1, k4.
Row 2: Knit.
Row 3: K2, m1, k2 tog, m1, p12, k3.
Row 4: Knit.
Row 5: K2, m1, k2 tog, m1, k16.
Row 6: K3, p13, k5.
Row 7: Cast off 3 sts, k to end of row.
Row 8: K3, p13, k2.
Repeat rows 1–8 until length desired. Join cast on and cast off edges. Sew garter st edge to centre of doily.

Doily 5: ELSA

Cast on 12 sts; 4 sts on each of 3 needles. Join in ring. Mark beginning of row.

Round 1: Knit.

Round 2: *M1, k2. Repeat from * to end of round (18 sts).

Round 3 and following alternate rows, unless otherwise stated: Knit, but k1, p1 into each m1 (24 sts).

Round 4: K1 to right, *m1, k4. Repeat from * to end of round (30 sts)

Round 5: (36 sts).

Round 6: K1 to right, *m1, k6. Repeat from * to end of round (42 sts).

Round 7: (48 sts).

Round 8: K1 to right, *m1, k8. Repeat from * to end of round (54 sts).

Round 9: (60 sts).

Round 10: K1 to right, *m1, k10. Repeat from * to end of round (66 sts).

Round 11: (72 sts).

Round 12: K1 to right, *m1, k12. Repeat from * to end of round (78 sts).

Round 13: (84 sts).

Round 14: K1 to right, *m1, k14. Repeat from * to end of round (90 sts).

Round 15: (96 sts).

Round 16: K1 to right, *m1, k16. Repeat from * to end of round (102 sts).

Round 17: (108 sts).

Round 18: K1 to right, *m1, k18. Repeat from * to end of round (114 sts).

Round 19: (120 sts).

Round 20: K1 to right, *m1, k20. Repeat from * to end of round (126 sts).

Round 21: As round 3 (132 sts).

Round 22 to 27: Knit.

Cast off.

Border or Edging:

Cast on 31 sts.

Knit one row.

Row 1: (Wrong side of work) k21, m1, k2 tog, k2, k2 tog, m1, k2 tog, m2, k2 (32 sts).

Row 2: Cast on 1 st, k2, k1, p1, k1, in m2 of previous row, k6, p19, k3 (34 sts).

Row 3: K22, m1, (k2 tog, k2) 3 times (32 sts).

Row 4: Cast off 2 sts, k6, (7 sts on R.H. needle) p20, turn, leave 3 sts on needle.

Row 5: Sl 1, k1, (m1, k2 tog) 7 times, k4, m1, k2 tog, k5.

Row 6: K7, p20, k3, (30 sts).

Row 7: K21, k2 tog, m1, k7 (30 sts).

Row 8: K8, p19, turn, leave 3 sts on needle.

Row 9: Sl 1, k16, k2 tog, m1, k4, m1, k2 tog, m2, k2.

Row 10: Cast on 1 st, k2, k1, p1, k1, in m2 of previous row, k7, p18, k3 (34 sts).

Row 11: K3, p16, p2 tog, m1, k4, (m1, k2 tog) twice, k5 (34 sts).

Row 12: Cast off 2 sts, k to last 3 sts, turn.

Row 13: Sl 1, p14, p2 tog, m1, k4, (m1, k2 tog) 3 times, m2, k2.

Row 14: Cast on 1 st, k2, k1, p1, k1, in m2 of previous row, k to end (36 sts).

Row 15: K3, p14, p2 tog, m1, k4, (m1, k2 tog) 4 times, k5, (36 sts).

Row 16: As row 12.

Row 17: Sl 1, p12, p2 tog, m1, k4, (m1, k2 tog) 5 times, m2, k2.

Row 18: As row 14 (38 sts).

Row 19: K3, p12, p2 tog, m1, k4, (m1, k2 tog) 6 times, k5 (38 sts).

Row 20: As row 12.

Row 21: Sl 1, k10, k2 tog, m1, k4, (m1, k2 tog) 7 times, m2, k2.

Row 22: Cast on 1 st, k2, k1, p1, k1, in m2 of previous row, k19, p12, k3 (40 sts).

Row 23: K13, k2 tog, m1, k4, (m1, k2 tog) 8 times, k5 (40 sts).

Row 24: Cast off 2 sts, k23, (24 sts on R.H. needle), p11, turn.

Row 25: Sl 1, k1, (m1, k2 tog) 3 times, m1, k3 tog, m1, k4, (m1, k2 tog) 9 times, m2, k2.

Row 26: Cast on 1 st, k2, k1, p1, k1, in m2 of previous row, k22, p11, k3 (42 sts).

Row 27: K14, m1, k2 tog, k2, k2 tog, (m1, k2 tog) 8 times, k2 tog, k4 (40 sts).

Row 28: Cast off 2 sts, k22, (23 sts on R.H. needle), p12, turn.

Row 29: Sl 1, k11, m1, k2 tog, k2, k2 tog, (m1, k2 tog) 7 times, m2, k2 tog, k1.

Row 30: Cast on 1 st, k2, k1, p1, k1 in m2 of previous row, k18, p13, k3 (40 sts).

Row 31: K3, p13, m1, k2 tog, k2, k2 tog, (m1, k2 tog) 6 times, k2 tog, k4 (38 sts).

Row 32: As row 12.

Row 33: Sl 1, p13, m1, k2 tog, k2, k2 tog, (m1, k2 tog) 5 times, m2, k2 tog, k1.

Row 34: Cast on 1 st, k2, k1, p1, k1, in m2 of previous row, k to end (38 sts).

Row 35: K3, p15, m1, k2 tog, k2, k2 tog, (m1, k2 tog) 4 times, k2 tog, k4 (36 sts).

Row 36: As row 12.

Row 37: Sl 1, p15, m1, k2 tog, k2, k2 tog, (m1, k2 tog) 3 times, m2, k2 tog, k1.

Row 38: As row 34 (36 sts).

Row 39: K3, p17, m1, k2 tog, k2, k2 tog, (m1, k2 tog) twice, k2 tog, k4, (34 sts).

Row 40: As row 12.

Row 41: Sl 1, k17, m1, k2 tog, k2, k2 tog, m1, k2 tog, m2, k2 tog, k1.

Repeat rows 2–41 until length desired, ending with row 39. Cast off.

Doily 6: ISOLDE

Cast on 8 sts; 2 sts on 2 needles, 4 sts on 3rd. Join into ring. Mark beginning of round.

Round 1: Knit.

Round 2: *M1, k1. Repeat from * to end of round.

Round 3 *and following alternate rounds*: Knit.

Round 4: *M1, k3, m1, k1 tbl. Repeat from * to end of round.

Round 6: *M1, k5, m1, k1 tbl. Repeat from * to end of round.

Round 8: *M1, k7, m1, k1 tbl. Repeat from * to end of round.

Round 10: *M1, k3, k2 tog, m1, k4, m1, k1 tbl. Repeat from * to end of round.

Round 12: *M1, k3, k2 tog, m1, k1, m1, sl 1, k1, psso, k3, m1, k1 tbl. Repeat from * to end of round.

Round 14: *M1, k3, k2 tog, m1, k3, m1, sl 1, k1, psso, k3, m1, k1 tbl. Repeat from * to end of round.

Round 16: *M1, k3, (k2 tog, m1) twice, k1, (m1, sl 1, k1, psso) twice, k3, m1, k1 tbl. Repeat from * to end of round.

Round 18: *M1, k3, (k2 tog, m1) twice, k3, (m1, sl 1, k1, psso) twice, k3, m1, k1 tbl. Repeat from * to end of round.

Round 20: As round 16. Repeat between brackets 3 times.

Round 22: As round 18. Repeat between brackets 3 times.

Round 24: As round 16. Repeat between brackets 4 times.

Round 26: *K3, (k2 tog, m1) 4 times, k3, (m1, sl 1, k1, psso) 4 times, k3, m1, k1 tbl, m1. Repeat from * to end of round.

Round 28: *Sl 1, k1, psso, k3, (m1, sl 1, k1, psso) 3 times, (m1, k1) 3 times, (m1, k2 tog) 3 times, m1, k3, k2 tog, m1, k3, m1. Repeat from * to end of round.

Round 30: *Sl 1, k1, psso, k3, (m1, sl 1, k1, psso) 3 times, m1, k2 tog, m1, k1, m1, sl 1, k1, psso (m1, k2 tog) 3 times, m1, k3, k2 tog, m1, k5, m1. Repeat from * to end of round.

Round 32: *Sl 1, k1, psso, k3, (m1, sl 1, k1, psso) 3 times, m1, k2 tog, m1, k1, m1, sl 1, k1, psso, (m1, k2 tog) 3 times, m1, k3, k2 tog, m1, k7, m1. Repeat from * to end of round.

Round 34: *Sl 1, k1, psso, k3, (m1, sl 1, k1, psso) 3 times, m1, k2 tog, m1, k1, m1, sl 1, k1, psso, (m1, k2 tog) 3 times, m1, k3, k2 tog, m1, k9, m1. Repeat from * to end of round.

Round 36: *Sl 1, k1, psso, k3, (m1, sl 1, k1, psso) 4 times, k1, (k2 tog, m1) 4 times, k3, k2 tog, m1, sl 1, k1, psso, (m1, k1 tbl) 7 times, m1, k2 tog, m1. Repeat from * to end of round.

Round 38: *Sl 1, k1, psso, k3, (m1, sl 1, k1, psso) 3 times, m1, sl 1, k2 tog, psso, (m1, k2 tog) 3 times, m1, k3, k2 tog, m1, sl 1, k1, psso, k1, (m1, k1 tbl, m1, k3) 3 times, m1, k1 tbl, m1, k1, k2 tog, m1. Repeat from * to end of round.

Round 40: *Sl 1, k1, psso, k3, (m1, sl 1, k1, psso) 3 times, k1, (k2 tog, m1) 3 times, k3, k2 tog, m1, sl 1, k2 tog, psso, k1, (m1, k1 tbl, m1, k1, k2 tog, k2) 3 times, m1, k1 tbl, m1, k1, k3 tog, m1. Repeat from * to end of round.

Round 42: *Sl 1, k1, psso, k3, (m1, sl 1, k1, psso) twice, m1, sl 1, k2 tog, psso, (m1, k2 tog) twice, m1, k3, k2 tog, m1, sl 1, k1, psso, k2, (m1, k1 tbl, m1, k6) 3 times, m1, k1 tbl, m1, k2, k2 tog, m1. Repeat from * to end of round.

Round 44: *Sl 1, k1, psso, k3, (m1, sl 1, k1, psso) twice, k1, (k2 tog, m1) twice, k3, k2 tog, m1, sl 1, k2 tog, psso, k2, (m1, k1 tbl, m1, k2, k2 tog, sl 1, k1, psso, k2) 3 times, m1, k1 tbl, m1, k2, k3 tog, m1. Repeat from * to end of round.

Round 46: *Sl 1, k1, psso, k3, m1, sl 1, k1, psso, m1, sl 1, k2 tog, psso, m1, k2 tog, m1, k3, k2 tog, m1, sl 1, k1, psso, k3, (m1, k1 tbl, m1, k8) 3 times, m1, k1 tbl, m1, k3, k2 tog, m1. Repeat from * to end of round.

Round 48: *Sl 1, k1, psso, k3, m1, sl 1, k1, psso, k1, k2 tog, m1, k3, k2 tog, m1, sl 1, k2 tog, psso, k3, (m1, k1 tbl, m1, k3, k2 tog, sl 1, k1, psso, k3) 3 times, m1, k1 tbl, m1, k3, k3 tog, m1. Repeat from * to end of round.

Round 50: *Sl 1, k1, psso, k3, m1, sl 1, k2 tog, psso, m1, k3, k2 tog, m1, sl 1, k1, psso, k10, (m1, k11) twice, m1, k10, k2 tog, m1. Repeat from * to end of round.

Round 52: *Sl 1, k1, psso, k7, k2 tog, m1, k1, p1, in next st, m1. Repeat from * to end of round.

Round 54: *Sl 1, k1, psso, k5, k2 tog, m1, k4, m1. Repeat from * to end of round.

Round 56: *Sl 1, k1, psso, k3, k2 tog, m1, k1, k2 tog, m2, sl 1, k1, psso, k1, m1. Repeat from * to end of round.

Round 57: Knit—k1, p1, k1 in each m2 of previous round.

Round 58: *Sl 1, k1, psso, k1, k2 tog, m1, sl 1, k1, psso, k5, k2 tog, m1. Repeat from * to end of round.

Round 59: Knit.

Edging

K1 to right, using crochet hook * pick up 3 sts, yarn round hook, pull yarn through all 3 sts, 12 ch. Repeat from * to end of round. Join with sl st. Cast off.

4. Bath Robe Edgings

Lace trim your towelling bath robes.

Materials

Robe 1: EDNA: Trimmed with a fairly wide lace knitted on 2¾ mm needles, with 4 ply cotton.

Robe 2: DOREEN Trimmed with a tiny pleated frill. This edging is perfect for bath robes, as it is extremely hard wearing. Use 1.75 mm needles and 4 ply cotton.

Robe 3: ROSE An eyelet lace with bold clear eyelets. This gives a crisp appearance to the lace. Use 2 mm needles and 4 ply cotton.

The quantity of cotton will depend on gown size. Buy extra and make a matching towel. Edging is attached to gown with firm fine stitches. Embroider if desired.

Robe 1: EDNA

Cast on 18 sts.

Row 1: Sl 1, k2, m1, k2 tog, k4, m1, sl 1, k1, psso, m1, sl 1, k1, psso. k5.

Row 2: K5, p10, k3.

Row 3: Sl 1, k2, m1, k2 tog, k2, k2 tog, m1, k2 tog, m1, k3, m2, k2 tog, m2, k2.

Row 4: K3, (p1, k2) twice, p9, k3 (21 sts on needle).

Row 5: Sl 1, k2, m1, k2 tog, k1, k2 tog, m1, k2 tog, m1, k11.

Row 6: K2, m2, k2 tog, k1, k2 tog, m2, k2 tog, k1, p8, k3.

Row 7: Sl 1, k2, m1, (k2 tog) twice, m1, k2 tog, m1, k5, p1, k4, p1, k2.

Row 8: K12, p7, k3.

Row 9: Sl 1, k2, m1, k2 tog, k2, m1, sl 1, k1, psso, m1, sl 1, k1, psso, k2, k2 tog, m2, sl 1, k2 tog, psso, m2, (k2 tog) twice.

Row 10: K3, p1, k2, p1, k3, p8, k3.
Row 11: Sl 1, k2, m1, k2 tog, k3, m1, sl 1, k1, psso, m1, sl 1, k1, psso, k9.
Row 12: Cast off 3, k5, p9, k3.
Repeat 1–12 until length desired.

Robe 2: DOREEN

Cast on 9 sts.
Row Knit.
Row 2: P7, turn.
Row 3: K7.
Row 4: P7, k2.
Row 5: K2, p7.
Row 6: K7, turn.
Row 7: P7.
Row 8: Knit.
Repeat rows 1–8 until length desired.

Robe 3: ROSE

Cast on 9 sts.
Row 1: Sl 2, k2, m1, k2 tog, m3, k2 tog, k1.
Row 2: M1, k2 tog, k1, p1, k3, m1, k2 tog, p2.
Row 3: Sl 2, k2, m1, k2 tog, k5.
Row 4: M1, k2 tog, k5, m1, k2 tog, p2.
Row 5: As row 3.
Row 6: As row 4.
Row 7: Sl 2, k2, m1, k2 tog, k2, m3, k2 tog, k1.
Row 8: M1, k2 tog, k1, p1, k5, m1, k2 tog, p2.
Row 9: Sl 2, k2, m1, k2 tog, p2, k5.
Row 10: K9, m1, k2 tog, p2.
Row 11: Sl 2, k2, m1, k2 tog, m3, k2 tog. Cast off last 5 sts as follows: Sl 3 sts on to R.H. needle, pass 5th st over 4th st, 4th st over 3rd, 3rd st over 2nd st until 1 st remains. Knit the remaining st.
Repeat Rows 2–11 until length desired.

5. Preserve Covers

Dainty covers for the preserves in your kitchen.

The centres with stitched floral motif are available in craft shops. The little circles could be made from scraps of material left over from the bread cloths. Turn in a tiny rolled hem or crochet around the circle, before attaching the knitted edging.

Preserve Cover No. 1 was designed to fit a large stone jar. Knit them in quality yarn, and they will last for years. The lovely lace edgings can be used on matching kitchen towels or anything needing a lace edging trim.

Preserve Cover 1: CLOVE

Cast on 260 sts.
Row 1: *M1, k2 tog, k1, k2 tog, m1, k5. Repeat from * to end of row.
Row 2 and every even numbered row: Purl.
Row 3: K1, *m1, sl 1, k2 tog, psso, m1, k7. Repeat from * to end of row.
Row 5: K5, *m1, k2 tog, k1, k2 tog, m1, k5. Repeat from * to end of row.
Row 7: K6, *m1, sl 1, k2 tog, psso, m1, k7. Repeat from * to end of row.
Row 9: *M1, k2 tog, k1, k2 tog, m1, k5. Repeat from * to end of row.
Row 11: K1, *m1, sl 1, k2 tog, psso, m1, k7. Repeat from * to end of row.
Row 13: K5, *m1, k2 tog, k1, k2 tog, m1, k5. Repeat from * to end of row.

Row 15: K6, *m1, sl 1, k2 tog, m1, k7. Repeat from * to end of row.
Row 17: M1, k2 tog, k1, k2 tog, m1, k5. Repeat from * to end of row.
Row 19: K1, *m1, sl 1, k2 tog, psso, m1, k7. Repeat from * to end of row.
Row 21: K5, k2 tog, k1, k2 tog. Repeat to end of row.
Row 23: K5, sl 1, k2 tog, psso. Repeat to end of row.
Row 25: K1, k2 tog. Repeat to end of row.
Row 27: K2 tog, m1. Repeat to end of row.
Row 28: Purl.
Row 29: Knit.
Row 30: Purl.
Row 31: K2 tog, m1. Repeat to end of row.
Row 32: Purl.
Row 33: Knit.
Row 34: Purl.
Row 35: K1, m1. Repeat to end of row.
Row 36: Purl.
Cast off.
Sew both ends together. Attach to material centre.

Preserve Cover 2: LILAC

Cast on 18 sts.
Row 1: M1, k1, m1, k2, (k2 tog) twice, k2, (m1, k2 tog) 4 times, k1.

Row 2: Sl 1, k1, p16.
Row 3: M1, k3, m1, k1, (k2 tog) twice, k1, (m1, k2 tog) 4 times, k1.
Row 4: Sl 1, k1, p16.
Row 5: M1, k5, m1, (k2 tog) twice, (m1, k2 tog) 4 times, k1.
Row 6: Sl 1, k1, p16.
Row 7: M1, k3, k2 tog, k2, (m1, k2 tog) 5 times, k1.
Row 8: Sl 1, k1, p16.
Repeat 1–8 until length desired.

Preserve Cover 3: CHERRY

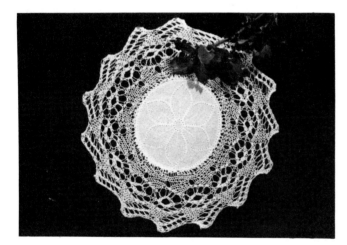

Cast on 15 sts.
Row 1: Sl 1, k4, k2 tog, m1, k1, m1, k2 tog, k1, m1, k2 tog, m1, k2.
Row 2: P16.
Row 3: Sl 1, k3, k2 tog, m1, k3, m1, k2 tog, k1, m1, k2 tog, m1, k2.
Row 4: Purl.
Row 5: Sl 1, k2, m1, (k2 tog) twice, m2, k2 tog, k1, m1, k2 tog, k1, m1, k2 tog, m1, k2.
Row 6: Purl—in m2, k and p.
Row 7: Sl 1, k4, m1, k2 tog, k1, k2 tog, m1, k4, m1, k2 tog, m1, k2.
Row 8: Purl.
Row 9: Sl 1, k5, m1, sl 1, k2 tog, psso, m1, k6, m1, k2 tog, m1, k2.
Row 10: Purl.
Row 11: Knit.
Row 12: Cast off 5 sts, p14.
Repeat rows 1–12 until length desired.

Preserve Cover 4: CUMQUAT

Cast on 14 sts.
Row 1: Sl 1, k2, m1, k2 tog, k1, (m2, k2 tog) 4 times.
Row 2: (K2, p1) 4 times, k3, m1, k2 tog, k1.
Row 3: Sl 1, k2, m1, k2 tog, k13.
Row 4: K15, m1, k2 tog, k1.
Row 5: Sl 1, k2, m1, k2 tog, k13.
Row 6: Cast off 4 sts, k11, m1, k2 tog, k1.
Repeat until length desired.

Preserve Cover 5: DAMSON

Cast on 9 sts.
Row 1: Sl 1, k1, m1, k2 tog, (m1, k1) 3 times, m1, k2.
Row 2: P11, k2.
Row 3: Sl 1, k1, m1, k2 tog, m1, k3, m1, k1, m1, k3, m1, k2.
Row 4: P15, k2.
Row 5: Sl 1, k1, m1, k2 tog, m1, sl 2, k3 tog, psso, m1, k1, m1, sl 2, k3 tog, psso, m1, k2.
Row 6: Cast off 6 sts, p6, k2.
Repeat rows 1–6 until length desired.

6. Shelf Edgings

Complement your ceramics with beribboned edgings. This kitchen corner displays three designs.

Top Shelf: STAMEN
A 19th century pattern featuring a woven type of knitting, edged with tiny pleats. A ribbon has been threaded through the eyelets.

Middle Shelf: HOLLY
The familiar holly pattern seems ideal for the kitchen shelf. The knobs, or berries, given an interesting texture to the edging.

Bottom Shelf: SPIRAL
An easy effective trim for shelves. Spiral can be used in many projects. Also shown edging the bread cloth in the corner.

Materials:

The width of your shelves will determine the amount of cotton. The shelves illustrated used:
2 balls 4 ply cotton (50 gm)
Pair of 2 mm needles.
Narrow ribbon to trim.
The edgings were attached to the shelves with double-sided adhesive tape.

Shelf Edging 1: STAMEN

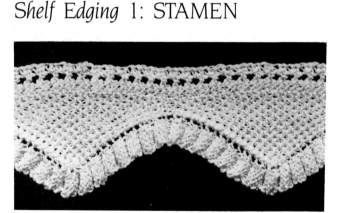

Cast on 16 sts.
Sl 1—worked purlwise in this pattern
Row 1: Sl 1, k2 tog, m2, k2 tog, k1 (p1, sl 1) twice, p1, m1, p5, turn, k5, turn, p5.
Row 2: P11, k3, p1, k2.

Row 3: Sl 1, k5, (sl 1, p1) 3 times, m1, k5, turn, p5, turn, k5.
Row 4: K5, p7, k6.
Row 5: Sl 1, k2 tog, m2, k2 tog, k1, (p1, sl 1) 3 times, p1, m1, p5, turn, k5, turn, p5.
Row 6: P13, k3, p1, k2.
Row 7: Sl 1, k5, (sl 1, p1) 4 times, m1, k5, turn, p5, turn, k5.
Row 8: K5, p9, k6.
Row 9: Sl 1, k2 tog, m2, k2 tog, k1, (p1, sl 1) 4 times, p1, m1, p5, turn, k5, turn, p5.
Row 10: P15, k3, p1, k2.
Row 11: Sl 1, k5, (sl 1, p1) 5 times, m1, k5, turn, p5, turn, k5.
Row 12: K5, p11, k6.
Row 13: Sl 1, k2 tog, m2, k2 tog, k1, (p1, sl 1) 5 times, p1, m1, p5, turn, k5, turn, p5.
Row 14: P17, k3, p1, k2.
Row 15: Sl 1, k5, (sl 1, p1) 6 times, m1, k5, turn, p5, turn, k5.
Row 16: K5, p13, k6.
Row 17: Sl 1, k2 tog, m2, k2 tog, k1, (p1, sl 1) 6 times, p1, m1, p5, turn, k5, turn, p5.
Row 18: P19, k3, p1, k2.
Row 19: Sl 1, k5, (sl 1, p1) 7 times, m1, k5, turn, p5, turn, k5.
Row 20: K5, p15, k6.
Row 21: Sl 1, k2 tog, m2, k2 tog, k1, (p1, sl 1) 7 times, p1, m1, p5, turn, k5, turn, p5.
Row 22: P21, k3, p1, k2.
Row 23: Sl 1, k5, (sl 1, p1) 8 times, m1, k5, turn, p5, turn, k5.
Row 24: K5, p17, k6.
Row 25: Sl 1, k2 tog, m2, k2 tog, k1, (p1, sl 1) 8 times, p1, m1, p5, turn, k5, turn, p5.
Row 26: P23, k3, p1, k2.
Row 27: Sl 1, k5, (sl 1, p1) 9 times, m1, k5, turn, p5, turn, k5.
Row 28: K5, p19, k6.
Row 29: Sl 1, k2 tog, m2, k2 tog, k1 (p1, sl 1) 9 times, p1, m1, p5, turn, k5, turn, p5.
Row 30: P25, k3, p1, k2.
Row 31: Sl 1, k5, (sl 1, p1) 10 times, m1, k5, turn, p5, turn, k5.
Row 32: K5, p1, p3 tog, p17, k6.
Row 33: Sl 1, k2 tog, m2, k2 tog, k1, (p1, sl 1) 9 times, p1, m1, p5, turn, k5, turn, p5.
Row 34: P6, p3 tog, p16, k3, p1, k2.
Row 35: Sl 1, k5, (sl 1, p1) 9 times, m1, k5, turn, p5, turn, k5.
Row 36: K5, p1, p3 tog, p15, k6.
Row 37: Sl 1, k2 tog, m2, k2 tog, k1, (p1, sl 1) 8 times, p1, m1, p5, turn, k5, turn, p5.
Row 38: P6, p3 tog, p14, k3, p1, k2.
Row 39: Sl 1, k5, (sl 1, p1) 8 times, m1, k5, turn, p5, turn, k5.
Row 40: K5, p1, p3 tog, p13, k6.

Row 41: Sl 1, k2 tog, m2, k2 tog, k1, (p1, sl 1) 7 times, p1, m1, p5, turn, k5, turn, p5.
Row 42: P6, p3 tog, p12, k3, p1, k2.
Row 43: Sl 1, k5, (sl 1, p1) 7 times, m1, k5, turn, p5, turn, k5.
Row 44: K5, p1, p3 tog, p11, k6.
Row 45: Sl 1, k2 tog, m2, k2 tog, k1, (p1, sl 1) 6 times, p1, m1, p5, turn, k5, turn, p5.
Row 46: P6, p3 tog, p10, k3, p1, k2.
Row 47: Sl 1, k5, (sl 1, p1) 6 times, m1, k5, turn, p5, turn, k5.
Row 48: K5, p1, p3 tog, p9, k6.
Row 49: Sl 1, k2 tog, m2, k2 tog, k1, (p1, sl 1) 5 times, p1, m1, p5, turn, k5, turn, p5.
Row 50: P6, p3 tog, p8, k3, p1, k2.
Row 51: Sl 1, k5, (sl 1, p1) 5 times, m1, k5, turn, p5, turn, k5.
Row 52: K5, p1, p3 tog, p7, k6.
Row 53: Sl 1, k2 tog, m2, k2 tog, k1, (p1, sl 1) 4 times, p1, m1, p5, turn, k5, turn, p5.
Row 54: P6, p3 tog, p6, k3, p1, k2.
Row 55: Sl 1, k5, (sl 1, p1) 4 times, m1, k5, turn, p5, turn, k5.
Row 56: K5, p1, p3 tog, p5, k6.
Row 57: Sl 1, k2 tog, m2, k2 tog, k1, (p1, sl 1) 3 times, p1, m1, p5, turn, k5, turn, p5.
Row 58: P6, p3 tog, p4, k3, p1, k2.
Row 59: Sl 1, k5, (sl 1, p1) 3 times, m1, k5, turn, p5, turn, k5.
Row 60: K5, p1, p3 tog, p3, k6.
Repeat rows 1–60 until length desired.

Shelf Edging 2: HOLLY

Cast on 16 sts.
Row 1: M1, k1, k2 tog, m1, k9, k2 tog, m1, k2.
Row 2: P4, k13.
Row 3: M1, k1, k2 tog, m1, k11, m1, k2 tog, k1.
Row 4: P4, k14.
Row 5: M1, k1, k2 tog, m1, k5, mb. (Each bobble is made thus—k3 in 1 st, turn, m1, p3, turn, m1, k4, turn, p5, turn, k2 tog, k1, k2 tog, turn, p3, turn, sl 1, k2 tog, psso), k5, k2 tog, m1, k2.
Row 6: P4, k15.
Row 7: M1, k1, k2 tog, m1, k13, m1, k2 tog, k1.
Row 8: P4, k16.
Row 9: M1, k1, k2 tog, m1, k13, k2 tog, m1, k2.
Row 10: P4, k17.

Row 11: M1, k1, k2 tog, m1, k5, mb, k9, m1, k2 tog, k1.
Row 12: P4, k18.
Row 13: M1, k1, k2 tog, m1, k15, k2 tog, m1, k2.
Row 14: P4, k19.
Row 15: M1, k1, k2 tog, m1, k17, m1, k2 tog, k1.
Row 16: P4, k20.
Row 17: M1, k1, k2 tog, m1, k5, mb, k11, k2 tog, m1, k2.
Row 18: P4, k21.
Row 19: M1, k2 tog twice, m1, k2 tog, k16, m1, k2 tog, k1.
Row 20: P4, k20.
Row 21: M1, k2 tog twice, m1, k2 tog, k14, k2 tog, m1, k2.
Row 22: P4, k19.
Row 23: M1, k2 tog twice, m1, k2 tog, k4, mb, k9, m1, k2 tog, k1.
Row 24: P4, k18.
Row 25: M1, k2 tog twice, m1, k2 tog, k12, k2 tog, m1, k2.
Row 26: P4, k17.
Row 27: M1, k2 tog twice, m1, k2 tog, k12, m1, k2 tog, k1.
Row 28: P4, k16.
Row 29: M1, k2 tog twice, m1, k2 tog, k4, mb, k5, k2 tog, m1, k2.
Row 30: P4, k15.
Row 31: M1, k2 tog twice, m1, k2 tog, k10, m1, k2 tog, k1.
Row 32: P4, k14.
Row 33: M1, k2 tog twice, m1, k2 tog, k8, k2 tog, m1, k2.
Row 34: P4, k13.
Row 35: M1, k2 tog twice, m1, k2 tog, k4, mb, k3, m1, k2 tog, k1.
Row 36: P4, k12.
Repeat 1–36.

Shelf Edging 3: SPIRAL

Cast on 24 sts.
Row 1: K2 (m1, k2 tog, k2) 5 times, m1, k2.
Wrong side of work:
Row 2 and alternate rows: Knit.
Row 3: K3, (m1, k2 tog, k2) 5 times, m1, k2.
Row 5: K4, (m1, k2 tog, k2) 5 times, m1, k2.
Row 7: K5, (m1, k2 tog, k2) 5 times, m1, k2.
Row 8: Cast off 4 sts, knit to end of row.
Repeat rows 1–8 until length desired.

7. Basket Lids

Basket lids have many uses. The ones illustrated are very elegant. These are suitable to cover picnic baskets. The lids are an attractive way to cover the clutter in work or magazine baskets. Try knitted lids as an alternative to gingham in a country decor.

The patterns for the basket lids would also make attractive tray cloths.

Materials:

Use either 4 ply cotton or, for a finer lid, 20 cotton.

Basket Lid 1: REED

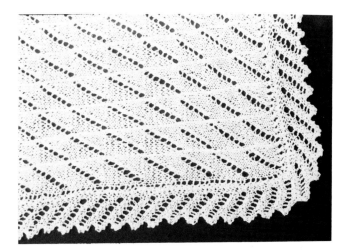

Cast on 139 sts.
Row 1: Right side of work, k1, *m1, k2 tog* to end of row.
Row 2: Purl.
Row 3: K2 tog, m1, *k6, k2 tog, m1, p1. Repeat from * until last 2 sts, m1, k2 tog.
Row 4: K2 tog, m1, *k1, p8. Repeat from * until last 2 sts, m1, k2 tog.
Row 5: K2 tog, m1, *k5, k2 tog, m1, p2. Repeat from * until last 2 sts, m1, k2 tog.
Row 6: K2 tog, m1, *k2, p7. Repeat from * until last 2 sts, m1, k2 tog.
Row 7: K2 tog, m1, *k4, k2 tog, m1, p3. Repeat from * until last 2 sts, m1, k2 tog.
Row 8: K2 tog, m1, *k3, p6. Repeat from * until last 2 sts, m1, k2 tog.

Row 9: K2 tog, m1, *k3, k2 tog, m1, p4. Repeat from * until last 2 sts, m1, k2 tog.
Row 10: K2 tog, m1, *k4, p5. Repeat from * until last 2 sts, m1, k2 tog.
Row 11: K2 tog, m1, *k2, k2 tog, m1, p5. Repeat from * until last 2 sts, m1, k2 tog.
Row 12: K2 tog, m1, *k5, p4. Repeat from * until last 2 sts, m1, k2 tog.
Row 13: K2 tog, m1, *k1, k2 tog, m1, p6. Repeat from * until last 2 sts, m1, k2 tog.
Row 14: K2 tog, m1, *k6, p3. Repeat from * until last 2 sts, m1, k2 tog.
Row 15: K2 tog, m1, *k2 tog, m1, p7. Repeat from * until last 2 sts, m1, k2 tog.
Row 16: K2 tog, m1, *k7, p2. Repeat from * until last 2 sts, m1, k2 tog.
Repeat rows 3–16 until 12 patterns have been worked then repeat rows 1 and 2 once.
Cast off.

Edging:

Cast on 8 sts.
Row 1: (Wrong side of work) k2, m1, k2 tog, k2, m1, k2.
Row 2 and alternate rows: Knit.
Row 3: K3, m1, k2 tog, k2, m1. k2.
Row 5: K4, m1, k2 tog, k2, m1. k2.
Row 7: K5, m1, k2 tog, k4.
Row 8: Cast off 3 sts, k8.
Continue these 8 rows until length desired.
Cast off.
Sew edging to centre, allowing fullness at the corners.
Press lightly.

Basket Lid 2: PLAIT

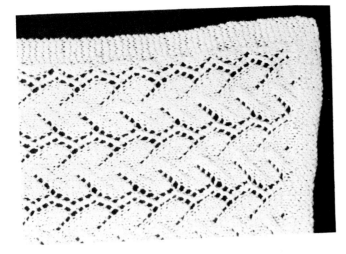

Cast on 109 sts.
Knit 9 rows.
Row 10: K6, purl to last 6 sts, k6.
Pattern
Row 1: Right side of lid. K7, *k2 tog, m1, k5, m1, k1, sl 1, k1, psso, k2 tog, k1, m1. Repeat from * to last 11 sts, k2 tog, m1, k9.
Row 2 and alternate rows: K6, purl to last 6 sts, k6.
Row 3: K7, m1, *sl 1, k1, psso, m1, k1, sl 1, k1, psso, k4, k2 tog, (k1, m1) twice. Repeat from * to last 11 sts, sl 1, k1, psso, m1, k1, sl 1, k1, psso, k6.
Row 5: K8, *m1, sl 1, k1, psso, m1, k1, sl 1, k1, psso, k2, k2 tog, k1, m1, k3. Repeat from * to last 10 sts, (m1, sl 1, k1, psso) twice, k6.
Row 7: K9, *m1, sl 1, k1, psso, m1, k1, sl 1, k1, psso, k2 tog, k1, m1, k5. Repeat from * to last 9 sts, m1, k2 tog, k7.
Row 9: K6, k2 tog, k1, *m1, k2 tog (m1, k1) twice, sl 1, k1, psso, k4, k2 tog, k1. Repeat from * to last 9 sts, m1, k2 tog, m1, k7.
Row 11: K6, k2 tog, *m1, k2 tog, m1, k3, m1, k1, sl 1, k1, psso, k2, k2 tog, k1. Repeat from * to last 10 sts, m1, k2 tog, m1, k8.
Row 12: K6, purl to last 6 sts, k6.
These 12 rows form the pattern. Repeat 15 times, then work rows 1–4. Knit 9 rows. Cast off. Press lid under damp cloth.

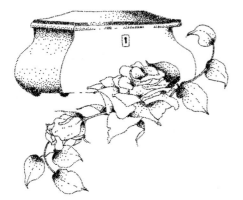

Basket Lid 3: TREFOIL

Cast on 95 sts. Purl one row. Knit 7 rows stocking stitch.
Row 8: K6, (m1, sl 1, k2 tog, psso, m1, k1) 20 times, m1, sl 1, k2 tog, psso, m1, k6.
Row 9: Purl.
Row 10: K13, sl 1, k2 tog, psso, (m1, k1, m2, k1, m2, k1, m1, sl 1, k2 tog, psso, k11, sl 1, k2 tog, psso) 3 times, m1, k1, (m2, k1) twice, m1, sl 1, k2 tog, psso, k13.
Row 11 and every alternate row, unless otherwise stated: P, work k1, p1, in m2 of previous row.
Row 12: K5, k2 tog, m1, k1, (m1, sl 1, k2 tog, psso) twice, (m1, sl 1, k1, psso, k1, m2, k3, m2, k1, k2 tog, m1, sl 1, k2 tog, psso, m1, sl 1, k2 tog, psso, m1, k1, m1, sl 1, k2 tog, psso, m1, sl 1, k2 tog, psso) 3 times, m1, sl 1, k1, psso, k1, m2, k3, m2, k1, k2 tog, (m1, sl 1, k2 tog, psso) twice, m1, k1, m1, sl 1, k1, psso, k5.
Row 14: K9, sl 1, k2 tog, psso, (m1, sl 1, k1, psso, k2, m2, k5, m2, k2, k2 tog, m1, sl 1, k2 tog, psso, k3, sl 1, k2 tog, psso) 3 times, m1, sl 1, k1, psso, k2, m2, k5, m2, k2, k2 tog, m1, sl 1, k2 tog, psso, k9.
Row 16: K6, m1, sl 1, k2 tog, psso, m1, k1, (m1, sl 1, k1, psso, k3, m2, k7, m2, k3, k2 tog, m1, k1, m1, sl 1, k2 tog, psso, m1, k1) 3 times, m1, sl 1, k1, psso, k3, m2, k7, m2, k3, k2 tog, m1, k1, m1, sl 1, k2 tog, psso, m1, k6.
Row 18: K7, sl 1, k2 tog, psso, (m1, sl 1, k1, psso, k4, m2, k9, m2, k4, k2 tog, m1, sl 1, k1, psso, k1, k2 tog) 3 times, m1, sl 1, k1, psso, k4, m2, k9, m2, k4, k2 tog, m1, sl 1, k2 tog, psso, k7.
Row 20: K6, m1, k2 tog, (m1, sl 1, k1, psso, k3, k2 tog, m1, sl 1, k1, psso, k7, k2 tog, m1, sl 1, k1, psso, k3, k2 tog, m1, sl 1, k2 tog, psso) 3 times, m1, sl 1, k1, psso, k3, k2 tog, m1, sl 1, k1, psso, k7, k2 tog, m1, sl 1, k1, psso, k3, k2 tog, m1, sl 1, k1, psso, m1, k6.
Row 21 and next eleven alternate rows: Purl.
Row 22: K6, m1, sl 1, k1, psso, (m1, sl 1, k1, psso, k2, k2 tog, m1, k1, m1, sl 1, k1, psso, k5, k2 tog, m1, k1, m1, sl 1, k1, psso, k2, k2 tog, m1, k1 tbl) 3 times, m1, sl 1, k1, psso, k2, k2 tog, m1, k1, m1, sl 1, k1, psso, k5, k2 tog, m1, k1, m1, sl 1, k1, psso, k2, k2 tog, m1, k2 tog, m1, k6.
Row 24: K6, m1, sl 1, k1, psso, (m1, sl 1, k1, psso, k1, k2

tog, m1, k3, m1, sl 1, k1, psso, k3, k2 tog, m1, k3, m1, sl 1, k1, psso, k1, k2 tog, m1, k1 tbl) 3 times, m1, sl 1, k1, psso, k1, k2 tog, m1, k3, m1, sl 1, k1, psso, k3, k2 tog, m1, k3, m1, sl 1, k1, psso, k1, k2 tog, m1, k2 tog, m1, k6.

Row 26: K6, m1, sl 1, k1, psso, (m1, sl 1, k1, psso, k2 tog, m1, sl 1, k1, psso, k1, k2 tog, m1, sl 1, k1, psso, k1, k2 tog, m1, sl 1, k1, psso, k1, k2 tog, m1, sl 1, k1, psso, k2 tog, m1, k1 tbl) 3 times, m1, sl 1, k1, psso, k2 tog, (m1, sl 1, k1, psso, k1, k2 tog) 3 times, m1, sl 1, k1, psso, k2 tog, m1, k2 tog, m1, k6.

Row 28: K6, m1, sl 1, k1, psso, *(M1, sl 1, k2 tog, psso, m1, k1) 4 times, m1, sl 1, k2 tog, psso, m1, k1 tbl. Repeat from * twice, m1, sl 1, k2 tog, psso, (m1, k1, m1, sl 1, k2 tog, psso) 4 times, m1, k2 tog, m1, k6.

Row 30: Knit.

Row 32: As row 8.

Row 34: K13, sl 1, k2 tog, psso, m1, (k1, m2) twice, k1, m1, sl 1, k2 tog, psso, k51, sl 1, k2 tog, psso, m1, k1, (m2, k1) twice, m1, sl 1, k2 tog, psso, k13.

Row 36: K5, k2 tog, m1, k1, (m1, sl 1, k2 tog, psso) twice, m1, sl 1, k1, psso, k1, m2, k3, m2, k1, k2 tog, m1, sl 1, k2 tog, psso, (m1, sl 1, k2 tog, psso, m1, k1) 11 times, (m1, sl 1, k2 tog, psso) twice, m1, sl 1, k1, psso, k1, m2, k3, m2, k1, k2 tog, (m1, sl 1, k2 tog, psso) twice, m1, k1, m1, sl 1, k1, psso, k5.

Row 38: K9, sl 1, k2 tog, psso, m1, sl 1, k1, psso, k2, m2, k5, m2, k2, k2 tog, m1, sl 1, k2 tog, psso, k43, sl 1, k2 tog, psso, m1, sl 1, k1, psso, k2, m2, k5, m2, k2, k2 tog, m1, sl 1, k2 tog, psso, k9.

Row 40: K6, m1, sl 1, k2 tog, psso, m1, k1, m1, sl 1, k1, psso, k3, m2, k7, m2, k3, k2 tog, (m1, k1, m1, sl 1, k2 tog, psso) 11 times, m1, k1, m1, sl 1, k1, psso, k3, m2, k7, m2, k3, k2 tog, m1, k1, m1, sl 1, k2 tog, psso, m1, k6.

Row 42: K7, sl 1, k2 tog, psso, m1, sl 1, k1, psso, k4, m2, k9, m2, k4, k2 tog, m1, sl 1, k2 tog, psso, k39, sl 1, k2 tog, psso, m1, sl 1, k1, psso, k4, m2, k9, m2, k4, k2 tog, m1, sl 1, k2 tog, psso, k7.

Row 44: K6, m1, k2 tog, m1, sl 1, k1, psso, k3, k2 tog, m1, sl 1, k1, psso, k7, k2 tog, m1, sl 1, k1, psso, k3, k2 tog, m1, sl 2, k2 tog, psso, (m1, k1, m1, sl 1, k2 tog, psso) 8 times, m1, k1, m1, sl 2, k2 tog, psso, m1, sl 1, k1, psso, k3, k2 tog, m1, sl 1, k1, psso, k7, k2 tog, m1, sl 1, k1, psso, k3, k2 tog, m1, sl 1, k1, psso, m1, k6.

Row 45 *and every alternate row, unless otherwise stated:* Purl.

Row 46: K6, (m1, sl 1, k1, psso) twice, k2, k2 tog, m1, k1, m1, sl 1, k1, psso, k5, k2 tog, m1, k1, m1, sl 1, k1, psso, k2, k2 tog, m1, sl 1, k1, psso, k33, k2 tog, m1, sl 1, k1, psso, k2, k2 tog, m1, k1, m1, sl 1, k1, psso, k5, k2 tog, m1, k1, m1, sl 1, k1, psso, k2, k2 tog, m1, sl 1, k1, psso, m1, k6.

Row 48: K6, (m1, sl 1, k1, psso) twice, k1, k2 tog, m1, k3, m1, sl 1, k1, psso, k3, k2 tog, m1, k3, m1, sl 1, k1, psso, k1, k2 tog, (m1, sl 1, k2 tog, psso, m1, k1) 8 times, m1, sl 1, k2 tog, psso, m1, sl 1, k1, psso, k1, k2 tog, m1, k3, m1, sl 1, k1, psso, k3, k2 tog, m1, k3, m1, sl 1, k1, psso, k1, k2 tog, m1, sl 1, k1, psso, m1, k6.

Row 50: K6 (m1, sl 1, k1, psso) twice, k2 tog, (m1, sl 1, k1, psso, k1, k2 tog) 3 times, m1, sl 1, k1, psso, k2 tog, m1, k33, m1, sl 1, k1, psso, k2 tog, (m1, sl 1, k1, psso, k1, k2

tog) 3 times, m1, sl 1, k1, psso, k2 tog, m1, sl 1, k1, psso, m1, k6.

Row 52: K6, m1, sl 1, k1, psso, (m1, sl 1, k2 tog, psso, m1, k1) 17 times, m1, sl 1, k2 tog, psso, m1, sl 1, k1, psso, m1, k6.

Row 54: Knit.

Row 56: K6, (m1, sl 1, k2 tog, psso, m1, k1) 18 times, m1, sl 1, k2 tog, psso, m1, k6.

Row 58: K13, sl 1, k2 tog, psso, m1, k1, (m2, k1) twice, m1, k49, m1, k1, (m2, k1) twice, m1, sl 1, k2 tog, psso, k13.

Row 59: Purl, work k1, p1 into m2 of previous row.

Row 60: K5, k2 tog, m1, k1, (m1, sl 1, k2 tog, psso) twice, m1, sl 1, k1, psso, k1, m2, k3, m2, k1, k2 tog, (m1, k1, m1, sl 1, k2 tog, psso) 12 times, m1, k4, m1, sl 1, k1, psso, k1, m2, k3, m2, k1, k2 tog, (m1, sl 1, k2 tog, psso) twice, m1, k1, m1, sl 1, k1, psso, k5.

Row 61: As row 59.

Row 62 *to* 109: Repeat rows 38 to 61, twice.

Row 110 *to* 129: Repeat rows 38 to 57 twice.

Row 130: K13, sl 1, k2 tog, psso, m1, k1, (m2, k1) twice, m1, k13, m1, k1, (m2, k1) twice, m1, sl 1, k2 tog, psso, k11, sl 1, k2 tog, psso, m1, k1, (m2, k1) twice, m1, k13, m1, k1, (m2, k1) twice, m1, sl 1, k2 tog, psso, k13.

Row 131 *to* 151: Repeat rows 11 to 31.

Row 152: As row 8.

Row 153: As row 9.

Work 6 rows st st.

Cast off loosely.

Edging: Cast on 7 sts.

Row 1: K3, m1, k2 tog tbl, m2, k2.

Row 2: K3, p1, k2, m1, k2 tog tbl, k1 tbl.

Row 3: K3, m1, k2 tog tbl, k4.

Row 4: Cast off 2 sts, k4, m1, k2 tog tbl, k1 tbl.

Repeat rows 1–4 until length desired.

Basket Lid 4: WILLOW

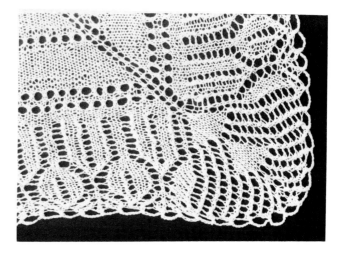

Using 2 needles, cast on 18 sts. Knit one row into back of sts, rearranging the sts on to 3 needles (6 sts on each needle).

Round 1: *K1, m1, k7, m1, k1. Repeat from * to end of round.

Round 2 and every alternate round unless otherwise stated: Knit.

Round 3: *M1, k1, m1, k9, m1, k1. Repeat from * to end of round.

Round 5: *(M1, k1) twice, m1, k11, m1, k1. Repeat from * to end of round.

Round 7: *M1, k3, m1, k1, m1, k13, m1, k1. Repeat from * to end of round.

Round 8: Knit.

Repeat rows 7 and 8, 6 times, working 2 more sts in each st st section on the pattern row.

Round 21: *M1, k17, m1, k1, m1, k27, m1, k1. Repeat from * to end of round.

Round 22: Purl.

Round 23: *M1, k19, m1, k1, m1, k29, m1, k1. Repeat from * to end of round.

Round 24: Purl.

Round 25: *M1, (k2 tog, m1) 5 times, k1, (m1, k2 tog) 5 times, m1, k1, m1, (k2 tog, m1) 7 times, sl 1, k2 tog, psso, (m1, k2 tog) 7 times, m1, k1.Repeat from * to end of round.

Round 26: Purl.

Round 27: *M1, k23, m1, k1, m1, k15, k3 in next st, k15, m1, k1. Repeat from * to end of round.

Round 28: Purl.

Round 29: *M1, k25, m1, k1, m1, k35, m1, k1. Repeat from * to end of round.

Round 30: Knit, rearranging the sts on to 4 needles (28, 38, 28, 38 sts).

Round 31: *M1, k27, m1, k1, m1, k37, m1, k1. Repeat from * to end of round.

Round 32: Knit.

Repeat rows 31–32 twice, working 2 sts more in st st section as before.

Round 37: *M1, k33, m1, k1, m1, k43, m1, k1. Repeat from * to end of round.

Round 38: Purl.

Round 39: *M1, k35, m1, k1, m1, k45, m1, k1. Repeat from * to end of round.

Round 40: Purl.

Round 41: *M1, (k2 tog, m1) 9 times, k1, (m1, k2 tog) 9 times, m1, k1, m1, (k2 tog, m1) 11 times, sl 1, k2 tog, psso, (m1, k2 tog) 11 times, m1, k1. Repeat from * to end of round.

Round 42: Purl.

Round 43: *M1, k39, m1, k1, m1, k23, k3 in next st, k23, m1, k1. Repeat from * to end of round.

Round 44: Purl.

Round 45: *M1, k41, m1, k1, m1, k51, m1, k1. Repeat from * to end of round.

Round 46: Knit.

Repeat rows 45–46 3 times, working 2 sts more in st st section as before.

Round 53: *M1, k49, m1, k1, m1, k59, m1, k1. Repeat from * to end of round.

Round 54: Purl.

Round 55: *M1, k51, m1, k1, m1, k61, m1, k1. Repeat from * to end of round.

Round 56: Purl.

Round 57: *M1, k53, m1, k1, m1, k63, m1, k1. Repeat from * to end of round.

Round 58: Purl.

Round 59: *M1, (k2 tog, m1) 13 times, sl 1, k2 tog, psso, (m1, k2 tog) 13 times, m1, k1, m1, (k2 tog, m1) 16 times, k1, (m1, k2 tog) 16 times, m1, k1. Repeat from * to end of round.

Round 60: Purl.

Round 61: *M1, k27, k3 in next st, k27, m1, k1, m1, k67, m1, k1. Repeat from * to end of round.

Round 62: Purl.

Round 63: *M1, (k2 tog, m1) 14 times, sl 1, k2 tog, psso, (m1, k2 tog) 14 times, m1, k1, m1, (k2 tog, m1) 17 times, k1, (m1, k2 tog) 17 times, m1, k1. Repeat from * to end of round.

Round 64: Purl.

Round 65: *M1, k29, k3 in next st, k29, m1, k1, m1, k71, m1, k1. Repeat from * to end of round.

Round 66: Purl.

Round 67: *M1, k63, m1, k1, m1, k73, m1, k1. Repeat from * to end of round.

Round 68: Purl.

Round 69: *M1, k65, m1, k1, m1, k75, m1, k1. Repeat from * to end of round.

Round 70: *K33, k2 tog, k111. Repeat from * to end of round.

From now on—where pattern is included in the instructions work thus—(k1, m1, k2 tog, m1, k2 tog, m1, k2, sl 1, k1, psso, m1, k1) stated times.

Round 71: *M1, work 6 patterns, m1, k1, m1, work 7 patterns, m1, k1. Repeat from * to end of round.

Round 73: *K1, m1, work 6 patterns, m1, k3, m1, work 7 patters, m1, k2. Repeat from * to end of round.

Round 75: *K2, m1, work 6 patterns, m1, k5, m1, work 7 patterns, m1, k3. Repeat from * to end of round.

Round 77: *K3, m1, work 6 patterns, m1, k1, m1, work 7 patterns, m1, k4. Repeat from * to end of round.

Round 79: *K4, m1, work 6 patterns, m1, k9, m1, work 7 patterns, m1, k5. Repeat from * to end of round.

Round 81: *K5, m1, work 6 patterns, m1, k11, m1, work 7 patterns, m1, k6. Repeat from * to end of round.

Round 83: *M1, (k2 tog, m1) 3 times, work 6 patterns, (m1, k2 tog) 3 times, m1, k1, (m1, k2 tog) 3 times, m1, work 7 patterns, m1, (k2 tog, m1) 3 times, k1. Repeat from * to end of round.

Round 85: *K1, m1, (k2 tog, m1) 3 times, work 6 patterns, (m1, k2 tog) 3 times, m1, k3, (m1, k2 tog) 3 times, m1, work 7 patterns, m1, (k2 tog, m1) 3 times, k2. Repeat from * to end of round.

Round 87: *K2, m1, (k2 tog, m1) 3 times, **(k2, m1, (k2 tog) twice, m1, k1, sl 1, k1, psso, m1, k2)** 6 times, (m1, k2 tog) 3 times, m1, k5, m1, (k2 tog, m1) 3 times. Repeat **—** 7 times, (m1, k2 tog) 3 times, m1, k3. Repeat from * to end of round.

Round 89: *K3, m1, (k2 tog, m1) 3 times, **(k3, m1, k2 tog, k1, sl 1, k1, psso, m1, k3)** 6 times, (m1, k2 tog) 3 times, m1, k7, (m1, k2 tog) 3 times, m1. Repeat **—** 7 times, (m1, k2 tog) 3 times, m1, k4. Repeat from * to end of round.

Round 91: *K4, (m1, k2 tog) 3 times, m1, k4, **(m1, sl 1, k2 tog, psso, m1, k2 tog, k2, m1, k2, sl 1, k1, psso)** 5 times, m1, sl 1, k2 tog, psso, m1, k4, (m1, k2 tog) 3 times, m1, k9, (m1, k2 tog) 3 times, m1, k4. Repeat from **—** 6 times, m1, sl 1, k2 tog, psso, m1, k4, (m1, k2 tog) 3 times, m1, k5. Repeat from * to end of round.

Round 93: *K5 (m1, k2 tog) 4 times, k3, m1, **(k1, m1, k2 tog, k1, k2 tog, m1, k2, sl 1, k1, psso, m1)** 5 times, k1, m1, k3, (k2 tog, m1) 4 times, k11, (m1, k2 tog) 4 times, k3, m1. Repeat from **—** 6 times, k1, m1, k3 (k2 tog, m1) 4 times, k6. Repeat from * to end of round.

Round 95: *(M1, k2 tog) 7 times, k3, m1, **(k1, m1, k2 tog, k1, k2 tog, m1, k2, sl 1, k1, psso, m1)** 5 times, k1, m1, k3, (k2 tog, m1) 7 times, k1, (m1, k2 tog) 7 times, k3, m1. Repeat from **—** 6 times, k1, m1, k3, (k2 tog, m1) 7 times, k1. Repeat from * to end of round.

Round 97: *K1, (m1, k2 tog) 7 times, k3, m1, **(k1, m1, k2 tog, k1, k2 tog, m1, k2, sl 1, k1, psso, m1)** 5 times, k1, m1, k3, (k2 tog, m1) 7 times, k3, (m1, k2 tog) 7 times, k3, m1. Repeat from **—** 6 times, k1, m1, k3, (k2 tog, m1) 7 times, k2. Repeat from * to end of round.

Round 99: *(M1, k2 tog) 8 times, k2, **(m1, k3, m1, (k2 tog) twice, m1, k1, sl 1, k1, psso)** 6 times, m1, k3, m1, k2, (k2 tog, m1) 8 times, k1, (m1, k2 tog) 8 times, k2. Repeat from **—** 6 times, m1, k3, m1, k2, (k2 tog, m1) 8 times, k1. Repeat from * to end of round.

Round 101: *K1, (m1, k2 tog) 8 times, k1, **(m1, k2 tog, m1, k1, m1, sl 1, k1, psso, m1, k2 tog, k1, sl 1, k1, psso)** 5 times, m1, k2 tog, m1, k1, m1, sl 1, k1, psso, m1, k1, (k2 tog, m1) 8 times, k3, (m1, k2 tog) 8 times, k1. Repeat **—** 6 times, m1, k2 tog, m1, k1, m1, sl 1, k1, psso, m1, k1, (k2 tog, m1) 8 times, k2. Repeat from * to end of round.

Round 103: *(M1, k2 tog) 10 times, **(m1, k3, m1, sl 1, k1, psso, m1, sl 1, k2 tog, m1, k2 tog)** 5 times, m1, k3, m1, sl 1, k1, psso, (m1, k2 tog) 9 times, m1, k1, (m1, k2 tog) 10 times. Repeat **—** 6 times, m1, k3, m1, sl 1, k1, psso, (m1, k2 tog) 9 times, m1, k1. Repeat from * to end of round.

Round 105: *K1, (m1, k2 tog) 8 times, k1, **(k2 tog, m1, k2 tog, m1, k1, m1, sl 1, k1, psso, m1, sl 1, k1, psso, k1)** 6 times, (k2 tog, m1) 8 times, k3, (m1, k2 tog) 8 times, k1. Repeat **—** 7 times, (k2, m1) 8 times, k2. Repeat from * to end of round.

Round 106: Knit.

Cast off with crochet hook as follows:

Slip last 3 and first 2 sts on to hook, draw thread through, *(8 ch, 1 dc into next 2 sts, slip off) 7 times, (8 ch, 1 dc into next 3 sts, slip off, 8 ch, 1 dc into next 2 sts, slip off) 13 times, (8 ch, 1 dc into next 2 sts, slip off) 6 times, 8 ch, 1 dc, into next 5 sts, slip off. Repeat from * to end. Work 2nd bracketed section 15 times instead of 13 on larger sides, omitting 1 dc at end of last repeat, 1 sl st in 1st st.

Cast off. Sew centre cast-on sts.

Press work with damp cloth.

8. Table Centres

Three attractive designs for your table.

Materials

Knitting on 2.75 mm needles, with 20 cotton, you will require approx. 50 gm of yarn.
The size of the centres will depend on your choice of cotton, and needles.

Table Centre 1: HYACINTH

Cast on 8 sts; 3 sts on each of two needles, 2 sts on 3rd needle. Join. Mark beginning of round.

Before proceeding read this note:
Where sl 1 to left appears at beginning of a round unpick last st on R.H. needle, slip on to beginning of L.H. needle. Also pass the last st off remaining 2 needles on to beginning of next needle. Where k1, k3, or k4 to right appears at beginning of round k the 1st 1, 3, or 4 sts from L.H needle on to R.H. needle.
Pass the same number of sts off remaining 2 needles onto end of previous needle. This applies to the patterns for all table centres in this book.

Round 1: Knit.
Round 2: *M2. Repeat from * to end of round (16 sts).
Round 3 *and* 5: Knit.
Round 4: As round 2 (32 sts).
Round 6: *M1, sl 1, k1, psso. Repeat from * to end of round (32 sts).
Round 7: *Work k1, p1, in m1 of previous round, k1, work (k1, p1) 3 times in m1 of previous round, k1. Repeat from * to end of round (80 sts).
Round 8: K1 to right, *m1, sl 1, k1, psso, k6 tbl, k2 tog. Repeat from * to end of round (72 sts).
Round 9 and alternate rounds unless otherwise stated: Knit, but work k1, p1, into each m1 of previous round (80 sts).
Round 10 *and* 12: K1 to right, * m1, sl 1, k1, psso, k6, k2 tog. Repeat from * to end of round (72 sts).
Round 13: *Work (k1, p1) twice into m1 of previous round, k8. Repeat from * to end of round (96 sts).
Round 14: K1 to right, * m1, k2 tbl, m1, sl 1, k1, psso, k6, k2 tog. Repeat from * to end of round (96 sts).
Round 16: K1 to right, *(m1, k2 tbl) twice, m1, sl 1, k1, psso, k6, k2 tog. Repeat from * to end of round. (120 sts).

Round 18: K1 to right. *(m1, sl 1, k1, psso, k2 tog) twice, m1, sl 1, k1, psso, k6, k2 tog. Repeat from * to end of round (120 sts).
Round 20: K1 to right, *m1, sl 1, k1, psso, k2 tog, m2, sl 1, k1, psso, k2 tog, m1, sl 1, k1, psso, k6, k2 tog. Repeat from * to end of round (128 sts).
Round 21: Knit, work k1, p1, into each m1, and (k1, p1) twice into each m2, of previous round (160 sts).
Round 22: K1 to right, *m1, sl 1, k1, psso, k2 tog, m1, k2 tbl, m1, sl 1, k1, psso, k2 tog, m1, sl 1, k1, psso, k6, k2 tog. Repeat from * to end of round (144 sts).
Round 24: K1 to right, *m1, sl 1, k1, psso, k2 tog, (m1, k2 tbl) twice, m1, sl 1, k1, psso, k2 tog, m1, sl 1, k1, psso, k6, k2 tog. Repeat from * to end of round (168 sts).
Round 26: K1 to right, * (m1, sl 1, k1, psso, k2 tog) 4 times, m1, sl 1, k1, psso, k6, k2 tog. Repeat from * to end of round (168 sts).
Round 28: K1 to right, *(m1, sl 1, k1, psso, k2 tog) twice, m2, (sl 1, k1, psso, k2 tog, m1) twice, sl 1, k1, psso, k6, k2 tog. Repeat from * to end of round (176 sts).
Round 29: As round 21 (224 sts).
Round 30: K1 to right, *(m1, sl 1, k1, psso, k2 tog) twice, m1, k2 tbl, (m1, sl 1, k1, psso, k2 tog) twice, m1, sl 1, k1, psso, k6, k2 tog. Repeat from * to end of round (192 sts).
Round 32: K1 to right, *(m1, sl 1, k1, k2 tog) twice, (m1, k2 tbl) twice, (m1, sl , k1, psso, k2 tog) twice, m1, sl 1, k1, psso, k6, k2 tog. Repeat from * to end of round (216 sts).
Round 34: K1 to right, * (m1, sl 1, k1, psso, k2 tog) 6 times, m1, sl 1, k1, psso, k6, k2 tog. Repeat from * to end of round (216 sts).
Round 36: K1 to right, *(m1, sl 1, k1, psso, k2 tog) 3 times, m2, (sl 1, k1, psso, k2 tog, m1) 3 times, (sl 1, k1, psso, k1, k2 tog) twice. Repeat from * to end of round (208 sts).
Round 37: As round 21 (272 sts).
Round 38: K1 to right, *(m1, sl 1, k1, psso, k2 tog) 3 times, m1, k2 tbl, (m1, sl 1, k1, psso, k2 tog) 4 times, sl 1, k1, psso, k2 tog. Repeat from * to end of round (208 sts).
Round 40: K1 to right, *(m1, sl 1, k1, psso, k2 tog) 3 times, m1, k1 tbl, k2, k1 tbl, (m1, sl 1, k1, psso, k2 tog) 3 times, m1, (sl 1, k2 tog, psso) twice. Repeat from * to end of round (208 sts).
Round 42: K1 to right, *(m1, sl 1, k1, psso, k2 tog) 3 times, m1, k1 tbl, k4, k1 tbl, (m1, sl 1, k1, psso, k2 tog) 4 times. Repeat from * to end of round (224 sts).
Round 44: K1 to right, *(m1, sl 1, k1, psso, k2 tog) 3 times, m1, k1 tbl, k6, k1 tbl, (m1, sl 1, k1, psso, k2 tog) 4 times. Repeat from * to end of round (240 sts).
Round 46: Sl 1 to left, *m2, sl 1, k1, psso, (sl 1, k1, psso,

Above: Basket lids and breadcloths (sections 7, p.47 and 9, p.57).

Left: Basket lids: Trefoil and Reed designs, and Bread cloths (sections 7, p.47, and 9, p.57).

Top left: Bath towel: Gillian, and Handtowel: Florence (sections 10, p.59, and 11, p.63).
Top right: Bath towel: Rina, and Handtowels Regent and Clover (sections 10, p.59, and 11, p.63).

Above: Handtowels: Hendra Vale, Domino and Ella (section 11, p.63).

Bottom: Bath towels: Josephine and Abelia (section 10, p.59).

k2 tog, m1) 3 times, k1 tbl, k4, m2, k4, k1 tbl, (m1, sl 1, k1, psso, k2 tog) 3 times, k2 tog. Repeat from * to end of round (272 sts).

Round 47: As round 21 (352 sts). Change to circular needle.

Round 48: K1 to right, *m1, k2 tbl, m1, sl 1, k2 tog, psso, k2 tog, m1, (sl 1, k1, psso, k2 tog) twice, m1, k1 tbl, k5, k4 tbl, k5, k1 tbl, m1, (sl 1, k1, psso, k2 tog) twice, m1, sl 1, k1, psso, sl 1, k2 tog, psso. Repeat from * to end of round (288 sts).

Round 50: K1 to right, * m1, k4, m1, (sl 1, k1, psso) twice, (sl 1, k2 tog, psso) twice, m1, k1 tbl, k2, (k1, p1 in next st) 12 times, k2, k1 tbl, m1, (sl 1, k2 tog, psso) twice, (k2 tog) twice. Repeat from * to end of round (368 sts).

Round 52: K1 to right, *m1, k6, m1, (sl 1, k2 tog, psso) twice, m1, k1 tbl, k30, k1 tbl, m1, (sl 1, k2 tog, psso) twice. Repeat from * to end of round (368 sts).

Round 54: K1 to right, *(m1, sl 1, k1, psso, k2 tog) 3 times, m1, sl 1, k1, psso, k30, k2 tog, m1, sl 1, k1, psso, k2 tog. Repeat from * to end of round (360 sts).

Round 56: K1 to right, *m1, k2, m1, sl 1, k1, psso, k2 tog, m1, k2, m1, sl 1, k1, psso, k2 tog, m1, sl 1, k1, psso, k5, k2 tog, m1, sl 1, k1, psso, k6, m1, k6, k2 tog, m1, sl 1, k1, psso, k5, k2 tog, m1, sl 1, k1, psso, k2 tog. Repeat from * to end of round (376 sts).

Round 58: K1 to right, *m1, k2, (m1, sl 1, k1, psso, k2 tog) twice, m1, k2, m1, sl 1, k1, psso, k2 tog, (m1, sl 1, k1, psso, k2, sl 1, k1, psso, k1, k2 tog) 4 times, m1, sl 1, k1, psso, k2 tog. Repeat from * to end of round (368 sts).

Round 60: Sl 1 to left, *m1, sl 1, k1, psso, k2 tog. Repeat from * to end of round (336 sts).

Round 62: K1 to right, *k2 tog, m1, sl 1, k1, psso. Repeat from * to end of round (336 sts).

Round 64: *M1, sl 1, k1, psso, k2 tog. Repeat from * to end of round (336 sts).

Round 66, 70, 74 and 78: As round 62.

Round 68, 72 and 76: As round 64.

Round 80: *M2, sl 1, k1 psso, k2 tog, m1, sl 1, k1, psso, k2 tog. Repeat from * to end of round (392 sts).

Round 81: *Work (k1, p1) 4 times in m2 of previous round, k2, work k1, p1 into m1 of previous round, k2. Repeat from * to end of round (784 sts).

Round 82: K1 to right, *m1, k6 tbl, m1 (sl 1, k1, psso) twice, (k2 tog) twice. Repeat from * to end of round (672 sts).

Round 84: K1 to right, *m1, k1 tbl, k6, k1 tbl, m1, (sl 1, k2 tog, psso) twice. Repeat from * to end of round (672 sts).

Round 85: *Work k1, p1, into each m1, k12, sl 1, k1, psso. Repeat from * to end of round (728 sts).

Cast off. Pin work into shape, spray lightly and leave to dry.

Table Centre 2: COSMOS

Cast on 8 sts; 3 sts on each of 2 needles, 2 sts on 3rd needle. Join into ring. Mark beginning of round.

Round 1: Knit.

Round 2: *K1, p1, into next st. Repeat from * to end of round (16 sts).

Round 3: Knit.

Round 4: As round 2 (32 sts).

Round 5, 6 and 7: Knit.

Round 8: As round 2 (64 sts).

Round 9, 10 and 11: Knit.

Round 12: *M1, sl 1, k1, psso, k4, k2 tog. Repeat from * to end of round (56 sts).

Round 13: *Work (k1, p1) 3 times into m1 of previous round, k6. Repeat from * to end of round (96 sts).

Round 14: *K6 tbl, k6. Repeat from * to end of round (96 sts).

Round 15, 16, 17 and18: Knit (96 sts).

Round 19: K3 to right, * m1, k6. Repeat from * to end of round (112 sts).

Round 20: K, work k1, p1, into m1 of previous round (128 sts).

Round 21: K1 to right, *m1, k1 tbl, k6, k1 tbl. Repeat from * to end of round (144 sts).

Round 22: As round 20 (160 sts).

Round 23: K1 to right, *m1, k1 tbl, k8, k1 tbl. Repeat from * to end of round (176 sts).

Round 24: *Work (k1, p1) twice into m1 of previous round, k10. Repeat from * to end of round (224 sts).

Round 25: *M1, k4 tbl, m1, (sl 1, k1, psso, k1, k2 tog) twice. Repeat from * to end of round (192 sts).

Round 26 and alternate rounds unless otherwise stated: Knit, working k1, p1, into each m1 of previous round (224 sts).

Round 27: K1 to right, *m1, k1 tbl, k4, k1 tbl, m1, (sl 1, k1, psso, k2 tog) twice. Repeat from * to end of round (192 sts).

Round 29: K1 to right, *m1, k1 tbl, k6, k1 tbl, m1, (sl 1, k2 tog, psso) twice. Repeat from * to end of round (192 sts).

Round 31: K1 to right, *m1, k1 tbl, k8, k1 tbl, m1, sl 1, k1, psso, k2 tog. Repeat from * to end of round (224 sts).

Round 32: As round 26 (256 sts).

Round 33: K1 to right, *m1, k1 tbl, k5, m1, k5, k1 tbl, m1, sl 1, k1, psso, k2 tog. Repeat from * to end of round (272 sts).

Round 34, 36 and 38: As round 26 (320 sts).

Round 35: Sl 1 to left, *m1, sl 1, k1, psso, k6, k2 tog. Repeat from * to end of round (288 sts).

Round 37: K1 to right, then work as for round 35 from * to end of round (288 sts).

Round 39: K1 to right, *m1, (sl 1, k1, psso, k1, k2 tog) twice. Repeat from * to end of round (224 sts).

Round 40: As round 26 (256 sts).

Round 41: K1 to right, *m1, (sl 1, k1, psso, k4, k2 tog) twice. Repeat from * to end of round (208 sts).

Round 42: *Work (k1, p1) 4 times in m1 of previous round, k12. Repeat from * to end of round (320 sts).

Round 43: K1 to right, *m1, k6 tbl, m1, (sl 1, k1, psso, k3, k2 tog) twice. Repeat from * to end of round (288 sts).

Round 44: As round 26 (320 sts).

Round 45: K1 to right, *(m1, sl 1, k1, psso) 4 times, m1, (sl 1, k1, psso, k2, k2 tog) twice. Repeat from * to end of round (272 sts). Now use circular needle.

Round 46: As round 26 (352 sts).

Round 47: K1 to right, *m2, (sl 1, k2 tog, psso, m1) 3 times. sl 1, k2 tog, psso, m2, (sl 1, k1, psso, k1, k2 tog) twice. Repeat from * to end of round (272 sts).

Round 48: Knit, work k1, p1 into each m1, and (k1, p1) twice into each m2, of previous round (384 sts).

Round 49: K1 to right, *m1, k2 tbl, (m1, sl 1, k2 tog, psso) 4 times, m1, k2 tbl, m1, (sl 1, k1 psso, k2 tog) twice. Repeat from * to end of round (304 sts).

Round 50: Work k1, p1, into m1 of previous round. *Sl 1, k1, psso, k1, p1, into m1 of previous round, k14, sl 1, k1, psso, k8. Repeat from * to end of round, ending last repeat with k6. (384 sts).

Round 51: K1 to right, *(m1, sl 1, k2 tog, psso) 7 times, sl 1, K2 tog, psso. Repeat from * to end of round (240 sts).

Round 52: *Work k1, p1 into m1 of previous round, k20, k2 tog. Repeat from * to end of round (336 sts).

Round 53 and 55: K1 to right, * m1, sl 1, k2 tog, psso. Repeat from * to end of round (224 sts).

Round 54 and 56: As round 26 (336 sts).

Round 57: K1 to right, (m1, sl 1, k2 tog, psso) 3 times, *m2, sl 1, k2 tog, psso, (m1, sl 1, k2 tog, psso) 6 times. Repeat from * until 12 sts remain. M2, sl 1, k2 tog, psso, (m1, sl 1, k2 tog, psso) 3 times (240 sts).

Round 58: As round 48 (368 sts).

Round 59: K1 to right, *(m1, sl 1, k2 tog, psso) 3 times, m1, k2 tbl, (m1, sl 1, k2 tog, psso) 4 times. Repeat from * to end of round (272 sts).

Round 60: As round 26 (400 sts).

Round 61: K1 to right, *(m1, sl 1, k2 tog, psso) twice, sl 1, k2 tog, psso, m1, (work k1, p1 into next st) 4 times, m1, (sl 1, k2 tog, psso) twice, (m1, sl 1, k2 tog, psso) twice. Repeat from * to end of round (336 sts).

Round 62: Work k1, p1, into m1 of previous round, k5, *k2 tog, k12, k2 tog, k11. Repeat from * to end of round, ending last repeat with k6 (400 sts).

Round 63: K1 to right, *(m1, sl 1, k2 tog, psso) twice, m1, k1 tbl, k8, k1 tbl, (m1, sl 1, k2 tog, psso) 3 times. Repeat from * to end of round (336 sts).

Round 64: As round 26 (432 sts).

Round 65: K4 to right, *m1, sl 1, k2 tog, psso, m1, k1 tbl, k10, k1 tbl, (m1, sl 1, k2 tog, psso) twice, (sl 1, k2 tog, psso) twice. Repeat from * to end of round (336 sts).

Round 66: *Work k1, p1 into m1 of previous round, k22, sl 1, k2 tog, psso. Repeat from * to end of round (368 sts).

Round 67: K1 to right, *m1, sl 1, k2 tog, psso, m1, k1 tbl, k6, m1, k6, k1 tbl, (m1, sl 1, k2 tog, psso) twice. Repeat from * to end of round (352 sts).

Round 68: As round 26 (432 sts).

Round 69: K4 to right, *(m1, sl 1, k1, psso, k5, k2 tog) twice, m1, sl 1, k1, psso, k5 tbl, k2 tog. Repeat from * to end of round (384 sts).

Round 70: As round 26 (432 sts).

Round 71: K1 to right, * m2, (sl 1, k1, psso) twice, k1, (k2 tog) twice. Repeat from * to end of round (336 sts).

Round 72: *Work (k1, p1) 4 times into m2 of previous round, sl 1, k1, psso, k1, k2 tog. Repeat from * to end of round (528 sts).

Round 73: *K8 tbl, sl 1, k2 tog, psso. Repeat from * to end of round (432 sts).

Cast off. Lightly starch centre, pin out to shape *using rustless pins*. Leave to dry.

Table Centre 3: PANSY

Cast on 8 sts; 3 sts on each of 2 needles, 2 sts on 3rd needle. Work with 4th. **Repeat pattern instructions 8 times.** Alternate rounds are knit, unless otherwise indicated.

Round 1: K1, m1.
Round 3: K2, m1.
Round 5: K3, m1.
Round 7: K4, m1.
Round 9: K5, m1.
Round 11: K6, m1.
Round 13: K2 tog, k1, k2 tog, m2, k2 tog, m1.
Round 14: Knit. (K5 out of m2 of previous round), k1, p1, to end of round.
Round 15: K3 tog, m1, k5, m1, k2 tog, m1.
Round 17: Transfer 1st st from L.H. to R.H. needle, m2, k2, k3 tog, k2, m1, k3 tog.
Round 18: As round 14.
Round 19: M1, k5, m1, k1, k3 tog, k1, m1, k2 tog.
Round 21: M1, k7, m1, k3 tog, m1, k2 tog.
Round 23: M1, k9, m1, k3 tog.
Round 25: K4, k3 tog, k4, m2, tw st, m1.
Round 26: As round 14.
Round 27: K3, k3 tog, k3, m1, k5, m1, k2 tog, m1.
Round 29: K2, k3 tog, k2, m1, k7, m1, k2 tog, m1.
Round 31: K1, k3 tog, k1, m1, k9, m1, k2 tog, m1.
Round 33: K3 tog, m1, k11, m1, k2 tog, m1.
Round 35: Transfer 1st st from L.H. to R.H. needle. M1, k13, m1, k3 tog.
Round 37: M2, k8, m2, k8.
Round 38: As round 14.
From now on repeat the pattern 16 times, 4 times on each needle.
Round 39: M1, k5, m1, k8.
Round 41: M1, k7, m1, k3, k2 tog, k3.
Round 43: M1, k9, m1, k2, k3 tog, k2.
Round 45: M1, k11, m1, k1, k3 tog, k1.
Round 47: M1, k13, m1, k3 tog.
Round 49: K14, k2 tog, m2.
Round 50: Knit. Out of m2 of previous round k7 sts.
Round 51: K6, k3 tog, k6, m1, k7, m1.
Round 53: K5, k3 tog, k5, m1, k9, m1.
Round 55: K4, k3 tog, k4, m1, k11, m1.
Round 57: K3, k3 tog, (k3, m1) 3 times, k1, m1, (k3, m1) twice.
Round 59: K2, k3 tog, k2, m1, (k2 tog, m1) twice, k3, m1, (k2 tog, k2, m1) twice.
Round 61: K1, k3 tog, k1, (m1, k2, k2 tog) twice, m1, k5, m1, (k2 tog, k2, m1) twice.
Round 62: Knit.
Crochet together in dc groups of 3.4.4.7.4.4. with 8 ch between each group. Fasten off.

Lightly starch. Pin out to shape with rustless pins. Leave to dry.

9. Bread Cloths

These useful cloths can be made in any size. Originally the unworn pieces of damask cloth, huckaback, and pieces of towel were trimmed with coarse cotton knitting. The cloths have a variety of uses—but were mainly used to protect food from dust and flies. These utility kitchen cloths can still be used to wrap bread, or to cover food.

Materials

Any size of thread would be suitable to knit these edgings. The cloths are easily washed and cared for. Their use conserves material which otherwise would be discarded.

Bread Cloth 1: RYE

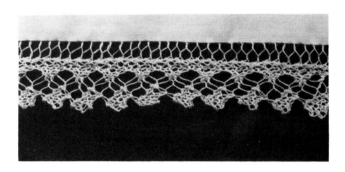

Cast on 11 sts.
Row 1: K4, m1, p2 tog, k4, m1, inc in last st.
Row 2: K3, m1, p2 tog, k4, m1, p2 tog, k1, sl 1.
Row 3: K4, m1, p2 tog, k1, p2 tog, m1, k4.
Row 4: K5, m1, p2 tog, k2, m1, p2 tog, k1, sl 1.
Row 5: K4, m1, p2 tog, k2, m1, p2 tog, k3.
Row 6: Cast off 3 sts, m1, k5, m1, p2 tog, k1, sl 1.
Repeat rows 1–6 until length desired.

Bread Cloth 2: WHEAT

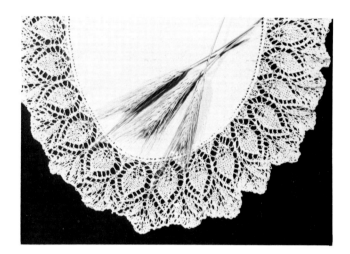

Cast on 174 sts.
Special Abbreviation: K1b = k into next st one row below, then k st on needle.
Row 1: Purl (wrong side of work).
Row 2: K4, *m1, k1, m1, k5. Repeat from *, ending last repeat with k4.
Row 3: Purl.
Row 4: K2, *k2 tog, m1, k3, m1, sl 1, k1, psso, k1. Repeat from * to last st, k1.
Row 5: Purl.
Row 6: K1, k2 tog, *m1, k2 tog, m1, k1, m1, sl 1, k1, psso, m1, sl 1, k2 tog, psso. Repeat from *, ending last repeat with sl 1, k1, psso, k1, instead of sl 1, k2 tog, psso.
Row 7: P4, *k1 tbl, p1, k1 tbl, p5. Repeat from *, ending last repeat with p4 instead of p5.
Row 8: K2, *m1, k2 tog, (k1, m1) twice, k1, sl 1, k1, psso, m1, k1. Repeat from * to last st, k1.
Row 9: P5, *k1 tbl, p1, k1 tbl, p7. Repeat from *, ending last repeat with p5 instead of p7.
Row 10: K1, k2 tog, *m1, k3, m1, k1, m1, k3, m1, sl 1, k2 tog, psso. Repeat from * ending last repeat with sl 1, k1, psso, k1, instead of sl 1, k2 tog, psso.
Row 11: P6, *k1 tbl, p1, k1 tbl, p9. Repeat from *, ending last repeat with p6 instead of p9.
Row 12: K1, k2 tog, *m1, k9, m1, sl 1, k2 tog, psso. Repeat from *, ending last repeat with sl 1, k1, psso, k1, instead of sl 1, k2 tog, psso.
Row 13: Purl.

Row 14: K3, *m1, sl 1, k1, psso, k5, k2 tog, m1, k3. Repeat from * to end.
Row 15: Purl.
Row 16: K2, *(m1, sl 1, k1, psso) twice, k3, (k2 tog, m1) twice, k1. Repeat from * to last st, k1.
Row 17: Purl.
Row 18: K1, *k1b, k1, (m1, sl 1, k1, psso) twice, k1, (k2 tog, m1) twice, k1. Repeat from * to last 2 sts, k1b, k1.
Row 19: Purl.
Row 20: K2, *m1, k3, m1, sl 1, k1, psso, m1, sl 1, k2 tog, psso, m1, k2 tog, m1, k3. Repeat from *, ending last repeat with k2 instead of k3.
Row 21: Purl.
Row 22: K3, *m1, k4, m1, sl 1, k1, psso, k1, k2 tog, m1, k4, m1, k1. Repeat from * to last 2 sts, k2.
Row 23: Purl.
Row 24: K3, *m1, k1, m1, k3, m1, sl 1, k1, psso, m1, sl 1, k2 tog, psso, m1, k2 tog, m1, k3, (m1, k1) twice. Repeat from * to last 2 sts, k2.
Row 25: Purl.
Row 26: K3, *m1, k3, m1, sl ·1, k2 tog, psso, m1, k1, m1, sl 1, k1, psso, k1, k2 tog, m1, k1, m1, sl 1, k2 tog, psso, m1, k3, m1, k1. Repeat from * to last 2 sts, k2.
Row 27: Purl.
Row 28: K3, *m1, k5, (m1, sl 1, k2 tog, psso, m1, k1) twice, m1, k3 tog, m1, k5, m1, k1. Repeat from * to last 2 sts, k2. Cast off knitwise.
Press with slightly damp cloth.

Bread Cloth 3: OATS

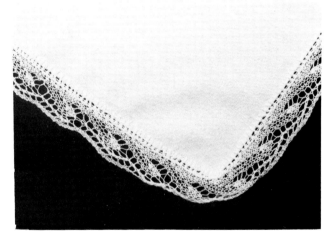

Cast on 13 sts.
Row 1: Purl (wrong side).
Row 2: Sl 1, k1, m1, p2 tog, k1, (m1, sl 1, k1, psso) 3 times, m2, k2 tog.
Row 3: M1, k2 tog, p9, m1, p2 tog, k1.
Row 4: Sl 1, k1, m1, p2 tog, k2, (m1, sl 1, k1, psso) 3 times, m2, k2 tog.
Row 5: M1, k2 tog, p10, m1, p2 tog, k1.

Row 6: Sl 1, k1, m1, p2 tog, k3, (m1, sl 1, k1, psso) 3 times, m2 k2 tog.
Row 7: M1, k2 tog, p11, m1, p2 tog, k1.
Row 8: Sl 1, k1, m1, p2 tog, k4, (m1, sl 1, k1, psso) 3 times, m2, k2 tog.
Row 9: M1, k2 tog, p12, m1, p2 tog, k1.
Row 10: Sl 1, k1, m1, p2 tog, k5, (m1, sl 1, k1, psso) 3 times, m2, k2 tog.
Row 11: M1, k2 tog, p13, m1, p2 tog, k1.
Row 12: Sl 1, k1, m1, p2 tog, k6, (m1, sl 1, k1, psso) 3 times, m2, k2 tog.
Row 13: M1, k2 tog, p14, m1, p2 tog, k1.
Row 14: Sl 1, k1, m1, p2 tog, k7, (m1, sl 1, k1, psso) 3 times, m2, k2 tog.
Row 15: M1, k2 tog, p15, m1, p2 tog, k1.
Row 16: Sl 1, k1, m1, p2 tog, k8, m1, k1. Return last st to L.H. needle, lift next 7 sts over, one at a time, then sl st on to R.H. needle.
Row 17: P2 tog, p9, m1, p2 tog, k1.
Repeat rows 2–17 until length desired.

Bread Cloth 4: CORN

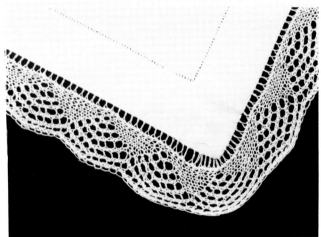

Cast on 14 sts.
Row 1: (Wrong side) k2, m1, k2 tog, k5, m1, k2 tog, m1, k3.
Row 2 and every alternate row: K1, m1, k2 tog, knit to end of row.
Row 3: K2, m1, k2 tog, k4, (m1, k2 tog) twice, m1, k3.
Row 5: K2, m1, k2 tog, k3, (m1, k2 tog) 3 times, m1, k3.
Row 7: K2, m1, k2 tog, k2, (m1, k2 tog) 4 times, m1, k3.
Row 9: K2, m1, k2 tog, k1, (m1, k2 tog) 5 times, m1, k3.
Row 11: K2, m1, k2 tog, k1, k2 tog, (m1, k2 tog) 5 times, k2.
Row 13: K2, m1, k2 tog, k2, k2 tog, (m1, k2 tog) 4 times, k2.
Row 15: K2, m1, k2 tog, k3, k2 tog, (m1, k2 tog) 3 times, k2.
Row 17: K2, m1, k2 tog, k4, k2 tog, (m1, k2 tog) twice, k2.
Row 19: K2, m1, k2 tog, k5, k2 tog, m1, k2 tog, k2.
Row 20: K1, m1, k2 tog, knit to end of row.
Repeat 1–20 until length desired.

10. Bath Towel Edgings

Six wide edgings for your bath towels. The extra width of the lace gives a large towel a luxurious appearance.

Materials

Each towel will require the following materials.
2 balls 4 ply cotton (50 g)
pair 2 mm (14) needles
fine sewing needle, and cotton, for attaching the lace
All towels in this book have been finished with a white feather stitch trim, worked with D.M.C. no. 8 cotton.

Bath Towel 1: JOSEPHINE

Cast on 33 sts.
Row 1: [K1, p1 (m1, k2 tog) 4 times] twice, p1, k1, m1, p2 tog, k1, (m2, k2 tog) twice, k4.
Row 2: K6, p1, k2, p1, k1, m1, p2 tog, k1, p1, k1, p8, k1, p10.
Row 3: K1, p1, k1, (m1, k2 tog) 3 times, (p1, k1) twice, (m1, k2 tog) 3 times, k1, p1, k1, m1, p2 tog, k11.
Row 4: K11, m1, p2 tog, k1, p1, k1, p6, (k1, p1) twice, k1, p5, k1, p2.
Row 5: (K1, p1) twice, (m1, k2 tog) twice, (k1, p1) 3 times, (m1, k2 tog) twice, (p1, k1) twice, m1, p2 tog, k1, (m2, k2 tog) 3 times, k4.
Row 6: K6, (p1, k2) twice, p1, k1, m1, p2 tog, (k1, p1) twice, k1, p4, (k1, p1) twice, k1, p5, k1, p2.
Row 7: (K1, p1) twice, k1, m1, k2 tog, (p1, k1) 4 times, m1, k2 tog, (k1, p1) twice, k1, m1, p2 tog, k14.

Row 8: Cast off 5 sts, k8, m1, p2 tog, (k1, p1) twice, k1, p2, (k1, p1) 6 times, k1, p2.
Row 9: (K1, p1) twice, (m1, k2 tog) twice, (k1, p1) 3 times, (m1, k2 tog) twice, (p1, k1) twice, m1, p2 tog, k1, (m2, k2 tog) twice, k4.
Row 10: K6, p1, k2, p1, k1, m1, p2 tog, (k1, p1) twice, k1, p4, (k1, p1) twice, k1, p5, k1, p2.
Row 11: K1, p1, k1, (m1, k2 tog) 3 times, (p1, k1) twice, (m1, k2 tog) 3 times, k1, p1, k1, m1, p2 tog, k11.
Row 12: K11, m1, p2 tog, k1, p1, k1, p6, (k1, p1) twice, k1, p5, k1, p2.
Row 13: K1, p1, (m1, k2 tog) 4 times, k1, p1, (m1, k2 tog) 4 times, p1, k1, m1, p2 tog, k1, (m2, k2 tog) 3 times, k4.
Row 14: K6, p1, (k2, p1) twice, k1, m1, p2 tog, k1, p1, k1, p8, k1, p10.
Row 15: K1, (m1, k2 tog) 10 times, k1, m1, p2 tog, k14.
Row 16: Cast off 5 sts, k8, m1, p2 tog, k1, p21.
Repeat rows 1–16 until length desired.

Bath Towel 2: ABELIA

Cast on 36 sts.
Row 1: [K1, p1 (m1, k2 tog) 4 times] twice, p1, k1, m1, p2 tog, k1, (m2, k2 tog) twice, k4.
Row 2: K3, p1, k2, k1, p1, k1, p1, in m4 of previous row, k17, m1, k2 tog, k8, m1, k2 tog, k1.
Row 3: Sl 1, k2, m1, k2 tog, k1, k2 tog, m2, sl 1, k1, psso, k3, m1, k2 tog, k3, k2 tog, m2, sl 1, k1, psso, k5, (m1, k2 tog) twice, k4, k2 tog, m2, k2 tog, k1.

Row 4: K3, p1, k16, p1, k6, m1, k2 tog, k3, p1, k4, m1, k2 tog, k1.

Row 5: Sl 1, k2, m1, k2 tog, k8, m1, k2 tog, k1, k2 tog, m2, sl 1, k1, psso, k2 tog, m2, sl 1, k1, psso, k4, (m1, k2 tog) twice, k3, k2 tog, m2, k2 tog, k1.

Row 6: K3, p1, k14, p1, k3, p1, k4, m1, k2 tog, k8, m1, k2 tog, k1.

Row 7: Sl 1, k2, m1, k2 tog, k1, k2 tog, m2, sl 1, k1, psso, k3, m1, k2 tog, k3, k2 tog, m2, sl 1, k1, psso, k7, (m1, k2 tog) twice, k2, k2 tog, m2, k2 tog, k1.

Row 8: K3, p1, k16, p1, k6, m1, k2 tog, k3, p1, k4, m1, k2 tog, k1.

Row 9: Sl 1, k2, m1, k2 tog, k8, m1, k2 tog, k1, k2 tog, m2, sl 1, k1, psso, k2 tog, m2, sl 1, k1, psso, k6, (m1, k2 tog) twice, k1, k2 tog, m2, k2 tog, k1.

Row 10: K3, p1, k14, p1, k3, p1, k4, m1, k2 tog, k8, m1, k2 tog, k1.

Row 11: Sl 1, k2, m1, k2 tog, k1, k2 tog, m2, sl 1, k1, psso, k3, m1, k2 tog, k3, k2 tog, m2, sl 1, k1, psso, k9, (m1, k2 tog) twice, k2 tog, m2, k2 tog, k1.

Row 12: K3, p1, k16, p1, k6, m1, k2 tog, k3, p1, k4, m1, k2 tog, k1.

Row 13: Sl 1, k2, m1, k2 tog, k8, m1, k2 tog, k17, (m1, k2 tog) twice, k4.

Row 14: Cast off 4 sts, k22, m1, k2 tog, k8, m1, k2 tog, k1.
Repeat rows 1–14 until length desired.

Bath Towel 3: RINA

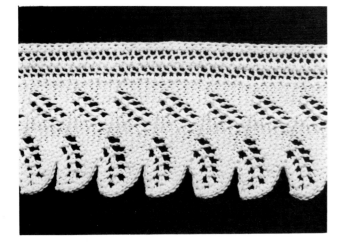

Cast on 24 sts.

Row 1: Sl 1, k2, m1, k2 tog, k1, m1, k2 tog, k2, (m1, k2 tog) twice, k5, (m2, k2 tog) twice, k1.

Row 2: K3, p1, k2, p1, k13, m1, k2 tog, k1, m1, k2 tog, k1.

Row 3: Sl 1, k2, m1, k2 tog, k1, m1, k2 tog, k3, (m1, k2 tog) twice, k6, (m2, k2 tog) twice, k1.

Row 4: K3, p1, k2, p1, k15, m1, k2 tog, k1, m1, k2 tog, k1.

Row 5: Sl 1, k2, m1, k2 tog, k1, m1, k2 tog, k4, (m1, k2 tog) twice, k7, (m2, k2 tog) twice, k1.

Row 6: K3, p1, k2, p1, k17, m1, k2 tog, k1, m1, k2 tog, k1.

Row 7: Sl 1, k2, m1, k2 tog, k1, m1, k2 tog, k5, (m1, k2 tog) twice, k8 (m2, k2 tog) twice, k1.

Row 8: K3, p1, k2, p1, k19, m1, k2 tog, k1, m1, k2 tog, k1.

Row 9: Sl 1, k2, m1, k2 tog, k1, m1, k2 tog, k6 (m1, k2 tog) twice, k9, (m2, k2 tog) twice, k1.

Row 10: K3, p1, k2, p1, k21, m1, k2 tog, k1, m1, k2 tog, k1.

Row 11: Sl 1, k2, m1, k2 tog, k1, m1, k2 tog, k26.

Row 12: Cast off 10, k17, m1, k2 tog, k1, m1, k2 tog, k1.
Repeat rows 1–12 until length desired.

Bath Towel 4: DIANE

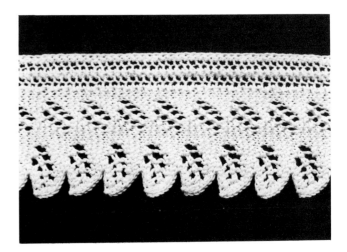

Cast on 24 sts.

Row 1: Sl 1, k2, m1, k2 tog, k1, m1, k2 tog, k2, (m1, k2 tog) twice, k5, (m2, k2 tog) twice, k1.

Row 2: K3, p1, k2, p1, k13, m1, k2 tog, k1, m1, k2 tog, k1.

Row 3: Sl 1, k2, m1, k2 tog, k1, m1, k2 tog, k3, (m1, k2 tog) twice, k6, (m2, k2 tog) twice, k1.

Row 4: K3, p1, k2, p1, k15, m1, k2 tog, k1, m1, k2 tog, k1.

Row 5: Sl 1, k2, m1, k2 tog, k1, m1, k2 tog, k4, (m1, k2 tog) twice, k7, (m2, k2 tog) twice, k1.

Row 6: K3, p1, k2, p1, k17, m1, k2 tog, k1, m1, k2 tog, k1.

Row 7: Sl 1, k2, m1, k2 tog, k1, m1, k2 tog, k5, (m1, k2 tog) twice, k8, (m2, k2 tog) twice, k1.

Row 8: K3, p1, k2, p1, k19, m1, k2 tog, k1, m1, k2 tog, k1.

Row 9: Sl 1, k2, m1, k2 tog, k1, m1, k2 tog, k24.

Row 10: Cast off 8 sts, k17, m1, k2 tog, k1, m1, k2 tog, k1.
Repeat rows 1–10 until length desired.

Bath Towel 5: DENYSE

Cast on 27 sts.

Row 1: Sl 1, k2, (m1, k2 tog) twice, k3, m1, k2 tog, k5, m1, k2 tog, m1, k1, (m1, k2 tog) twice, m2, k2 tog, k1.

Row 2: M1, k2 tog, k1, p1, k1, p21, k3.

Row 3: Sl 1, k2, m1, k2 tog, k1, m1, k2 tog, k2, m1, k2 tog, k3, k2 tog, m1, k2 tog, m1, k3, (m1, k2 tog) twice, k1, m2, k2.

Row 4: M1, k2 tog, k1, p1, k2, p22, k3.

Row 5: Sl 1, k2, m1, k2 tog, k2, m1, k2 tog, k1, m1, k2 tog, k2, k2 tog, m1, k2 tog, m1, k5, (m1, k2 tog) twice, m2, k2 tog, m2, k2.

Row 6: M1, k2 tog, k1, p1, k2, p1, k1, p23, k3.

Row 7: Sl 1, k2, m1, k2 tog, k3, (m1, k2 tog) twice, k3, (m1, k2 tog) twice, k2, k2 tog, (m1, k2 tog) twice, *m2, k2 tog. Repeat from * twice, k1.

Row 8: M1, k2 tog, k1, p1, *k2, p1. Repeat from * once, k1, p22, k3.

Row 9: Sl 1, k2, m1, (k2 tog) twice, m2, k2 tog, k1, m1, k2 tog, k4, (m1, k2 tog) twice, k1, k2 tog, (m1, k2 tog) twice, *m2, k2 tog. Repeat from * 3 times, k1.

Row 10: M1, k2 tog, k1, p1, *k2, p1. Repeat from * twice, k1, p18, k1, p3, k3.

Row 11: Sl 1, k2, (m1, k2 tog, k5) twice, (m1, k2 tog) twice, m1, sl 1, k2 tog, psso, m1, k2 tog, k13.

Row 12: Cast off 11 sts, k2, p21, k3.

Repeat rows 1–12 until length desired.

Bath Towel 6: GILLIAN

Cast on 32 sts.

Row 1: Sl 1, k2, m1, (k2 tog) twice, m2, k2 tog, k2, m1, k2 tog, k2, (k2 tog, m2, k2 tog) 3 times, k3, m1, k2 (33 sts).

Row 2: M1, k2 tog, k6, p1, (k3, p1) twice, k5, p2, k2, p1, k3, m1, k2 tog, k1.

Row 3: Sl 1, k2, m1, k2 tog, k7, m1, k2 tog, k3, (k2 tog, m2, k2 tog) twice, k4, m1, k2 tog, m1, k2 (34 sts).

Row 4: M1, k2 tog, k9, p1, k3, p1, k6, p3, k6, m1, k2 tog, k1 (34 sts).

Row 5: Sl 1, k2, m1, (k2 tog) twice, m2, k2 tog, k2, (m1, k2 tog) twice, k4, k2 tog, m2, k2 tog, k5, (m1, k2 tog) twice, m1, k2 (35 sts).

Row 6: M1, k2 tog, k12, p1, k9, p2, k2, p1, k3, m1, k2 tog, k1 (35 sts).

Row 7: Sl 1, k2, m1, k2 tog, k7, (m1, k2 tog) twice, k11, (m1, k2 tog) 3 times, m1, k2 (36 sts).

Row 8: M1, k2 tog, k22, p3, k6, m1, k2 tog, k1 (36 sts).

Row 9: Sl 1, k2, m1, (k2 tog) twice, m2, k2 tog, k4, (m1, k2 tog) twice, k9, (m1, k2 tog) twice, k2, m1, k2 tog, m1, k2 (37 sts).

Row 10: M1, k2 tog, k4, p2, k16, p4, k2, p1, k3, m1, k2 tog, k1 (37 sts).

Row 11: Sl 1, k2, m1, k2 tog, k9, (m1, k2 tog) twice, k7, (m1, k2 tog) twice, k4, m1, k2 tog, m1, k2 (38 sts).

Row 12: M1, k2 tog, k4, p4, k14, p5, k6, m1, k2 tog, k1 (38 sts).

Row 13: Sl 1, k2, m1, (k2 tog) twice, m2, k2 tog, k6, (m1, k2 tog) twice, k5, (m1, k2 tog) twice, k6, m1, k2 tog, m1, k2 (39 sts).

Row 14: M1, k2 tog, k4, p6, k12, p6, k2, p1, k3, m1, k2 tog, k1 (39 sts).

Row 15: Sl 1, k2, m1, k2 tog, k11, (m1, k2 tog) twice, k3, (m1, k2 tog) twice, k8, m1, k2 tog, m1, k2 (40 sts).

Row 16: M1, k2 tog, k4, p8, k10, p7, k6, m1, k2 tog, k1 (40 sts).

Row 17: Sl 1, k2, m1, (k2 tog) twice, m2, k2 tog, k5, (k2 tog, m1) twice, k5, (k2 tog, m1) twice, k6, (k2 tog, m1) twice, k2 tog, k1 (39 sts).

Row 18: M1, k2 tog, k4, p6, k12, p6, k2, p1, k3, m1, k2 tog, k1 (39 sts).

Row 19: Sl 1, k2, m1, k2 tog, k8, (k2 tog, m1) twice, k7, (k2 tog, m1) twice, k4, (k2 tog, m1) twice, k2 tog, k1 (38 sts).
Row 20: M1, k2 tog, k4, p4, k14, p5, k6, m1, k2 tog, k1, (38 sts).
Row 21: Sl 1, k2, m1, (k2 tog) twice, m2, k2 tog, k3, (k2 tog, m1) twice, k9, (k2 tog, m1) twice, k2, (k2 tog, m1) twice, k2 tog, k1 (37 sts).
Row 22: M1, k2 tog, k4, p2, k16, p4, k2, p1, k3, m1, k2 tog, k1 (37 sts).
Row 23: Sl 1, k2, m1, k2 tog, k6, (k2 tog, m1) twice, k11, (k2 tog, m1) 4 times, k2 tog, k1 (36 sts).
Row 24: M1, k2 tog, k22, p3, k2, p1, k3, m1, k2 tog, k1 (36 sts).
Row 25: Sl 1, k2, m1, (k2 tog) twice, m2, k2 tog, k1, (k2 tog, m1) twice, k5 k2 tog, m2, k2 tog, k4, (k2 tog, m1) 3 times, k2 tog, k1 (35 sts).

Row 26: M1, k2 tog, k12, p1, k9, p2, k2, p1, k3, m1, k2 tog, k1 (35 sts).
Row 27: Sl 1, k2, m1, k2 tog, k6, k2 tog, m1, k4, (k2 tog, m2, k2 tog) twice, k3, (k2 tog, m1) twice, k2 tog, k1 (34 sts).
Row 28: M1, k2 tog, k9, p1, k3, p1, k6, p3, k6, m1, k2 tog, k1 (34 sts).
Row 29: Sl 1, k2, m1, (k2 tog) twice, m2, k2 tog, k1, k2 tog, m1, k3, (k2 tog, m2, k2 tog) 3 times, k2, k2 tog, m1, k2 tog, k1 (33 sts).
Row 30: M1, k2 tog, k6, p1, (k3, p1) twice, k5, p2, k2, p1, k3, m1, k2 tog, k1 (33 sts).
Row 31: Sl 1, k2, m1, k2 tog, k4, k2 tog, m1, k2, (k2 tog, m2, k2 tog) 4 times, k1, k2 tog, k1 (32 sts).
Row 32: M1, k2 tog, (k3, p1) 4 times, k11, m1, k2 tog, k1 (32 sts).
Repeat rows 1–32 until length desired.

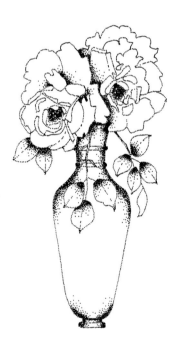

11. Handtowel Edgings

Handtowel edgings by the dozen! All the patterns are within scope of the average knitter. The illustration of ARLE clearly shows the row of feather stitching used on each towel in the book.

Materials

The edgings were knitted on 2 mm needles, with 4 ply cotton.

Handtowel 1: REGENT

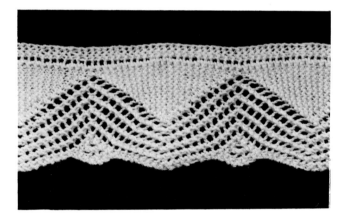

Cast on 21 sts.
Row 1: Sl 1, k2, m1, k2 tog, k3, k2 tog, (m1, k2 tog) 4 times, m1, k3.
Row 2 and alternate rows: Knit.
Row 3: Sl 1, k2, m1, k2 tog, k2, k2 tog, (m1, k2 tog) 4 times, m1, k4.
Row 5: Sl 1, k2, m1, k2 tog, k1, k2 tog, (m1, k2 tog) 4 times, m1, k3, m1, k2.
Row 7: Sl 1, k2, m1, k2 tog, k2 tog, (m1, k2 tog) 5 times, k1, m1, k2 tog, m1, k2.
Row 9: Sl 1, k2, m1, k2 tog, k2, (m1, k2 tog) 5 times, k2 tog, m1, k2 tog, k1.
Row 11: Sl 1, k2, m1, k2 tog, k3, (m1, k2 tog) 5 times, k3.
Row 13: Sl 1, k2, m1, k2 tog, k4, (m1, k2 tog) 5 times, k2 tog.
Row 15: Sl 1, k2, m1, k2 tog, k5, (m1, k2 tog) 4 times, m1, k2.
Row 17: Sl 1, k2, m1, k2 tog, k6, (m1, k2 tog) 4 times, m1, k2.
Row 19: Sl 1, k2, m1, k2 tog, k7, (m1, k2 tog) 4 times, m1, k2.
Row 21: Sl 1, k2, m1, k2 tog, k8, (m1, k2 tog) 4 times, m1, k2.
Row 23: Sl 1, k2, m1, k2 tog, k9, (m1, k2 tog) 4 times, m1, k2.
Row 25: Sl 1, k2, m1, k2 tog, k10, (m1, k2 tog) 4 times, m1, k2.
Row 27: Sl 1, k2, m1, k2 tog, k11, (m1, k2 tog) 4 times, m1, k2.
Row 29: Sl 1, k2, m1, k2 tog, k12, (m1, k2 tog) 4 times, m1, k2.
Row 31: Sl 1, k2, m1, k2 tog, k10, k2 tog, (m1, k2 tog) 5 times, k1.
Row 33: Sl 1, k2, m1, k2 tog, k9, k2 tog, (m1, k2 tog) 5 times, k1.
Row 35: Sl 1, k2, m1, k2 tog, k8, k2 tog, (m1, k2 tog) 5 times, k1.
Row 37: Sl 1, k2, m1, k2 tog, k7, k2 tog, (m1, k2 tog) 5 times, k1.
Row 39: Sl 1, k2, m1, k2 tog, k6, k2 tog, (m1, k2 tog) 5 times, k1.
Row 41: Sl 1, k2, m1, k2 tog, k5, k2 tog, (m1, k2 tog) 5 times, k1.
Row 43: Sl 1, k2, m1, k2 tog, k4, k2 tog, (m1, k2 tog) 5 times, k1.
Row 44: Knit.
Repeat rows 1–44 until length desired.
End with row 7 to make pattern even.

Handtowel 2: BUTTONS

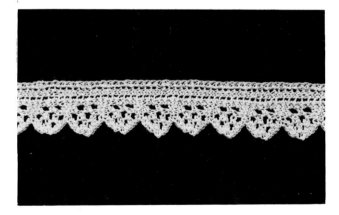

Cast on 12 sts. Knit one row.
Row 1: Sl 1 purlwise, k2 tog, m1, k2, m1, k2 tog, k1, m2, k2 tog, m2, k2.
Row 2: Sl 1 purlwise, k2, p1, k2, p1, k8.
Row 3: Sl 1, k2 tog, m1, k2, m1, k2 tog, k8.

Row 4: Sl 1 purlwise, k14.
Row 5: Sl 1 purlwise, k2 tog, m1, k2, m1, k2 tog, k1, (m2, k2 tog) 3 times, k1.
Row 6: Sl 1 purlwise, (k2, p1) 3 times, k8.
Row 7: Sl 1 purlwise, k2 tog, m1, k2, m1, k2 tog, k11.
Row 8: Sl 1 purlwise, k2 tog, k15.
Row 9: Sl 1 purlwise, k2 tog, m1, k2, m1, k2 tog, k4, (m2, k2 tog) twice, k2 tog.
Row 10: Sl 1 purlwise, (k2, p1) twice, k11.
Row 11: Sl 1 purlwise, k2 tog, m1, k2, m1, k2 tog, k11.
Row 12: Cast off 6 sts, k11.
Repeat rows 1–12.

Row 26: As row 24.
Row 27: Sl 1, k1, p2, k1, m1, sl 1, k1, psso, k1, p2, (m1, k1) 16 times, sl last st. K edge st of 7th row, psso.
Row 28: Sl 1, p32, k2, p4, k4.
Row 29: Sl 1, k1, p2, k2, m1, sl 1, k1, psso, p2, k1, (m1, k2 tog) 15 times, k edge st of row 5.
Row 30: Sl 1, p33, k2, p4, k4.
Row 31: Sl 1, k1, p2, k3, m1, p2 tog, p1, k to last st. Slip, knit edge st of 3rd row, psso.
Row 32: Cast off 32, k3, p4, k4.
Repeat 1–32 until length desired.

Handtowel 3: ARLE

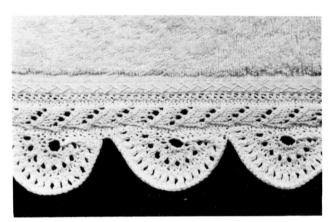

Cast on 12 sts. Knit one row.
Row 1: Sl 1, k1, p2, m1, sl 1, k1, psso, k2, p2, k2.
Row 2: Sl 1, k3, p4, k4.
Row 3: Sl 1, k1, p2, k1, m1, sl 1, k1, psso, k1, p2, k2.
Row 4: As row 2.
Row 5: Sl 1, k1, p2, k2, m1, sl 1, k1, psso, p2, k2.
Row 6: As row 2.
Row 7: Sl 1, k1, p2, k3, m1, p2 tog, p1, k2.
Row 8: As row 2.
Repeat these 8 rows once.
Row 17: Sl 1, k1, p2, m1, sl 1, k1, psso, k2, p2, k1, m2, k1.
Row 18: Sl 1, work in m2 of previous row—(k1, p1) 3 times, k3, p4, k4.
Row 19: Sl 1, k1, p2, k1, m1, sl 1, k1, psso, k1, p2, k7, sl the last st, k the edge st of row 15, psso.
Row 20: Sl 1, p7, k2, p4, k4.
Row 21: Sl 1, k1, p2, k2, m1, sl 1, k1, psso, p2, m1 (by picking up the thread that lies before the next st, and knitting it), k1, (m1, k1) 6 times, m1, sl the last stitch, pick up and knit the edge st of 13th row, psso.
Row 22: Sl 1, p15, k2, p4, k4.
Row 23: Sl 1, k1, p2, k3, m1, p2 tog, p1, k1, *m1, k2 tog*. Repeat from * 6 times, m1, sl last st, knit edge st of the 11th row, psso.
Row 24: Sl 1, p16, k2, p4, k4.
Row 25: Sl 1, k1, p2, m1, sl 1, k1, psso, k2, p2, k16, sl last st. K edge st of 9th row, psso.

Handtowel 4: OBLIQUE

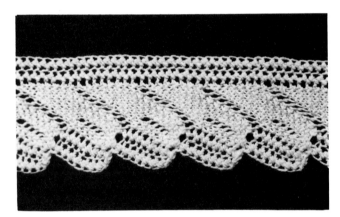

Cast on 17 sts.
Row 1: (M1, p2 tog) twice, k1, m1, k2 tog, k6, (m1, p2 tog) twice.
Row 2: (M1, p2 tog) twice, k9, (m1, p2 tog) twice.
Row 3: (M1, p2 tog) twice, k2, m1, k2 tog, k3, m1, k2, (m1, p2 tog) twice.
Row 4: (M1, p2 tog) twice, k10, (m1, p2 tog) twice.
Row 5: (M1, p2 tog) twice, k3, m1, k2 tog, k3, m1, k2, (m1, p2 tog) twice.
Row 6: (M1, p2 tog) twice, k11, (m1, p2 tog) twice.
Row 7: (M1, p2 tog) twice, k4, m1, k2 tog, k3, m1, k2, (m1, p2 tog) twice.
Row 8: (M1, p2 tog) twice, k12, (m1, p2 tog) twice.
Row 9: (M1, p2 tog) twice, k5, m1, k2 tog, k3, m1, k2, (m1, p2 tog) twice.
Row 10: (M1, p2 tog) twice, k13, (m1, p2 tog) twice.
Row 11: (M1, p2 tog) twice, k6, m1, k2 tog, k3, m1, k2, (m1, p2 tog) twice.
Row 12: (M1, p2 tog) twice, k14, (m1, p2 tog) twice.
Row 13: (M1, p2 tog) twice, k7, m1, k2 tog, k5, (m1, p2 tog) twice.
Row 14: (M1, p2 tog) twice, k14, (m1, p2 tog) twice.
Row 15: (M1, p2 tog) twice, k8, m1, (sl 1, k2 tog, psso) twice, (m1, p2 tog) twice.
Row 16: Cast off 3 sts, k1, m1, k10, (m1, p2 tog) twice.
Repeat rows 1–16 until length desired.

Handtowel 5: FLORENCE

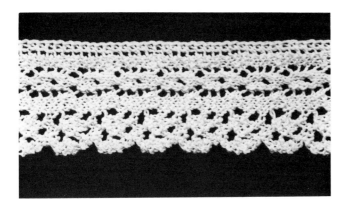

Cast on 17 sts.
Row 1: K2, m1, k2 tog, k1, m1, k2tog, k1, sl 1, k1, psso, m1, k3, m2, k2 tog, m2, k2.
Row 2: K3, p1, k2, p1, k3, p5, k5.
Row 3: K2, m1, k2 tog, k1, m1, k2 tog, k1, sl 1, k1, psso, m1, k10.
Row 4: K2, m2, k2 tog, k1, k2 tog, m2, k2 tog, k2, p3 k6.
Row 5: K2, m1, k2 tog, k2, m1, k3 tog, m1, k4, p1, k4, p1, k2.
Row 6: K12, p3, k6.
Row 7: K2, m1, (k2 tog) twice, m1, k3, m1, k2 tog, k2, m2, sl 1, k3 tog, psso, m2, (k2tog) twice.
Row 8: K3, p1, k2, p1, k3, p5, k5.
Row 9: As row 3.
Row 10: Cast off 3 sts, k6, p2, m1, p2 tog, p1, k5.
Repeat rows 1–10 until length desired.

Handtowel 6: ELLA

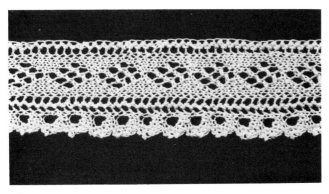

Cast on 16 sts.
Row 1: M1, p2 tog, k4, m1, k2 tog, k3, m1, p2 tog, k1, m2, k2.
Row 2: K2, k1, p1, k1 in m2 of previous row, k1, m1, p2 tog, k9, m1, p2 tog.
Row 3: M1, p2 tog, k3, (m1, k2 tog) twice, k2, m1, p2 tog, k6.
Row 4: K6, m1, p2 tog, k9, m1, p2 tog.
Row 5: M1, p2 tog, k2, (m1, k2 tog) 3 times, k1, m1, p2 tog, k6.

Row 6: Cast off 3 sts, k2, m1, p2 tog, k9, m1, p2 tog.
Row 7: M1, p2 tog, k3, (m1, k2 tog) twice, k2, m1, p2 tog, k1, m2, k2.
Row 8: K2, k1, p1, k1 in m2 of previous row, k1 m1, p2 tog, k9, m1, p2tog.
Row 9: M1, p2 tog, k4, m1, k2 tog, k3, m1, p2 tog, k6.
Row 10: K6, m1, p2 tog, k9, m1, p2 tog.
Row 11: M1, p2 tog, k9, m1, p2 tog, k6.
Row 12: Cast off 3 sts, k2, m1, p2 tog, k9, m1, p2 tog.
Repeat 1–12 until length desired.

Handtowel 7: DOMINO

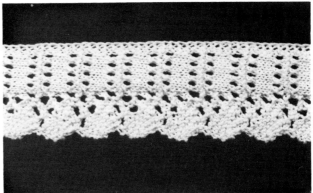

Cast on 21 sts.
Row 1: K3, (m1, k2 tog) 4 times, m2, k2 tog, k8.
Row 2: K10, p1. k11.
Row 3: K22.
Row 4: K22.
Row 5: K3, (m1, k2 tog) 4 times, k1, (m2, k2 tog) twice, k6.
Row 6: K7, p1, k2, p1, k13.
Row 7: K3, p8, k13.
Row 8: K24.
Row 9: K3, p8, k1, (m2, k2 tog) 3 times, sl next 4 sts, k2 tog, pass the 4 sl sts over last st.
Row 10: K2 tog, (k1, p1) twice, k1, p2, k13.
Repeat rows 1–10 until length desired.

Handtowel 8: GERTRUDE

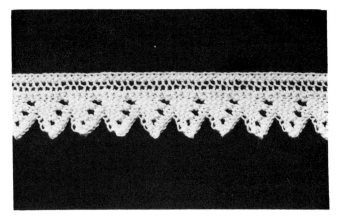

Cast on 10 sts.
Row 1: Sl 1, k2, m1, k2 tog, k5.
Row 2: M1, k7, m1, k2 tog, k1.
Row 3: Sl 1, k2, m1, k2 tog, k6.
Row 4: M1, k8, m1, k2 tog, k1.
Row 5: Sl 1, k2, m1, k2 tog, k7.
Row 6: M1, k9, m1, k2 tog, k1.
Row 7: Sl 1, k2, m1, k2 tog, k1, *m2, k2 tog. Repeat from * twice, k1.
Row 8: K3, (p1, k2) twice, p1, k3, m1, k2 tog, k1.
Row 9: Sl 1, k2, m1, k2 tog, k11.
Row 10: Cast off 6 sts, k6, m1, k2 tog, k1.
Repeat rows 1–10 until length desired.

Handtowel 9: HENDRA VALE

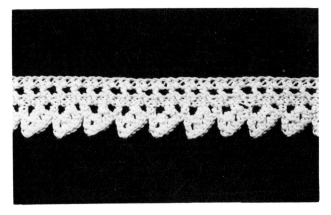

Cast on 8 sts.
Row 1: K1, k2 tog, m2, k2 tog, k1, m4, k2.
Row 2: K2, (k1, p1) twice in m4 of previous row, k3, p1, k2.
Row 3: K12.
Row 4: K12.
Row 5: K1, k2 tog, m2, k2 tog, k1, (m2, k2 tog) 3 times.
Row 6: (K2, p1) 3 times, k3, p1, k2.
Row 7: K15.
Row 8: Cast off 7 sts, k7.
Repeat rows 1–8 until length desired.

Handtowel 10: CLOVER

Cast on 16 sts.
Row 1: Sl 1, k2, (m2, k2 tog) twice, k6, m2, k2 tog, k1.
Row 2: K3, p1, k8, p1, k2, p1, k3.
Row 3: Sl 1, k18.
Row 4: Knit.
Row 5: Sl 1, k2, (m2, k2 tog) twice, k7, (m2, k2 tog) twice, k1.
Row 6: K3, p1, k2, p1, k9, p1, k2, p1, k3.
Row 7: Sl 1, k22.
Row 8: Knit.
Row 9: Sl 1, k2, (m2, k2 tog) twice, (m2, sl 1, k2 tog, psso) 5 times, k1.
Row 10: K3, p1, (k2, p1) 6 times, k3.
Row 11: Sl 1, k24.
Row 12: Cast off 9 sts, k15.
Repeat rows 1–12 until length desired.

Handtowel 11: ROSEMARY

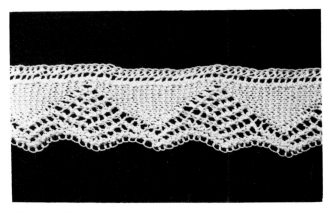

Cast on 15 sts.
Row 1: Sl 1, k1, m1, k2 tog, k5, (m1, k2 tog) twice, m1, k2.
Row 2 and all even numbered rows: M1, k2 tog, k to end of row.
Row 3: Sl 1, k1, m1, k2 tog, k4, (m1, k2 tog) 3 times, m1, k2.
Row 5: Sl 1, k1, m1, k2 tog, k3, (m1, k2 tog) 4 times, m1, k2.
Row 7: Sl 1, k1, m1, k2 tog, k2, (m1, k2 tog) 5 times, m1, k2.
Row 9: Sl 1, k1, m1, k2 tog, k1, (m1, k2 tog) 6 times, m1, k2.

Row 11: Sl 1, k1, m1, k2 tog, k1, k2 tog, (m1, k2 tog) 6 times, k1.
Row 13: Sl 1, k1, m1, k2 tog, k2, k2 tog, (m1, k2 tog) 5 times, k1.
Row 15: Sl 1, k1, m1, k2 tog, k3, k2 tog, (m1, k2 tog) 4 times, k1.
Row 17: Sl 1, k1, m1, k2 tog, k4, k2 tog, (m1, k2 tog) 3 times, k1.
Row 19: Sl 1, k1, m1, k2 tog, k5, k2 tog, (m1, k2 tog) twice, k1.
Row 21: Sl 1, k1, m1, k2 tog, k7, m1, k2 tog, m1, k2.
Row 23: Sl 1, k1, m1, k2 tog, k8, m1, k2 tog, m1, k2.
Row 25: Sl 1, k1, m1, k2 tog, k9, m1, k2 tog, m1, k2.
Row 27: Sl 1, k1, m1, k2 tog, k10, m1, k2 tog, m1, k2.
Row 29: Sl 1, k1, m1, k2 tog, k11, m1, k2 tog, m1, k2.
Row 31: Sl 1, k1, m1, k2 tog, k9, k2 tog, (m1, k2 tog) twice, k1.
Row 33: Sl 1, k1, m1, k2 tog, k8, k2 tog, (m1, k2 tog) twice, k1.
Row 35: Sl 1, k1, m1, k2 tog, k7, k2 tog, (m1, k2 tog) twice, k1.
Row 37: Sl 1, k1, m1, k2 tog, k6, k2 tog, (m1, k2 tog) twice, k1.
Row 39: Sl 1, k1, m1, k2 tog, k5, (k2 tog, m1) twice, k2 tog, k1.
Row 40: M1, k2 tog, k to end of row.
Repeat rows 1–40 until length desired.

Handtowel 12: TRIPLE POINT

Cast on 18 sts.
Row 1: Sl 1, k3, m1, k2 tog, k1, (m1, k2 tog) 3 times, m1, k2, m2, k2 tog, k1.
Row 2: K3, p1, k12, m1, k2 tog, k2.
Row 3: Sl 1, k3, m1, k2 tog, k2, (m1, k2 tog) 3 times, m1, k6.
Row 4: K17, m1, k2 tog, k2.
Row 5: Sl 1, k3, m1, k2 tog, k3, (m1, k2 tog) 3 times, m1, k2, m2, k2 tog, m2, k2.
Row 6: K3, p1, k2, p1, k14, m1, k2 tog, k2.
Row 7: Sl 1, k3, m1, k2 tog, k4, (m1, k2 tog) 3 times, m1, k9.
Row 8: K22, m1, k2 tog, k2.
Row 9: Sl 1, k3, m1, k2 tog, k5, (m1 k2 tog) 3 times, m1, k2, (m2, k2 tog) 3 times, k1.
Row 10: K3, p1, (k2, p1) twice, k16, m1, k2 tog, k2.

Row 11: Sl 1, k3, (m1, k2 tog, k2) twice, (m1, k2 tog) 3 times, m1, k12.
Row 12: Cast off 7 sts, k19, m1, k2 tog, k2.
Row 13: Sl 1, k3, m1, k2 tog, k3, m1, k2 tog, k2, (m1, k2 tog) 3 times, m1, k2, m2, k2 tog, k1.
Row 14: K3, p1, k18, m1, k2 tog, k2.
Row 15: Sl 1, k3, m1, k2 tog, k4, m1, k2 tog, k2, (m1, k2 tog) 3 times, m1, k6.
Row 16: K23, m1, k2 tog, k2.
Row 17: Sl 1, k3, m1, k2 tog, k2, m1, k2 tog, k1, m1, k2 tog, k2, (m1, k2 tog) 3 times, m1, k2, m2, k2 tog, m2, k2.
Row 18: K3, p1, k2, p1, k20, m1, k2 tog, k2.
Row 19: Sl 1, k3, m1, k2 tog, k25.
Row 20: K8, k2 tog, (m1, k2 tog) 4 times, k2, m1, k2 tog, k5, m1, k2 tog, k2.
Row 21: Sl 1, k3, m1, k2 tog, k17, (m2, k2 tog) 3 times, k1.
Row 22: K3, (p1, k2) twice, p1, k1, k2 tog, (m1, k2 tog) 4 times, k2, m1, k2 tog, k4, m1, k2 tog, k2.
Row 23: Sl 1, k3, m1, k2 tog, k26.
Row 24: Cast off 7 sts, k3, k2 tog, (m1, k2 tog) 4 times, k2, m1, k2 tog, k3, m1, k2 tog, k2.
Row 25: Sl 1, k3, m1, k2 tog, k15, m2, k2 tog, k1.
Row 26: K3, p1, k1, k2 tog, (m1, k2 tog) 4 times, k6, m1, k2 tog, k2.
Row 27: Sl 1, k3, m1, k2 tog, k18.
Row 28: K5, k2 tog, (m1, k2 tog) 4 times, k5, m1, k2 tog, k2.
Row 29: Sl 1, k3, m1, k2 tog, k13, m2, k2 tog, m2, k2.
Row 30: K3, p1, k2, p1, k1, k2 tog, (m1, k2 tog) 4 times, k4, m1, k2 tog, k2.
Row 31: Sl 1, k3, m1, k2 tog, k19.
Row 32: K8, k2 tog, (m1, k2 tog) 4 times, k3, m1, k2 tog, k2.
Row 33: Sl 1, k3, m1, k2 tog, k11, (m2, k2 tog) 3 times, k1.
Row 34: K3, p1, (k2, p1) twice, k1, k2 tog, (m1, k2 tog) 4 times, k2, m1, k2 tog, k2.
Row 35: Sl 1, k3, m1, k2 tog, k20.
Row 36: Cast off 7 sts, k3, k2 tog, k9, m1, k2 tog, k2.
Repeat rows 1–36 until length desired.

12. Face Washer Edgings

Six wider than usual face washer edgings.

Materials

Each edging was knitted on 2 mm needles using 4 ply cotton. Allow ample fullness when attaching edging to face washer. You will probably have left-over yarn from your towels to edge the washers. If not, one 50 gm ball will be sufficient for two face washers.

Face Washer 1: HEATH

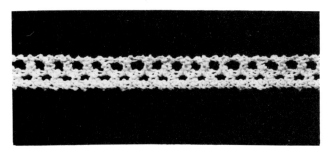

Cast on 7 sts.
Row 1: K2 tog, m3, sl 1, k2 tog, psso, m2, k2.
Row 2: K3, p1, k2, p1, k2.
Row 3: Knit.
Row 4: Cast off 2 sts, knit to end of row.
Repeat rows 1–4 until length desired.

Face Washer 2: FERN

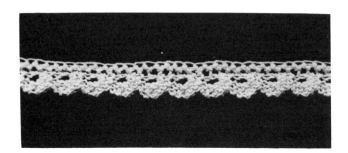

Cast on 5 sts.
Row 1: M1, p2 tog, k1, m1, k2.
Row 2: K2, (k1, p1, k1) in m1 of previous row, k1, m1, p2 tog.
Row 3: M1, p2 tog, k6.
Row 4: K6, m1, p2 tog.
Row 5: M1, p2 tog, k6.
Row 6: Cast off 3 sts, k2, m1, p2 tog.
Repeat rows 1–6 until length desired.

Face Washer 3: DAISY

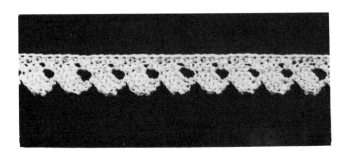

Cast on 5 sts.
Row 1: Sl 1, k1, k2 tog, m1, k1.
Row 2: K1, (k1, p1, k1, p1, k1) in next st, m1, k2 tog, k1.
Row 3: Sl 1, k1, m1, k2 tog, k5.
Row 4: K6, m1, k2 tog, k1.
Row 5: As row 3.
Row 6: As row 4.
Row 7: As row 3.
Row 8: Cast off 4 sts, k1, m1, k2 tog, k1.
Repeat row 1–8 until length desired.

Face Washer 4: COWSLIP

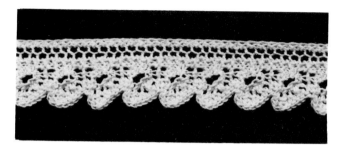

Cast on 11 sts.
Row 1: K3, m1, k2 tog, k1, sl 1, k1, psso, cast on 4 sts, k2 tog, k1.
Row 2: K10, m1, k2 tog, k1.
Row 3: K3, m1, k2 tog, sl 1, k1, psso, (m1, k1) 4 times, m1, k2 tog.
Row 4: K13, m1, k2 tog, k1.
Row 5: K3, m1, k2 tog, sl 1, k1, psso, (m1, k1) twice, m1, sl 1, k2 tog, psso, (m1, k1) twice, m1, k2 tog.
Row 6: K15, m1, k2 tog, k1.
Row 7: K3, m1, k2 tog, k11, k2 tog.
Row 8: Cast off 6 sts, k7, m1, k2 tog, k1.
Repeat row 1–8 until length desired.

Face Washer 6: FORGET-ME-NOT

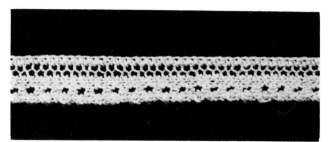

Cast on 8 sts.
Row 1: Sl 1, k2, m1, k2 tog, k1, m2, k2.
Row 2: K3, p1, k3, m1, k2 tog, k1.
Row 3: Sl 1, k2, m1, k2 tog, k5.
Row 4: Cast off 2 sts, k4, m1, k2 tog, k1.
Repeat rows 1–4 until length desired.

Face Washer 5: DANDELION

Cast on 9 sts.
Row 1: K2, (m1, k2 tog) twice, m1, k3.
Row 2 and every alternate row: Knit.
Row 3: K2, (m1, k2 tog) twice, m1, k4.
Row 5: K2, (m1, k2 tog) twice, m1, k5.
Row 7: K2, (m1, k2 tog) twice, m1, k6.
Row 9: K2, (m1, k2 tog) twice, m1, k7.
Row 11: K2, (m1, k2 tog) twice, m1, k8.
Row 12: Cast off 6 sts, knit to end of row.
Repeat rows 1–12 until length desired.

13. The Carinya Collection

Heirloom Bed Linen in Miniature

The *Carinya Coverlet*, motif, and edging, were knitted on 1.25 mm needles, using size ten cotton.

The *homespun sheets* feature incredibly fine, and intricate hemstitching. The lace edging on the top sheet was knitted with 60 cotton, with 1.25 mm needles.

The *matching pillowcases* are embroidered with tiny floral sprays, and dozens of French knots. The knitted edging complements the embroidery.

The *satin-bound blankets* are hand knitted in 1 ply French mohair. The ribbons are sewn with tiny stitches.

Carinya Coverlet: SOPHIE

Cast on 8 sts; 2 sts on each of 4 needles. Work with 5th.
Round 1 and alternate rounds: Knit.
Round 2: *M1, k1 * to end of round.
Round 4: *M1, k2 * to end of round.
Round 6: *M1, k3 * to end of round.
Round 8: *M1, k4 * to end of round.
Round 10: *M1, k5 * to end of round.
Round 12: *M1, k1, m1, k3, k2 tog* to end of round.
Round 14: *M1, k3, m1, k2, k2 tog* to end of round.
Round 16: *M1, k5, m1, k1, k2 tog* to end of round.
Round 18: *M1, k7, m1, k2 tog* to end of round.
Round 20: *M1, k1, m1, k5, k2 tog, m1, k2 tog* to end of round.
Round 22: *M1, k2 tog, m1, k1, m1, k4, k2 tog, m1, k2 tog* to end of round.
Round 24: *(M1, k2 tog) twice, m1, k1, m1, k3, k2 tog, m1, k2 tog* to end of round.
Round 26: *(M1, k2 tog) 3 times, m1, k1, m1, k2, k2 tog, m1, k2 tog* to end of round.
Round 28: *(M1, k2 tog) 4 times, (m1, k1) twice, k2 tog, m1, k2 tog* to end of round.
Round 30: *(M1, k2 tog) 5 times, m1, k1, (m1, k2 tog) twice* to end of round.
Round 32: Cast off to last 18 sts. These are worked on two needles to form square. You will have 17 sts on L.H. needle, and one st on R.H. needle. Continue square section of the motif thus.

Row 1: K2, (p3, k3) twice, p3.
Row 2: (K3, p3) 3 times.
Row 3 *and* 4: As row 2.
Row 5: (P3, k3) 3 times.
Row 6, 7 *and* 8: As row 5.
Row 9: (K3, p3) 3 times.
Row 10 11 *and* 12: As row 9.
Row 13: (P3, k3) 3 times.
Row 14, 15 *and* 16: As row 13.
Row 17: (K3, p3) 3 times.
Row 18, 19 *and* 20: As row 17.
Row 21: (P3, k3) 3 times.
Row 22, 23 *and* 24: As row 21.
Cast off.
To straighten edge of work, you will need to knit wedge shaped pieces.

Trapezoid or Wedge

Cast on 17 sts.
Row 1 *and alternate rows*: Purl.
Row 2: K1, (m1, k2 tog) 7 times, (m1, k1) twice.
Row 4: K1, (m1, k2 tog) 8 times, (m1, k1) twice.
Row 6: K1, (m1, k2 tog) 9 times, (m1, k1) twice.
Row 8: K1, (m1, k2 tog) 10 times, (m1, k1) twice.
Row 10: K1, (m1, k2 tog) 11 times, (m1, k1) twice.
Row 12: K1, (m1, k2 tog) 12 times, (m1, k1) twice.
Row 14: K1, (m1, k2 tog) 13 times, (m1, k1) twice.
Row 15: Purl cast off.
When joining the motifs for an article requiring a square corner, you will need a small **triangle**. Work as follows:
Cast on 17 sts.
Row 1: Purl.
Row 2: (K2 tog, m1) 8 times, k1.
Row 3: P2 tog, p to 2nd last st, p2 tog. *Work alternate rows thus.*
Row 4: (K2 tog, m1) 7 times, k1.
Row 6: (K2 tog, m1) 6 times, k1.
Row 8: (K2 tog, m1) 5 times, k1.
Row 10: (K2 tog, m1) 4 times, k1.
Row 12: (K2 tog, m1) 3 times, k1.
Row 14: (K2 tog, m1) twice, k1.
Row 15: P2 tog, p1, p2 tog.
Cast off.
Join motifs to your requirements. The coverlet illustrated was edged in the following pattern:

Above: The Carinya collection (section 13, p.70).

Right: Knitting tools on Carinya coverlet: Sophie (section 13, p.70).

Left: Six lace edged handkerchiefs (section 14, p.77).
Below left: Five exquisite collars (section 15, p.79).
Below right: Curtained corner (section 16, p.83) with cushions (section 2, p.26).

Filigree plate (section 19, p.94), shelf edgings (section 6, p.45), and lace edged handkerchiefs (section 14, p.77).

Cushion: Rosedale (section 1, p.19), Carinya coverlet (section 13, p.70) and Pomander ball (section 1, p.19).

Carinya collection (section 13, p.70).

Carinya Edging

Cast on 29 sts.
Row 1: K5, p18, k4, m1, k2.
Row 2: M1, k2 tog, k to end of row.
Row 3: K26, m1, k2 tog, m1, k2.
Row 4: M1, k2 tog, k6, p18. Turn.
Row 5: K1, (m1, k2 tog) 9 times, k1, (m1, k2 tog) twice, m1, k2.
Row 6: M1, k2 tog, k7, p18. Turn.
Row 7: K2, (m1, k2 tog) 8 times, k1, (m1, k2 tog) 3 times, m1, k2.
Row 8: M1, k2 tog, k8, p18, k5.
Row 9: K6, (m1, k2 tog) 9 times, (k2 tog, m1) 3 times, k2 tog, k1.
Row 10: M1, k2 tog, k7, p18, k5.
Row 11: K25, (k2 tog, m1) twice, k2 tog, k1.
Row 12: M1, k2 tog, k6, p18, turn.
Row 13: P18, k3, k2 tog, m1, k2 tog, k1.
Row 14: M1, k2 tog, k23, turn.
Row 15: P18, k4, k2 tog, k1.
Row 16: M1, k2 tog, k to end of row.
Repeat rows 1–16 until length required.
Sew edging on all sides of coverlet, allowing ample fullness at corners.

Sheet Edging: CARINYA

Cast on 23 sts.
Row 1: Sl 1, k3, m1, k2 tog, k2, m2, sl 1, k2 tog, psso, k2, (m1, k2 tog) 4 times, M1, k2.
Row 2: M1, k2 tog, k13, p1, k4, m1, k2 tog, K2.
Row 3: Sl 1, k3, m1, k2 tog, k4, k2 tog, k2, (m1, k2 tog) 4 times, m1, k2.
Row 4: M1, k2 tog, k18, m1, k2 tog, K2.
Row 5: Sl 1, k3, m1, k2 tog, m2, k2 tog, m2, sl 1, k2 tog, psso, k1, (m1, k2 tog) 4 times, m1, k2.

Row 6: M1, k2 tog, k12, p1, k2, p1, k4, m1, k2 tog, k2.
Row 7: Sl 1, k3, m1, k2 tog, k10, (m1, k2 tog) 4 times, m1, k2.
Row 8: M1, k2 tog, k21, m1, k2 tog, k2.
Row 9: Sl 1, k3, m1, k2 tog, k2, m2, k2 tog, (m2, sl 1, k2 tog, psso) twice, k1, (m1, k2 tog) 4 times, m1, k2.
Row 10: M1, k2 tog, k12, (p1, k2) twice, p1, k4, m1, k2 tog, k2.
Row 11: Sl 1, k3, m1, k2 tog, k13, (m1, k2 tog) 4 times, m1, k2.
Row 12: M1, k2 tog, k24, m1, k2 tog, k2.
Row 13: Sl 1, k3, m1, k2 tog, k2, m2, k2 tog, (m2, sl 1, k2 tog, psso) 3 times, k1, (m1, k2 tog) 4 times, m1, k2.
Row 14: M1, k2 tog, k12, (p1, k2) 3 times, p1, k4, m1, k2 tog, k2.
Row 15: Sl 1, k3, m1, k2 tog, k16, (m1, k2 tog) 4 times, m1, k2.
Row 16: M1, k2 tog, k27, m1, k2 tog, k2.
Row 17: Sl 1, k3, m1, k2 tog, k27.
Row 18: Cast off 10 sts, k18, m1, k2 tog, k2.
Repeat rows 1–18 until length desired.

Pillows: CARINYA

Cast on 7 sts.
Row 1: K5, m1, k2.
Row 2 *and alternate rows*: M1, k2 tog, k to end of row.
Row 3: K4, m1, k2 tog, m1, k2.
Row 5: K3, (m1, k2 tog) twice, m1, k2.
Row 7: K2, (m1, k2 tog) 3 times, m1, k2.
Row 9: K2, (k2 tog, m1) 3 times, k2 tog, k1.
Row 11: K3, (k2 tog, m1) twice, k2 tog, k1.
Row 13: K4, k2 tog, m1, k2 tog, k1.
Row 15: K5, k2 tog, K1.
Row 16: As row 2.
Repeat rows 1–16 until length desired.

14. Lace Edged Linen Handkerchiefs

Six exquisite tiny edgings to knit, using 100 cotton and 1.25 mm needles. One ball should make three handkerchiefs. However, the quantity will depend on your handkerchief size. Attach edging to handkerchief with tiny stitches. The handkerchiefs make an ideal gift for a bride.

Handkerchief 1: BERNICE

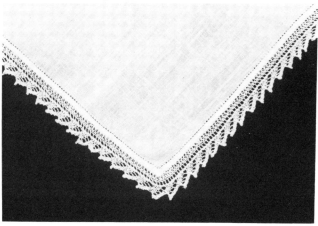

Cast on 8 sts.
Row 1: Sl 1, k2, m1, k2 tog, k1, m2, k2.
Row 2: K3, p1, k3, m1, k2 tog, k1.
Row 3: Sl 1, k2, m1, k2 tog, k5.
Row 4: Cast off 2 sts, k4, m1, k2 tog, k1.
Repeat rows 1–4 until length desired.

Handkerchief 2: DELPHA

Cast on 8 sts.
Row 1: Knit.
Row 2: Sl 1, k2, (m1, k2 tog) twice, inc in last st.
Row 3: Knit.
Row 4: Sl 1, k2, m1, k2 tog, k1, m1, k2 tog, inc in last st.
Row 5: Knit.
Row 6: Sl 1, k2, m1, k2 tog, k2, m1, k2 tog, inc in last st.
Row 7: Knit.
Row 8: Sl 1, k2, m1, k2 tog, k3, m1, k2 tog, inc in last st.
Row 9: Cast off 4 sts, k7.
Repeat rows 2–9 until length desired.

Handkerchief 3: NINA

Cast on 7 sts.
Row 1: Sl 1, k2, m2, k2 tog, m2, k2 tog.
Row 2: Sl 1, k1, p1, k2, p1, k3.
Row 3: Sl 1, k4, m2, k2 tog, m2, k2 tog.
Row 4: Sl 1, k1, p1, k2, p1, k5.
Row 5: Sl 1, k6, m2, k2 tog, m2, k2 tog.
Row 6: Sl 1, k1, p1, k2, p1, k7.
Row 7: Sl 1, k12.
Row 8: Cast off 6 sts, k6.
Repeat rows 1–8 until length desired.

Handkerchief 4: CAROL

Cast on 8 sts.
Row 1: K3, m1, k2 tog, m2, k tog, k1.
Row 2: K3, p1, k2, m1, k2 tog, k1.
Row 3: K3, m1, k2 tog, k1, m2, k2 tog, k1.
Row 4: K3, p1, k3, m1, k2 tog, k1.
Row 5: K3, m1, k2 tog, k2, m2, k2 tog, k1.
Row 6: K3, p1, k4, m1, k2 tog, k1.
Row 7: K3, m1, k2 tog, k6.
Row 8: Cast off 3 sts, k4, m1, k2 tog, k1.
Repeat rows 1–8 until length desired.

Handkerchief 5: SARAH

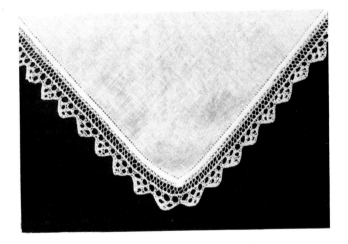

Cast on 7 sts.
Row 1: Knit.
Row 2: Purl.
Row 3: Sl 1, k2, m1, k2 tog, m2, k2 tog.
Row 4: M1, k2, p1, k2, m1, k2 tog, k1.
Row 5: Sl 1, k2, m1, k2 tog, k4.
Row 6: K6, m1, k2 tog, k1.
Row 7: Sl 1, k2, m1, k2 tog, (m2, k2 tog) twice.
Row 8: K2, p1, k2, p1, k2, m1, k2 tog, k1.

Row 9: Sl 1, k2, m1, k2 tog, k6.
Row 10: K8, m1, k2 tog, k1.
Row 11: Sl 1, k2, m1, k2 tog, (m2, k2 tog) 3 times.
Row 12: (K2, p1) 3 times, k2, m1, k2 tog, k1.
Row 13: Sl 1, k2, m1, k2 tog, k9.
Row 14: Cast off 7 sts, k3, m1, k2 tog, k1.
Repeat rows 3–14 until length desired.

Handkerchief 6: LUCY

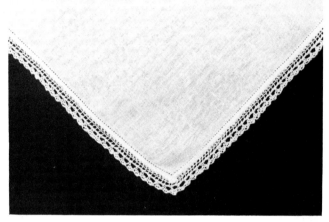

Cast on 6 sts.
Row 1: Sl 1, k1, m1, k2 tog, m2, k2.
Row 2: Sl 1, k2, p1, k4.
Row 3: Sl 1, k1, m1, k2 tog, k4.
Row 4: Cast off 2 sts, k5.
Repeat rows 1–4 until length desired.

15. Collars

Five exquisite collars to knit. Each one quite different and delicate.

The PRISCILLA (No. 5) is an exceptional piece of knitting. This intricate pattern bears the date 31 March 1849. The original collar was knitted on No. 19 needles, using cotton thread No. 120. The collar illustrated was knitted on 2 mm (14) needles, using cotton No. 40. The other four designs were knitted on 2.75 mm needles, using 20 cotton.

Collar 1: JULIE

Materials:

1 20 gm ball cotton No. 20
2.75 mm (or No. 12) knitting needles
1.25 (No. 3) crochet hook
1 metre 3 mm ribbon

Cast on 101 sts.
Row 1: Knit.
Row 2: Purl.
Row 3: As row 1.
Row 4: As row 2.
Row 5: K3, m1, k1, (m1, k2 tog, m1, k1) 14 times, (m1, k2 tog) 3 times, (m1, k1, m1, k2 tog) 16 times, k1 (132 sts on needle).
Row 6: P twice into 1st st. Purl to end.
Row 7: Knit.
Row 8: Purl.
Row 9: As row 7.
Row 10: As row 8
Row 11: K2, *m1, k2 tog, k1, k2 tog, m1, k1 *. Repeat from

* to last 11 sts, m1, k2 tog, k1, k2 tog, m1, (k3 tog) twice (129 sts on needle).
Row 12: P3, *m1, p3 tog, m1, p3 *. Repeat to end of row.
Row 13: K2, k2 tog, * m1, k1, m1, k2 tog, k1, k2 tog. Repeat from * to last 5 sts, m1, k1, m1, k2 tog, k2.
Row 14: P3, * m1, p3, m1, p3 tog. Repeat from * to last 6 sts, (m1, p3) twice (131 sts on needle).
Row 15: K3, *m1, k2 tog, k1, k2 tog, m1, k1. Repeat from * to last 2 sts, k2.
Row 16: P4, *m1, p3 tog, m1, p3. Repeat from * to last st, p1.
Row 17: K3, k2 tog, *m1, k1, m1, k2 tog, k1, k2 tog. Repeat from * to last 6 sts, m1, k1, m1, k2 tog, k3.
Row 18: P4, *m1, p3, m1, p3 tog. Repeat from * to last 7 sts, m1, p3, m1, p4 (133 sts on needle).
Row 19: Knit.
Row 20: Purl.
Row 21: As row 19.
Row 22: As row 20.
Row 23: K5, k2 tog, * m1, k1, m1, sl 1, k1, psso, k4, k2 tog. Repeat from * to last 9 sts, m1, k1, m1, sl 1, k1, psso, k6.
Row 24: Purl.
Row 25: *Sl 1, k1, psso, k2, k2 tog, m1, k3, m1. Repeat from * to last 7 sts, sl 1, k1, psso, k2, k3 tog (130 sts on needle).
Row 26: Purl.
Row 27: *Sl 1, k1, psso, k2 tog, m1, k1, m1, k3 tog, m1, k1, m1. Repeat from * to last 4 sts, sl 1, k1, psso, k2 tog (128 sts on needle).
Row 28: Purl.
Row 29: *K2 tog, m1, k3, m1, k1, m1, k3, m1. Repeat from * to last 2 sts, k2 tog.
Row 30: Purl.
Row 31: K2, *m1, k3 tog, m1, k3. Repeat from * to last 5 sts, m1, k3 tog, m1, k2.
Row 32: Purl.

Edging

Using crochet hook, work 1dc into 1st 2sts. Slip off knitting needle. * 6ch, 1dc into next 3sts. Slip off. Repeat from * to last 2sts. 6ch. 1dc into next 2sts. Work along row having eight 6ch loops evenly spaced. Fasten off.
With right side facing, attach thread to 1st row, and on other short side of collar 1dc into same place as join. Continue to work over row, ends having eight 6ch loops evenly spaced, ending with 1sl st into 1st dc. Fasten off. Work single crochet around neck edge. Press the collar. Thread ribbon through 5th row of work. Tie in bow.

Collar 2: DORA

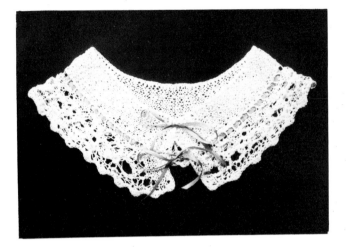

Materials:

1 ball cotton No 20.
Pair 2.75 (No. 12) needles

Cast on 20 sts. Knit 12 rows.
Row 1: Sl 1, k10, k2 tog, m1, k1, k2 tog, m3, k2 tog, m1, k2.
Row 2: K5, p1, k5, m1, k2 tog, k9.
Row 3: Sl 1, k12, m1, k2 tog, k3, k2 tog, m1, k2.
Row 4: K11, m1, k2 tog, k9.
Row 5: Sl 1, k13, m1, k2 tog, k1, k2 tog, k1, m1, k2.
Row 6: K2, turn, sl 1, k1, turn, k11, m1, k2 tog, k9.
Row 7: Sl 1, k12, k2 tog, m1, k3 tog, m1, k2 tog, m1, k2.
Row 8: K10, m1, k2 tog, k9.
Row 9: Sl 1, k12, k2 tog, k1, k2 tog, k1, m1, k2.
Row 10: K9, m1, k2 tog, k9.
Repeat 1–10 until you have desired length for collar, then finish with 12 rows of knitting. Cuffs can be made, omitting the 12 rows of knitting at beginning and end.
The collar is finished with a small picot **edge** worked thus: 2dc, 2ch, 2dc into same st, then 4dc into 4 sts. Repeat round lace edge. Work plain dc on neck edge.
Size of neck can be adjusted using needle and No. 20 cotton. Thread through knitting, then gather to size desired.

Collar 3: PRUDENCE

Materials:

1 ball cotton No. 20
Pair 2.75 (No. 12) needles

Cast on 23 sts.
Row 1: K3, p12, (m1, k2 tog) 3 times, m1, k2.
Row 2: K21, turn.
Row 3: P13, (m1, k2 tog) 3 times, m1, k2.
Row 4: Knit.
Row 5: K17, (m1, k2 tog) 3 times, m1, k2.
Row 6: K9, p14, turn.
Row 7: K1, (m1, k2 tog) 10 times, m1, k2.
Row 8: K9, p15, turn.
Row 9: Knit.
Row 10: Cast off 4 sts, k to end of row.
Repeat from 1–10 until length desired.
Press the collar lightly, thread ribbon through holes. Tie in bow.

Collar 4: DORCAS

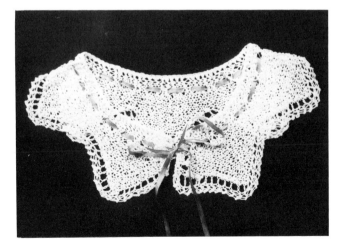

Materials:

1 ball cotton No. 20
Pair 2.75 (No. 12 needles)

Cast on 6 sts.
Row 1: Knit.
Row 2: K2, *ml, k1. Repeat from * to end of row (10 sts).
Row 3: Knit.
Row 4: K2, ml, k to end of row (11 sts).
Row 5: Knit.**
Row 6: K2, ml, k to end of row.
Row 7: Knit.
Row 8: K2, ml, k to end of row.
Row 9: Knit.
Row 10: K2, ml, k to last 3 sts, turn.
Row 11: Knit.
Repeat rows 6 to 11 inclusive, twice (20 sts).
Row 24: K2, ml, k3 tog, k to end of row.
Row 25: Knit.
Repeat rows 24 and 25 once.
Row 28: K2, ml, k3 tog, k to last 3 sts, turn.
Row 29: Knit.
Repeat rows 24 to 29 inclusive, twice (11 sts) **
Repeat from ** to ** four times, then from ** to end of 39th row (12 sts on needle, six points worked).
Next row: K2, ml, k3 tog, (ml, k2 tog) 3 times, k1.
Next row: Knit.
Cast off firmly, ending at neck edge.
Matching **cuffs** may be made thus: Work as for collar until three points have been worked, ending 27th row of 3rd point (12 sts on needle).
Next row: K2, ml, k3 tog, (ml, k2 tog) 3 times, k1.
Next row: Knit.
Cast off firmly.
Press. Thread length of ribbon through holes. Tie in bow.

Collar 5: PRISCILLA

Materials:

1 ball cotton No. 40
Pair 2 mm (No. 14) needles

Cast on 39 sts.
Row 1: K2, ml, p2 tog, k2, ml, k4, k2 tog, p1, k2 tog, k4, ml, p1, ml, k4, k2 tog, p1, k2 tog, k4, ml, k2, ml, p2 tog, k2.
Row 2: K2, ml, p2 tog, k2, p6, (k1, p6) 3 times, k2, ml, p2 tog, k2.
Row 3: K2, ml, p2 tog, k2, ml, k4, k2 tog, p1, k2 tog, k4, ml, p1, ml, k4, k2 tog, p1, k2 tog, k4, ml, k2, ml, p2 tog, k2.
Row 4: as row 2.
Row 5: K2, ml, p2 tog, k2, ml, k2 tog, k2, k2 tog, p1, k2 tog, k2, k2 tog, ml, p1, ml, k2 tog, k2, k2 tog, p1, k2 tog, k2, k2 tog, ml, k2, ml, p2 tog, k2.
Row 6: K2, ml, p2 tog, k2, p5, (k1, p5) 3 times, k2, ml, p2 tog, k2.
Row 7: K2, ml, p2 tog, k2, ml, k1, ml, k4, p1, k3, k2 tog, ml, p1, ml, k2 tog, k3, p1, k4, ml, k1, ml, k2, ml, p2 tog, k2.
Row 8: K2, ml, p2 tog, k2, p7, (k1, p5) twice, k1, p7, k2, ml, p2 tog, k2.
Row 9: K2, ml, p2 tog, k2, ml, k3, ml, k2, k2 tog, p1, k2 tog, k3, p1, k3, k2 tog, p1, k2 tog, k2, ml, k3, ml, k2, ml, p2 tog, k2.
Row 10: K2, ml, p2 tog, k2, p8, (k1, p4) twice, k1, p8, k2, ml, p2 tog, k2.
Row 11: K2, ml, p2 tog, k2, ml, k5, ml, k1, k2 tog, p1, (k2 tog) twice, p1, (k2 tog) twice, p1, k2 tog, k1, ml, k5, ml, k2, ml, p2 tog, k2.
Row 12: K2, ml, p2 tog, k2, p9, (k1, p2) twice, k1, p9, k2, ml, p2 tog, k2.
Row 13: K2, ml, p2 tog, k2, ml, k3, p1, k3, ml, k2 tog, (p1, k2 tog) 3 times, ml, k3, p1, k3, ml, k2, ml, p2 tog, k2.
Row 14: K2, ml, p2 tog, k2, p4, k1, p5, (k1, p1) twice, k1, p5, k1, p4, k2, ml, p2 tog, k2.
Row 15: K2, ml, p2 tog, k2, ml, k4, p1, k4, ml, k3 tog, p1, k3 tog, ml, k4, p1, k4, ml, k2, ml, p2 tog, k2.
Row 16: K2, ml, p2 tog, k2, p5, (k1, p6) twice, k1, p5, k2, ml, p2 tog, k2.
Row 17: K2, ml, p2 tog, k2, ml, k5, p1, k5, ml, k3 tog, ml, k5, p1, k5, ml, k2, ml, p2 tog, k2.
Row 18: K2, ml, p2 tog, k2, p6, k1, p13, k1, p6, k2, ml, p2 tog, k2.
Row 19: K2, ml, p2 tog, k2, ml, k4, k2 tog, p1, k2 tog, k4, ml, p1, ml, k4, k2 tog, p1, k2 tog, k4, ml, k2, ml, p2 tog, k2.
Row 20: as row 2.
Row 21: as row 1.
Row 22: as row 2.
Row 23: as row 1.
Row 24: as row 2.
Row 25: as row 1.
Row 26: as row 2.
Row 27: K2, ml, p2 tog, k2, ml, k2 tog, k2, k2 tog, p1, k2 tog, k2, k2 tog, ml, p1, ml, k2 tog, k2, k2 tog, p1, k2 tog, k2, k2 tog, ml, k2, ml, p2 tog, k2.
Row 28: K2, ml, p2 tog, k2, p5, (k1, p5) 3 times, k2, ml, p2 tog, k2.
Row 29: K2, ml, p2 tog, k2, ml, (k1, p1) in next st, ml, k4,

p1, k3, k2 tog, m1, p1, m1, k2 tog, k3, p1, k4, m1, (k1, p1) in next st, m1, k2, m1, p2 tog, k2.
Row 30: K2, m1, p2 tog, k6, p4, (k1, p5) twice, k1, p4, k6, m1, p2 tog, k2.
Row 31: K2, m1, p2 tog, k2, m1, p4, m1, k2, k2 tog, p1, k2 tog, k3, p1, k3, k2 tog, p1, k2 tog, k2, m1, p4, m1, k2, m1, p2 tog, k2.
Row 32: K2, m1, p2 tog, k8, p3, (k1, p4) twice, k1, p3, k8, m1, p2 tog, k2.
Row 33: K2, m1, p2 tog, k2, m1, (p2 tog) 3 times, m1, k1, k2 tog, p1, (k2 tog) twice, p1, (k2 tog) twice, p1, k2 tog, k1, m1, (p2 tog) 3 times, m1, k2, m1, p2 tog, k2.
Row 34: K2, m1, p2 tog, k7, p2, (k1, p2) 3 times, k7, m1, p2 tog, k2.
Row 35: K2, m1, p2 tog, k2, m1, (k1, p1) in next st, m1, p3 tog, m1, (k1, p1) in next st, m1, k2 tog, p1, k2 tog, (p1, k2 tog) twice, m1, (k1, p1) in next st, m1, p3 tog, m1, (k1, p1) in next st, m1, k2, m1, p2 tog, k2.
Row 36: K2, m1, p2 tog, k11, (p1, k1) 3 times, p1, k11, m1, p2 tog, k2.
Row 37: K2, m1, p2 tog, k2, m1, p4, m1, p1, m1, p4, m1, k3 tog, p1, k3 tog, m1, p4, m1, p1, m1, p4, m1, k2, m1, p2 tog, k2.
Row 38: K2, m1, p2 tog, k15, p1, k1, p1, k15, m1, p2 tog, k2.
Row 39: K2, m1, p2 tog, k2, m1, (p2 tog) 3 times, m1, p1, m1, (p2 tog) 3 times, m1, k3 tog, m1, (p2 tog) 3 times, m1, p1, m1, (p2 tog) 3 times, m1, k2, m1, p2 tog, k2.
Row 40: K2, m1, p2 tog, k27, m1, p2 tog, k2.
Row 41: K2, m1, p2 tog, k2, m1, (k1, p1) in next st, m1, (p3 tog, m1) 3 times, (k1, p1) in next st, m1, p1, m1, (k1, p1) in next st, (m1, p3 tog) 3 times, m1, (k1, p1) in next st, m1, k2, m1, p2 tog, k2.
Row 42: K2, m1, p2 tog, k31, m1, p2 tog, k2.
Row 43: K2, m1, p2 tog, k2, m1, p4, m1, p2 tog, p1, p2 tog, m1, p4, m1, k1, m1, p4, m1, p2 tog, p1, p2 tog, m1, p4, m1, k2, m1, p2 tog, k2.
Row 44: K2, m1, p2 tog, k8, k3 tog, k6, p1, k6, k3 tog, k8, m1, p2 tog, k2.
Row 45: K2, m1, p2 tog, k2, m1, (p2 tog) 3 times, m1, p1, m1, (p2 tog) 3 times, m1, k1, m1, (p2 tog) 3 times, m1, p1, m1, (p2 tog) 3 times, m1, k2, m1, p2 tog, k2.
Row 46: K2, m1, p2 tog, k13, p1, k13, m1, p2 tog, k2.
Row 47: K2, m1, p2 tog, k2, m1, p1, (m1, p3 tog) seven times, m1, p1, m1, k2, m1, p2 tog, k2.
Row 48: K2, m1, p2 tog, k2, p3, k2 tog, k1, k2 tog, m1, k3 tog, m1, k2 tog, k1, k2 tog, p3, k2, m1, p2 tog, k2.
Row 49: K2, m1, p2 tog, k2, m1, k3, m1, p3 tog, p3, p3 tog, m1, k3, m1, k2, m1, p2 tog, k2.
Row 50: K2, m1, p2 tog, k2, p5, k2 tog, k1, k2 tog, p5, k2, m1, p2 tog, k2.
Row 51: K2, m1, p2 tog, k2, m1, k5, m1, p3 tog, m1, k5, m1, k2, m1, p2 tog, k2.
Row 52: K2, m1, p2 tog, k2, p7, k1, p7, k2, m1, p2 tog, k2.
Row 53: K2, m1, p2 tog, k2, m1, k3, p1, k3, m1, p1, m1, k3, p1, k3, m1, k2, m1, p2 tog, k2.
Row 54: K2, m1, p2 tog, k2, p4, (k1, p4) 3 times, k2, m1, p2 tog, k2.
Row 55: K2, m1, p2 tog, k2, m1, k4, p1, k4, m1, k1, m1, k4, p1, k4, m1, k2, m1, p2 tog, k2.
Row 56: K2, m1, p2 tog, k2, p5, (k1, p5) 3 times, k2, m1, p2 tog, k2.
Row 57: K2, m1, p2 tog, k2, m1, k5, p1, k5, m1, p1, m1, k5, p1, k5, m1, k2, m1, p2 tog, k2.
Row 58: K2, m1, p2 tog, k2, p6, (k1, p6) 3 times, k2, m1, p2 tog, k2.
Row 59: K2, m1, p2 tog, k2, m1, k4, k2 tog, p1, k2 tog, k4, m1, p1, m1, k4, k2 tog, p1, k2 tog, k4, m1, k2, m1, p2 tog, k2.
Row 60: K2, m1, p2 tog, k2, p6, (k1, p6) 3 times, k2, m1, p2 tog, k2.
Repeat until length desired, ending on the 19th row.

Edging

Cast on 24 sts.
Row 1: K2, m1, p2 tog, k2, m1, k3, sl 1, k1, psso, m1, k3, m1, sl 1, k1, psso, k3, m1, k2 tog, m2, k2 tog, k1.
Row 2: K3, p1, k1, p15, k2, m1, p2 tog, k2.
Row 3: K2, m1, p2 tog, k2, m1, k2 tog, k2, k2 tog, m1, k3, m1, k2 tog, k2, k2 tog, m1, k1, m2, k1, m2, k2 tog, k1.
Row 4: K3, p1, k2, p1, k1, p2 tog, p3, p2 tog, p1, p2 tog, p3, p2 tog, k2, m1, p2 tog, k2.
Row 5: K2, m1, p2 tog, k2, m1, k2 tog, k2, m1, k3 tog, m1, k2, k2 tog, m1, k1, (m2, k2 tog) 3 times, k1.
Row 6: K3, p1, (k2, p1) twice, k1, p2 tog, p6, p2 tog, k3, m1, p2 tog, k2.
Row 7: K2, m1, p2 tog, k3, m1, k2 tog, k3, k3 tog, m1, k11.
Row 8: Cast off 7 sts, k4, p2 tog, p1, p2 tog, k4, m1, p2 tog, k2.
Row 9: K2, m1, p2 tog, k4, m1, (k1, p1, k1, in next st) 3 times, m1, k2 tog, m2, k2 tog, k1.
Row 10: K3, p1, k1, p10, k5, m1, p2 tog, k2.
Row 11: K2, m1, p2 tog, k5, (m1, k3) twice, m1, sl 1, k1, psso, k2, m1, k1, m2, k1, m2, k2 tog, k1.
Row 12: K3, p1, k2, p1, k1, p13, k2 tog, k3, m1, p2 tog, k2.
Row 13: K2, m1, p2 tog, k2, k2 tog, m1, k3, sl 1, k1, psso, m1, k3, m1, sl 1, k1, psso, k3, m1, k1, (m2, k2 tog) 3 times, k1.
Row 14: K3, (p1, k2) twice, p1, k1, p15, k2 tog, k1, m1, p2 tog, k2.
Row 15: K2, m1, p2 tog, k1, k2 tog, m1, k3, sl 1, k1, psso, m1, k3, m1, sl 1, k1, psso, k2, k2 tog, m1, k11.
Row 16: Cast off 7 sts, k4, p13, k2 tog, k1, m1, p2 tog, k2.
Repeat rows 1–16 until edging is the length required to edge collar. The neck edge can be neatened by a single row of crochet, or pick up sts, and k 4 rows.

16. Curtains

Knitted lace curtains provide a delicate filter of light in the room. The four patterns provided should encourage you to start knitting.

Materials

ELEPHANT EYE MOTIF: Approx. 40 cm square.
Use 4 ply cotton. Set on 4 needles size 2.75 mm.
WAGON WHEELS, EMERALD STAR *and* TRAILING VINES *Curtain Samples*: Use 20 cotton, 2 mm needles.
No quantities are given. Knit a sample motif, and work out yarn required. WAGON WHEELS gives the same effect as the pair of antique knitted curtains illustrated.

Curtain Motif 1: ELEPHANT EYE

Cast on 8 sts; 2 sts on each of 2 needles, 4 sts on 3rd needle.
Round 1: Knit.
Round 2: *K1, m1, k1. Repeat from * to end of round (12 sts).
Round 3: Knit.
Round 4: *K1, (m1, k1) twice. Repeat * to end of round (20 sts).
Round 5: Knit, work k1, p1, into each m1 of previous round (28 sts).
Round 6: *K2 tog, m1, k3, m1, sl 1, k1, psso. Repeat from * to end of round.
Round 7: As round 5 (36 sts).
Round 8: *K2 tog, m2, sl 1, k1, psso, k1, k2 tog, m2, sl 1, k1, psso. Repeat from * to end of row (36 sts).
Round 9, 11 *and* 13: Knit, work k1, p1, into m2 of previous round.
Round 10: *K2 tog, m2, k5, m2, sl 1, k1, psso. Repeat from * to end of round (44 sts).
Round 12: *K2 tog, m2, sl 1, k1, psso, k3, k2 tog, m2, sl 1, k1, psso. Repeat from * to end of round.
Round 14: *K2 tog, m3, k7, m3, sl 1, k1, psso. Repeat from * to end of round (52 sts).
Round 15, 17 *and* 19: Knit, work k1, p1, into m3 of previous round.
Round 16: *K2 tog, m3, sl 1, k1, psso, k5, k2 tog, m3, sl 1, k1, psso. Repeat from * to end of round.
Round 18: *K2 tog, m3, k9, m3, sl 1, k1, psso. Repeat from * to end of round (60 sts).
Round 20: *(K1, m1) 3 times, sl 1, k2 tog, psso, k3, k3 tog, (m1, k1) 3 times. Repeat from * to end of round (68 sts).
Round 21: Knit.
Round 22: *K1, (m1, k2 tog) twice, m1, k1, m1, sl 2, k3 tog, psso, m1, k1, m1, (sl 1, k1, psso, m1) twice, k1, m4. Repeat from * to end of round.
Round 23: Knit, work (k1, p1) 4 times, k1, into each m4 of previous round (104 sts).
Round 24: *K1, (m1, k2 tog) 3 times, (m1, k1) 3 times, m1, (sl 1, k1, psso, m1) 3 times, k1, (into next st, k1, p1) 9 times. Repeat from * to end of round (156 sts).
Round 25: Knit.
Round 26: *Sl 1, k2 tog, psso, (m1, k2 tog) 3 times, m1, sl

1, k2 tog, psso, m1, (sl 1, k1, psso, m1) 3 times, k3 tog, (k1, m1, k1) 9 times. Repeat from * to end of round (176 sts).

Round 27: *K18, (k1, p1 into m1, k2) 8 times, k1, p1, into m1, k1. Repeat from * to end of row (212 sts).

Round 28: *Sl 1, k2 tog, psso, (m1, k2 tog) twice, m1, sl 1, k2 tog, psso, m1, (sl 1, k1, psso, m1) twice, k3 tog, (k2 tog, m2, sl 1, k1, psso) 9 times. Repeat from * to end of round (196 sts).

Round 29 and 31: Knit, k1, p1, into m2 of previous round.

Round 30: *Sl 1, k2 tog, psso, m1, k2 tog, m1, sl 1, k2 tog, psso, m1, sl 1, k1, psso, m1, k3 tog, (k2 tog, m2, sl 1, k1, psso) 9 times. Repeat from * to end of round (180 sts).

Round 32: *(Sl 1, k2 tog, psso, m1) twice, k3 tog, (k2 tog, m3, sl 1, k1, psso) 9 times. Repeat from * to end of round.

Round 33: Knit, k1, p1, into m3 of previous round (164 sts).

Round 34: *Sl 1, k1, psso, k1, k2 tog, (k2 tog, m3, sl 1, k1, psso) 9 times. Repeat from * to end of round (192 sts).

Round 35: Knit, k1, p1, k1 into m3 of previous round.

Round 36: Knit.

The motifs are sewn together, taking care to keep seams fairly loose. Insert clip on curtain rings evenly to hang curtain. The motifs are suitable for *tablecloths, runners* or *cushions*.

Curtain Motif 2: WAGON WHEELS

Cast on 11 sts, 4 sts on each of 2 needles, 3 sts on 3rd needle. Work with 4th.

Rounds 1 and 2: Knit.

Round 3: K twice into every st (22 sts)..

Rounds 4 and 5: Knit.

Round 6: *M2, k2 tog. Repeat from * to end of round (33 sts).

Round 7: *K1, p1, into m2 of previous round, k1. Repeat from * to end of round (33 sts).

Round 8: *M2, sl 1, k2 tog, psso. Repeat from * to end of round.

Round 9 to 14: Repeat rounds 7 and 8 3 times.

Round 15: As round 7.

Round 16: K, arrange sts on 3 needles, 11 sts on each needle.

Round 17 to 19: Knit.

Round 20: K 1st st from L.H. needle on to R.H. needle. *M2, k2 tog, k1. Repeat from * to end of round (64 sts).

Round 21: K1, *p1, k3. Repeat from * to end, last repeat k2.

Round 22 to 24: Knit.

Round 25: *K2 tog, m2, k2 tog. Repeat from * to end of round (64 sts).

Round 26: K2, *p1, k3. Repeat from * to last 2 sts, p1, k1.

Round 27 to 29: Knit.

Round 30: *M2, (k2 tog) twice. Repeat from * to end of round (64 sts).

Round 31: As round 21.

Round 32: K1, *m1, k3. Repeat from * to end of round, k2 (80 sts).

Round 33 to 36: Knit **.

Using crochet hook proceed as follows:

Crochet 2 sts tog, 7 ch. Repeat until all sts are worked. Cast off.

Medallion 2

Knit as 1 st until **. Crochet 2 sts tog, 3 ch, 1 dc in middle of 7 ch loop of 1st medallion, 3 ch. Crochet 2 sts tog on 2nd medallion.

Connect in this way 5 loops from both medallions. Continue as 1st medallion. Knit and connect in this way six medallions.

Crochet 2 small **connecting medallions** as follows:

Row 1: 10 ch form loop.

Row 2: 3 ch (counts as 1st tr), 19 tr. Close with sl st.

Row 3: 3 ch (counts as 1st tr), 2 tr leaving last loops on hook. Finish 3 tr tog (making 3 tr puff st), 5 ch, skip 1st, 3 tr puff st in next tr, continue until end. Close with sl st (10 puffs)

Row 4: *5 ch, 1 dc in middle of 5 ch loop, 5 ch, 1 dc in top of puff st. Repeat from * to end of round. Close with sl st (20 loops).

Row 5: *Sl st to middle of loop. 7 ch, 1 dc into middle of next loop. Repeat from * to end of round. Close with sl st.

Row 6: **Connecting the knitted medallions.** Sl st to middle of next loop. 3 ch, 1 dc in middle loop of knitted medallion. 3 ch, 1 dc in middle loop of crocheted medallion. Continue until 20 loops have been connected. Close with sl st. Cast off.

Connect the 6 medallions with the 2 crochet medallions. WAGON WHEELS can be made larger by increasing the number of medallions.

Curtain Motif 3: EMERALD STAR

Cast on 8 sts; 2 sts on each of 2 needles, 4 sts on 3rd needle. Mark beginning of round.

Round 1 and 2: Knit.

Round 3: *M1, k1. Repeat from * to end of round (16 sts).

Round 4 and alternate rounds: Knit.

Round 5: As round 3 (32 sts).

Round 7: *M1, k3, m1, k1 tbl. Repeat from * to end of round (48 sts).

Round 9: *M1, k5, m1, k1 tbl. Repeat from * to end of round (64 sts).

Round 11: *M1, k7, m1, k1 tbl. Repeat from * to end of round (80 sts).

Change to 5 needles (20 sts on each of 4 needles).

Round 13: *M1, sl 1, k1, psso, k15, k2 tog, m1, k1 tbl. Repeat from * to end of round.

Round 15: *M1, k1, m1, sl 1, k1, psso, k5, sl 1, k2 tog, psso, k5, k2 tog, m1, k1, m1, k1 tbl. Repeat from * to end of round.

Round 17: *M1, k1, (m1, sl 1, k1, psso) twice, k3, sl 1, k2 tog, psso, k3, (k2 tog, m1) twice, k1, m1, k2 tbl. Repeat from * to end of round.

Round 19: *M1, k1, (m1, sl 1, k1, psso) 3 times, k1, sl 1, k2 tog, psso, k1, (k2 tog, m1) 3 times, k1, m1, k1 tbl. Repeat from * to end of round.

Round 21: *M1, k1, (m1, sl 1, k1, psso) 4 times, k1, (k2 tog, m1) 4 times, k1, m1, k1 tbl. Repeat from * to end of round (88 sts).

Round 23: *M1, k1, (m1, sl 1, k1, psso) 4 times, m1, sl 1, k2 tog, psso, m1, (k2 tog, m1) 4 times, k1, m1, k1 tbl. Repeat from * to end of round (96 sts).

Round 25: *M1, k1, (m1, sl 1, k1, psso) 5 times, k1, (k2 tog, m1) 5 times, k1, m1, k1 tbl. Repeat from * to end of round (104 sts).

Round 27: *M1, k3, (m1, sl 1, k1, psso) 4 times, m1, sl 1, k2 tog, psso, m1, (k2 tog, m1) 4 times, k3, m1, k1 tbl. Repeat from * to end of round (112 sts).

Round 29: *M1, k1, m1, sl 1, k1, psso, k2, (m1, sl 1, k1, psso) 4 times, k1, (k2 tog, m1) 4 times, k2, k2 tog, m1, k1, m1, k1 tbl. Repeat from * to end of round (120 sts).

Round 31: *K2, m1, k1, m1, sl 1, k1, psso, k2, (m1, sl 1, k1, psso) 3 times, m1, sl 1, k2 tog, psso, m1, (k2 tog, m1) 3 times, k2, k2 tog, m1, k1, m1, k3. Repeat from * to end of round (128 sts).

Round 33: *M1, k31, m1, k1 tbl. Repeat from * to end of round.

Round 35: *M1, k33, m1, k1 tbl. Repeat from * to end of round.

Round 36: Knit (144 sts).

Knit 1 st from L.H. needle on to R.H. needle.

Crochet Edge thus:

Row 1: dc in 3 sts, 9 ch, to end of row.

Row 2: **Connecting row with other medallions:**
Sl st to centre of 1st 9 st loop. 9 ch, 1 dc in centre of next loop.

When connecting medallions: 4 ch, 1 dc in centre of 9 st loop of 1st medallion, 4 ch, 1 dc in centre of 9 st loop of 2nd loop.

Continue thus until 8 medallions are connected.

EMERALD STAR can be made larger by increasing the number of medallions.

Curtain Motif 4: TRAILING VINES

Cast on 290 sts. Knit 1 row. Purl 1 row.

Row 1: K3, *m1, k1, sl 1, k1, psso, p1, k2 tog, k1, m1, p1, sl 1, k1, psso, p1, k2 tog, m1, k1, m1, k1, p1, (m1, sl 1, k1, psso) 5 times, p1.* Repeat from *—* 9 times. M1, k1, sl 1, k1, psso, p1, k2 tog, k1, m1, p1, sl 1, k1, psso, p1, k2 tog, m1, k1, m1, k3.

Row 2: K1, p1, *p5, k1, p1, k1, (p3, k1) twice, (m1, sl 1, k1, psso) 5 times, k1*. Repeat from *—* 9 times. P5, k1, p1, k1, p3, k1, p5, k1.

Row 3: K3, *m1, k1, sl 1, k1, psso, p1, k2 tog, k1, p1, sl 1, k2 tog, psso, m1, k3, m1, k1, p1, (m1, sl 1, k1, psso) 5 times, p1*. Repeat from *—* 9 times. M1, k1, sl 1, k1, psso, p1, k2 tog, k1, p1, sl 1, k2 tog, psso, (m1, k3) twice.

Row 4: K1, p1, *p7, k1, p2, k1, p3, k1, (m1, sl 1, k1, psso) 5 times, k1*. Repeat from *—* 9 times. P7, k1, p2, k1, p5, k1.

Row 5: K3, *m1, k1, m1, sl 1, k1, psso, p1, (k2 tog) twice, m1, k5, m1, k1, p1, (m1, sl 1, k1, psso) 5 times, p1*. Repeat from *—* 9 times. M1, k1, m1, sl 1, k1, psso, p1, (k2 tog, twice, m1, k5, m1, k3.

Row 6: K1, p1, *p8, k1, p1, k1, p4, k1, (m1, sl 1, k1, psso) 5 times, k1*. Repeat from *—* 9 times. P8, k1, p1, k1, p6, k1.

Row 7: K3, *m1, k3, m1, sl 1, k2 tog, psso, p1, m1, k1, sl 1, k1, psso, p1, k2 tog, k1, m1, k1, p1, (m1, sl 1, k1, psso) 5 times, p1*. Repeat from *—* 9 times. m1, k3, m1, sl 1, k2 tog, psso, p1, m1, k1, sl 1, k1, psso, p1, k2 tog, k1, m1, k3.

Row 8: K1, p1, *p4, k1, p3, k1, p6, k1, (m1, sl 1, k1, psso) 5 times, k1*. Repeat from *—* 9 times. P4, k1, p3, k1, p8, k1.

Row 9: K3, *m1, k5, m1, sl 1, k1, psso, k1, sl 1, k1, psso, p1, k2 tog, k1, m1, k1, p1, (m1, sl 1, p1, psso) 5 times, p1*. Repeat from *—* 9 times. M1, k5, m1, sl 1, k1, psso, k1, sl 1, k1, psso, p1, k2 tog, k1, m1, k3.

Row 10: K1, p1, *p4, k1, p2, k1, p7, k1 (m1, sl 1, k1, psso) 5 times, k1*. Repeat from *—* 9 times. P4, k1, p2, k1, p9, k1.

Repeat rows 1–10 17 times.

Cast off.

Using crochet hook 0.75, right side of work facing, begin in R.H. bottom corner. Work 1 row dc along 1 side of curtain, 3 dc in corner, 30 ch to form loop, 1 dc. Work dc until next pattern edge, 30 ch for next loop. Continue until 22 loops are made (one in each pattern edge, with dc between). 3 dc in next corner, dc other side of curtain. Turn work (wrong side facing).

1 ch to turn. *1 dc in next dc, 3 ch, 1 sl st into same dc (picot made). 1 dc into next dc*. Repeat from *—* until next corner, and 1st loop. Work 30 dc along 30 ch loops. 1 dc into dc. Repeat making picots between each loop. Work 30 dc along each 30 ch loop to strengthen loops. Repeat picot edge on other side. Fasten off.

17. Huckaback Towels

Three huckaback guest towels displaying the effect of the size of cotton used.

The towels illustrated have dainty hemstitch borders, tied with colourful ribbons. These beautiful linen towels make a charming gift.

Materials

Towel 1: PARIS 1 ball 60 cotton
Towel 2: EYELET 1 ball 40 cotton
Towel 3: JANE 1 ball 20 cotton
Needles, pair of 1.25 mm.

Huckaback Towel Edging 1: PARIS

Cast on 15 sts. Purl one row.
Row 1: Sl 1 purlwise, k2, m1, (k2 tog, m1) twice, k3, m1, k2 tog, m2, k3.
Row 2: K4, p11, m1, k2 tog, k1.
Row 3: Sl 1 purlwise, k2, m1, (k2 tog, m1) twice, k5, m1, k2 tog, m2, k2, m3, k2.
Row 4: K2, p1, k1, p1, k3, p13, m1, k2 tog, k1.
Row 5: Sl 1 purlwise, k2, m1, (k2 tog, m1) twice, k7, m1, k2 tog, m2, k2 tog, k6.
Row 6: Cast off 5 sts, k2, p15, m1, k2 tog, k1.
Row 7: Sl 1 purlwise, k2, m1, k3 tog, m1, k2 tog, m1, k2, sl 1, k2 tog, psso, k2, m1, k3 tog, m2, k3.

Row 8: K4, p13, m1, k2 tog, k1.
Row 9: Sl 1 purlwise, k2, m1, k3 tog, m1, k2 tog, m1, k1, sl 1, k2 tog, psso, k1, m1, k3 tog, m2, k2, m3, k2.
Row 10: K2, p1, k1, p1, k3, p11, m1, k2 tog, k1.
Row 11: Sl 1 purlwise, k2, m1, k3 tog, m1, k2 tog, m1, sl 1, k2 tog, psso, m1, k3 tog, m2, k2 tog, k6.
Row 12: Cast off 5 sts, k2, p9, m1, k2 tog, k1.
Repeat from 1 to 12.

Huckaback Towel Edging 2: EYELET

Cast on 8 sts.
Row 1: Sl 1, k2 tog, m2, k2 tog, k1, m4, k2.
Row 2: K2, (k1, p1) twice in m4 of previous row, k3, p1, k2.
Row 3: Sl 1, k11.
Row 4: K12.
Row 5: Sl 1, k2 tog, m2, k2 tog, k1, (m2, k2 tog) 3 times.
Row 6: (K2, p1) 3 times, k3, p1, k2.
Row 7: Sl 1, k14.
Row 8: Cast off 7 sts, k7.
Repeat rows 1–8 until length desired.

Huckaback Towel Edging 3: JANE

Cast on 18 sts.
Row 1: Sl 1, k2, m1, k2 tog, k1, (m1, k2 tog) 3 times, k3, k2 tog, m1, k1.
Row 2: M1, k2, p5, k11.
Row 3: Sl 1, k2, (m1, k2 tog) 4 times, k3, k2 tog, m1, k3.
Row 4: M1, k4, p5, k10.
Row 5: Sl 1, k2, m1, k2 tog, k1, (m1, k2 tog) twice, k3, (k2 tog, m1) twice, k3.
Row 6: M1, k6, p5, k9.
Row 7: Sl 1, k2, (m1, k2 tog) 3 times, k3, (k2 tog, m1) 3 times, k3.
Row 8: M1, k8, p5, k8.
Row 9: Sl 1, k2, m1, k2 tog, k1, m1, k2 tog, k3, (k2 tog, m1) 4 times, k3.
Row 10: M1, k10, p5, k7.
Row 11: Sl 1, k2, (m1, k2 tog) twice, k3, (k2 tog, m1) 5 times, k3.
Row 12: M1, k12, p5, k6.
Row 13: Sl 1, k3, m1, k2 tog, k3, (k2 tog, m1) 6 times, k3.
Row 14: M1, k14, p5, k5.
Row 15: Sl 1, k2, m1, k2 tog, k3, (k2 tog, m1) 7 times, k3.
Row 16: M1, k16, p5, k4.
Row 17: Sl 1, k6, (k2 tog, m1) 8 times, k3.
Row 18: K9, pass 8 sts, one by one, over 9th st, k9, p5, k3.
Repeat rows 1–18 until length desired.

18. Bed Linen

A bed linen group, featuring white embroidery and delicate drawn thread work, complemented by edgings of knitted lace.

White cotton *Cellular Blankets* are trimmed with wide luxurious borders.

Continental Pillows and Heirloom Sheets show the use of knitted lace to its full advantage. Fine linens require the use of finer threads and needles. The knitting will take longer, but the results will compensate for the extra effort. Quantities of yarn wil! depend on article being trimmed.

Cellular Blanket: SCROLL

Cast on 48 sts. Knit one row.

Row 1: Sl 1, k5, draw the st previous to the last st over. Draw the next previous st over, draw the next st over (3 sts drawn over one), m1, k6, m1, k2 tog, k1, m1, k2 tog, k9, draw the previous 3 sts over last st. M1, k11, k2 tog, m1, k2 tog, k1, m1, k1, m1, k2 tog, m2, k2 tog, k1.

Row 2: K3, p1, k19, k1, p1, k1 in loop, k17, k1, p1, k1 in loop, k3.

Row 3: Sl 1, k12, m1, k2 tog, k1, m1, k2 tog, k18, k2 tog, m1, k2 tog, k1, m1, k3, m1, k2 tog, m2, k2 tog, k1.

Row 4: K3, p1, k20. Draw the previous 3 sts over last st, m1, k20, draw the previous 3 sts over last st, m1, k6.

Row 5: Sl 1, k5, k1, p1, k1 in loop, k5, m1, k2 tog, k1, m1, k2 tog, k7, k1, p1, k1 in loop, k6, k2 tog, m1, k2 tog, k1, m1, k5, m1, k2 tog, m2, k2 tog, k1.

Row 6: K3, p1, k47.

Row 7: Sl 1, k5, draw the previous 3 sts over last st, m1, k9, m1, k2 tog, k1, m1, k2 tog, k6. Draw the previous 3 sts over last st, m1, k8, k2 tog, m1, k2 tog, k1, m1, k7, m1, k2 tog, m2, k2 tog, k1.

Row 8: K3, p1, k22, k1, p1, k1 in loop, k17, k1, p1, k1 in loop, k3.

Row 9: Sl 1, k15, m1, k2 tog, k1, m1, k2 tog, k12, k2 tog, m1, k2 tog, k1, m1, k9, m1, k2 tog, m2, k2 tog, k1.

Row 10: K3, p1, k23, draw the previous 3 sts over last st, m1, k20, draw the previous 3 sts over last st, m1, k6.

Row 11: Sl 1, k5, k1, p1, k1 in loop, k17, k1, p1, k1 in loop, k3, k2 tog, m1, k2 tog, k1, m1, k11, m1, k2 tog, m2, k2 tog, k1.

Row 12: K3, p1, k50.

Row 13: Sl 1, k5, draw the previous 3 sts over last st, m1, k6, m1, k2 tog, k1, m1, k2 tog, k9, draw the previous 3 sts over last st, m1, k5, k2 tog, m1, k2 tog, k5, k2 tog, m1, k2 tog, k1, m1, k2 tog, k1, m1, k2 tog, m2, (k2 tog) twice.

Row 14: K3, p1, k22, k1, p1, k1 in loop, k17, k1, p1, k1 in loop, k3.

Row 15: Sl 1, k12, m1, k2 tog, k1, m1, k2 tog, k14, m1, k2 tog, k4, k2 tog, m1, k2 tog, k1, m1, k2 tog, k1, m1, k2 tog, m2, (k2 tog) twice.

Row 16: K3, p1, k21, draw the previous 3 sts over last st, m1, k20, draw the previous 3 sts over last st, m1, k6.

Row 17: Sl 1, k5, k1, p1, k1 in loop, k5, m1, k2 tog, k1, m1, k2 tog, k7, k1, p1, k1 in loop, k4, m1, k2 tog, k2, k2 tog, m1, k2 tog, k1, m1, k2 tog, k1, m1, k2 tog, m2, (k2 tog) twice.

Row 18: K3, p1, k46.

Row 19: Sl 1, k5, draw the previous 3 sts over last st, m1, k9, m1, k2 tog, k1, m1, k2 tog, k6, draw the previous 3 sts over last st, m1, k8, m1, (k2 tog) twice, m1, k2 tog, k1, m1, k2 tog, k1, m1, k2 tog, m2, (k2 tog) twice.
Row 20: K3, p1, k19, k1, p1, k1 in loop, k17, k1, p1, k1 in loop, k3.
Row 21: Sl 1, k15, m1, k2 tog, k1, m1, k2 tog, k14, (m1, k2 tog) twice, (k1, m1, k2 tog) twice, m2, (k2 tog) twice.
Row 22: K3, p1, k19, draw the previous 3 sts over last st, m1, k20, draw the previous 3 sts over last st, m1, k6.
Row 23: Sl 1, k5, k1, p1, k1 in loop, k17, k1, p1, k1 in loop, k7, m1, sl 1, k2 tog, psso, k1, m1, k2 tog, k1, m1, k2 tog, m2, (k2 tog) twice.
Row 23: K3, p1, k44.
Repeat rows 1–24 until length desired.

Continental Pillow: PASTORAL LACE

Cast on 36 sts.
Row 1: Sl 1, k3, m1, k2 tog, k10, m1, k2 tog, k11, k2 tog, m1, k2, m2, k2 tog, k1. (The 2nd loop of the m2 at this end of the row is dropped in the next row.)
Row 2: M1, k2 tog, k18, m1, k2 tog, k10, m1, k2 tog, k2.
Row 3: Sl 1, k3, m1, k2 tog, k2, k2 tog, m2, k2 tog, k4, m1, k2 tog, k10, k2 tog, m1, k4, m2, k2.
Row 4: M1, k2 tog, k19, m1, k2 tog, k4, p1, k5, m1, k2 tog, k2.
Row 5: Sl 1, k3, m1, (k2 tog) twice, m2, (k2 tog) twice, m2, k2 tog, k2, m1, k2 tog, k9, k2 tog, m1, k6, m2, k2.
Row 6: M1, k2 tog, k20, m1, k2 tog, k2, p1, k3, p1, k3, m1, k2 tog, k2.
Row 7: Sl 1, k3, m1, k2 tog, k2, k2 tog, m2, k2 tog, k4, m1, k2 tog, k8, k2 tog, m1, k2, k2 tog, m2, k2 tog, k2, m2, k2.
Row 8: M1, k2 tog, k5, p1, k15, m1, k2 tog, k4, p1, k5, m1, k2 tog, k2.
Row 9: Sl 1, k3, m1, (k2 tog) twice, m2, (k2 tog) twice, m2, k2 tog. K2, m1, k2 tog, k7, k2 tog, m1, k1, k2 tog, m2, (k2 tog) twice, m2, k2 tog, k1, m2, k2.
Row 10: M1, k2 tog, k4, p1, k3, p1, k13, m1, k2 tog, k2, (p1, k3) twice, m1, k2 tog, k2.
Row 11: Sl 1, k3, m1, k2 tog, k2, k2 tog, m2, k2 tog, k4, m1, k2 tog, k6, k2 tog, m1, k4, k2 tog, m2, k2 tog, k4, m2, k2.
Row 12: M1, k2 tog, k7, p1, k15, m1, k2 tog, k4, p1, k5, m1, k2 tog, k2.
Row 13: Sl 1, k3, m1, k2 tog, k10, m1, k2 tog, k5, k2 tog, m1, k3, k2 tog, m2, (k2 tog) twice, m2, k2 tog, k3. m2, k2.
Row 14: M1, k2 tog, k6, p1, k3, p1, k13, m1, k2 tog, k10, m1, k2 tog, k2.
Row 15: Sl 1, k3, m1, k2 tog, k10, m1 , k2 tog, k4, k2 tog, m1, k6, k2 tog, m2, k2 tog, k6, m2, k2.
Row 16: M1, k2 tog, k9, p1, k15, m1, k2 tog, k10, m1, k2 tog, k2.

Row 17: Sl 1, k3, m1, k2 tog, k2, k2 tog, m2, k2 tog, k4, m1, k2 tog, k3, k2 tog, m1, k2, k2 tog, m2, k2 tog, k6, k2 tog, m2, k2 tog, k2, m2, k2.
Row 18: M1, k2 tog, k5, p1, k9, p1, k10, m1, k2 tog, k4, p1, k5, m1, k2 tog, k2.
Row 19: Sl 1, k3, m1, (k2 tog) twice, m2, (k2 tog) twice, m2, k2 tog, k2, m1, k2 tog, k2, k2 tog, m1, k1, k2 tog, m2, (k2 tog) twice, m2, k2 tog, k2, k2 tog, m2, (k2 tog) twice, m2, k2 tog, k1, m2, k2.
Row 20: M1, k2 tog, k4, p1, k3, p1, k5, p1, k3, p1, k8, m1, k2 tog, k2, (p1, k3) twice, m1, k2 tog, k2.
Row 21: Sl 1, *k3, m1, k2 tog, k2, k2 tog, m2, k2 tog, k4, m1, k2 tog, k1, k2 tog, m1, k4, k2 tog, m2, k2 tog, k6, k2 tog, m2, k2 tog, k4, m2, k2.
Row 22: M1, k2 tog, k7, p1, k9, p1, k10, m1, k2 tog, k4, p1, k5, m1, k2 tog, k2.
Row 23: Sl 1, k3, m1, (k2 tog) twice, m2, (k2 tog) twice, m2, k2 tog, k2, m1, k2 tog, k3, m1, (k2 tog) twice, m2, (k2 tog) twice, m2, k2 tog, k2, k2 tog, m2, (k2 tog) twice, m2, k2 tog, k1.
Row 24: M1, k2 tog, k4, p1, k3, p1, k5, p1, k3, p1, k8, m1, k2 tog, k2, (p1, k3) twice, m1, k2 tog k2.
Row 25: Sl 1, k3, m1, k2 tog, k2, k2 tog, m2, k2 tog, k4, m1, k2 tog, k4, m1, k2 tog, k1, k2 tog, m2, k2 tog, k6, k2 tog, m2, k2 tog, k1, k2 tog, m2, k2 tog, k1.
Row 26: M1, k2 tog, k5, p1, k9, p1, k10, m1, k2 tog, k4, p1, k5, m1, k2 tog, k2.
Row 27: Sl 1, k3, m1, k2 tog, k10, (m1, k2 tog, k5) twice, k2 tog, m2, k2 tog, k5, k2 tog, m2, k2 tog, k1.
Row 28: M1, k2 tog, k9, p1, k15, m1, k2 tog, k10, m1, k2 tog, k2.
Row 29: Sl 1, k3, m1, k2 tog, k10, m1, k2 tog, k6, m1, k2 tog, k2, k2 tog, m2, (k2 tog) twice, m2, k2 tog, k2, k2 tog, m2, k2 tog, k1.
Row 30: M1, k2 tog, k6, p1, k3, p1, k13, m1, k2 tog, k10, m1, k2 tog, k2.
Row 31: Sl 1, k3, m1, k2 tog, k2, k2 tog, m2, k2 tog, k4, m1, k2 tog, k7, m1, k2 tog, k3, k2 tog, m2, k2 tog, k3, k2 tog, m2, k2 tog, k1.
Row 32: M1, k2 tog, k7, p1, k15, m1, k2 tog, k4, p1, k5, m1, k2 tog, k2.
Row 33: Sl 1, k3, m1, (k2 tog) twice, m2, (k2 tog) twice, m2, k2 tog, k2, m1, k2 tog, k8, m1, (k2 tog) twice, m2, (k2 tog) twice, m2, (k2 tog) twice, m2, k2 tog, k1.
Row 34: M1, k2 tog, k4, p1, k3, p1, k13, m1, k2 tog, k2, p1, k3, p1, k3, m1, k2 tog, k2.
Row 35: Sl 1, k3, m1, k2 tog, k2, k2 tog, m2, k2 tog, k4, m1, k2 tog, k9, m1, k2 tog, k1, k2 tog, m2, k2 tog, k1, k2 tog, m2, k2 tog, k1.
Row 36: M1, k2 tog, k5, p1, k15, m1, k2 tog, k4, p1, k5, m1, k2 tog, k2.
Row 37: Sl 1, k3, m1, (k2 tog) twice, m2, (k2 tog) twice, m2, k2 tog, k2, m1, k2 tog, k10, m1, k2 tog, k4, k2 tog, m2, k2 tog, k1.
Row 38: M1, k2 tog, k20, m1, k2 tog, k2, (p1, k3) twice, m1, k2 tog, k2.
Row 39: Sl 1, k3, m1, k2 tog, k2, k2 tog, m2, k2 tog, k4, m1, k2 tog, k11, m1, k2 tog, k2, k2 tog, m2, k2 tog, k1.

Row 40: M1, k2 tog, k19, m1, k2 tog, k4, p1, k5, m1, k2 tog, k2.
Row 41: Sl 1, k3, m1, k2 tog, k10, m1, k2 tog, k12, m1, (k2 tog) twice, m2, k2 tog, k1.
Row 42: M1, k2 tog, k18, m1, k2 tog, k10, m1, k2 tog, k2.
Repeat rows 1–42 until length desired.

Sheet 1: BEACONSFIELD LACE

Cast on 30 sts.
Row 1: Sl 1, k2, m1, k2 tog, k1, k2 tog, m1, k1, (m1, k2 tog) twice, k7 (m1, k2 tog) 4 times, m1, k2.
Row 2: M1, k2 tog, k29.
Row 3: Sl 1, k2, m1, (k2 tog) twice, m1, k3, (m1, k2 tog) twice, k7, (m1, k2 tog) 4 times, m1, k2.
Row 4: M1, k2 tog, k30.
Row 5: Sl 1, k2, m1, k3 tog, m1, k2 tog, k1, k2 tog, (m1, k2 tog) twice, k7, (m1, k2 tog) 4 times, m1, k2.
Row 6: M1, k2 tog, k29.
Row 7: Sl 1, k2, m1, k2 tog, k1, m1, k3, m1, k1, (m1, k2 tog) twice, k7, (m1, k2 tog) 4 times, m1, k2.
Row 8: M1, k2 tog, k32.
Row 9: Sl 1, k2, m1, k2 tog, k2, m1, k3 tog, m1, k3, (m1, k2 tog) twice, k7, (m1, k2 tog) 4 times, m1, k2.
Row 10: M1, k2 tog, k33.
Row 11: Sl 1, k2, m1, k2 tog, k6, k2 tog, m1, k2 tog, m1, k1, m1, k2 tog, k4, k2 tog, (m1, k2 tog) 5 times, k1.
Row 12: M1, k2 tog, k32.
Row 13: Sl 1, k2, m1, k2 tog, k5, k2 tog, m1, k2 tog, m1, k3, m1, k2 tog, k2, k2 tog, (m1, k2 tog) 5 times, k1.
Row 14: M1, k2 tog, k31.
Row 15: Sl 1, k2, m1, k2 tog, k4, k2 tog, (m1, k2 tog) twice, k1, k2 tog, m1, (k2 tog) twice, (m1, k2 tog) 5 times, k1.
Row 16 M1, k2 tog, k28.
Row 17: Sl 1, k2, m1, k2 tog, k3, k2 tog, m1, k2 tog, m1, k1, m1, k3, m1, k1, k2 tog, (m1, k2 tog) 5 times, k1.
Row 18: M1, k2 tog, k29.
Row 19: Sl 1, k2, m1, k2 tog, k2, k2 tog, m1, k2 tog, m1, k3, m1, k3 tog, m1, k1, k2 tog, (m1, k2 tog) 5 times, k1.
Row 20: M1, k2 tog, k28.
Repeat rows 1–20 until length desired.

Sheet 2: BARBARA ANNE LACE

Cast on 10 sts.
Row 1: Knit.
Row 2: Sl 1, *k2, m1, k1, m1, k2, m1, p1, k3.
Row 3: Sl 1, k2, m1, p2 tog, k2, m1, k3, m1, k1, m2, k2.
Row 4: Sl 1, k2, p1, k1, p5, k2, m1, p2 tog, k3.
Row 5: Sl 1, k2, m1, p2 tog, k2, m1, k5, m1, k1, m2, k2 tog, m2, k2.
Row 6: Sl 1, k2, p1, k2, p1, k1, p7, k2, m1, p2 tog, k3.
Row 7: Sl 1, k2, m1, p2 tog, k2, m1, k1, sl 1, k1, psso, p1, k2 tog, k1, m1, k1, m2, k3 tog, m2, k2 tog, m2, k2.
Row 8: Sl 1, (k2, p1) 3 times, (k1, p3) twice, k2, m1, p2 tog, k3.
Row 9: Sl 1, k2, m1, p2 tog, k2, m1, k1, sl 1, k1, psso, p1, k2 tog, k1, m1, k11.
Row 10: Cast off 8 sts, k2, p3, k1, p3, k2, m1, p2 tog, k3.
Row 11: Sl 1, k2, m1, p2 tog, k2, m1, k1, m1, sl 1, k1, psso, p1, k2 tog, (m1, k1) twice, m2, k2.
Row 12: Sl 1, k2, p1, (k1, p4) twice, k2, m1, p2 tog, k3.
Row 13: Sl 1, k2, m1, p2 tog, k2, m1, k3, m1, sl 1, k2 tog, psso, m1, k3, m1, k1, m2, k2 tog, m2, k2.
Row 14: Sl 1, k2, p1, k2, p1, k1, p11, k2, m1, p2 tog, k3.
Row 15: Sl 1, k2, m1, p2 tog, k2, m1, k5, m1, k1, m1, k5, m1, k1, m2, k3 tog, m2, k2 tog, m2, k2.
Row 16: Sl 1, (k2, p1) 3 times, k1, p15, k2, m1, p2 tog, k3.
Row 17: Sl 1, k2, m1, p2 tog, k2, m1, k1, sl 1, k1, psso, p1, k2 tog, (k1, m1) twice, k1, sl 1, k1, psso, p1, k2 tog, k1, m1, k11.
Row 18: Cast off 8 sts, k2, p3, k1, p7, k1, p3, k2, m1, p2 tog, k3.
Row 19: Sl 1, k2, m1, p2 tog, k2, m1, k1, sl 1, k1, psso, p1, k2 tog, (k1, m1) twice, k1, sl 1, k1, psso, p1, k2 tog, k1, m1, k1, m2, k2.
Row 20: Sl 1, k2, p1, k1, p3, k1, p7, k1, p3, k2, m1, p2 tog, k3.
Row 21: Sl 1, k2, m1, p2 tog, k2, m1, k1, m1, sl 1, k1, psso, p1, k3 tog, m1, k1, m1, sl 1, k2 tog, psso, p1, k2 tog, (m1, k1) twice, m2, k2 tog, m2, k2.
Row 22: Sl 1, (k2, p1) twice, k1, p4, k1, p5, k1, p4, k2, m1, p2 tog, k3.
Row 23: Sl 1, k2, m1, p2 tog, k2, m1, k3, m1, (k2 tog) twice. Pass one st over. M1, k1, m1, (k2 tog) twice, pass one st over, m1, k3, m1, k1, m2, k3 tog, m2, k2 tog, m2, k2.
Row 24: Sl 1, (k2, p1) 3 times, k1, p6, (p2 tog) twice, p5, k2, m1, p2 tog, k3.
Row 25: Sl 1, k2, m1, p2 tog, k2, m1, k5, (m1, k1) 3 times, m1, k5, m1, k11.

Above left: Beaconsfield lace (section 18, p.88), and two miniature cushions (section 1, p.19).
Above right: Pence jug (section 23, p.103), Pomander ball (section 1, p.19), Sheet edging (section 18, p.88) and Miniature cushion (section 1, p.19).
Right: Display of white knitted lace.

Right: The Botham bed (section 20, p.97).
Below: Traycloth (section 25, p.105).

Row 26: Cast off 8 sts, k2, p8, (p2 tog) twice, p7, k2, m1, p2 tog, k3.

Row 27: Sl 1, k2, m1, p2 tog, k2, m1, k1, sl 1, k1, psso, p1, k2 tog, k1, m1, k3 tog, m1, k1, sl 1, k1, psso, p1, k2 tog, k1, m1, k1, m2, k2.

Row 28: Sl 1, k2, p1, k1, p3, k1, p7, k1, p3, k2, m1, p2 tog, k3.

Row 29: Sl 1, k2, m1, p2 tog, k2, m1, k1, sl 1, k1, psso, p1, k2 tog, (k1, m1) twice, k1, sl 1, k1, psso, p1, k2 tog, k1, m1, k1, m2, k2 tog, m2, k2.

Row 30: Sl 1, (k2, p1) twice, k1, p3, k1, p7, k1, p3, k2, m1, p2 tog, k3.

Row 31: Sl 1, k2, m1, p2 tog, k2, m1, sl 1, k2 tog, psso, p1, k3 tog, m1, k1, m1, sl 1, k2 tog, psso, p1, k3 tog, m1, k1, m2, k3 tog, m2, k2 tog, m2, k2.

Row 32: Sl 1, (k2, p1) 3 times, (k1, p2 tog) twice, p1, p2 tog, k1, p2 tog, k2, m1, p2 tog, k3.

Row 33: Sl 1, k2, m1, p2 tog, k2, m1, sl 1, k2 tog, psso, m1, k1, m1, sl 1, k2 tog, psso, m1, k11.

Row 34: Cast off 8 sts, k2, (p2 tog) twice, p3 tog, k2, m1 p2 tog, k3.

Row 35: Sl 1, k2, m1, p2 tog, k2, m1, k3 tog, m1, k1, m2, k2.

Row 36: Sl 1, k2, p1, k1, p3 tog, k2, m1, p2 tog, k3.

Row 37: Sl 1, k2, m1, p2 tog, k2, (m1, k1) twice, m2, k2 tog, m2, k2.

Row 38: Sl 1, (k2, p1) twice, k1, p3 tog, k2, m1, p2 tog, k3.

Row 39: Sl 1, k2, m1, p2 tog, k2, (m1, k1) twice, m2, k3 tog, m2, k2 tog, m2, k2.

Row 40: Sl 1, (k2, p1) 3 times, k1, p3 tog, k2, m1, p2 tog, k3.

Row 41: Sl 1, k2, m1, p2 tog, k2, m1, k1, m1, k11.

Row 42: Cast off 8 sts, k7, m1, p2 tog, k2.

Repeat rows 3–42 until length desired.

Sheet 3: JANELLE LACE

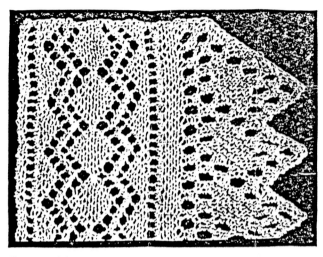

Cast on 36 sts.

Row 1: Sl 1, k1, m1, k2 tog, k3, m1, k2 tog, m1, sl 1, k2 tog, psso, m1, k2 tog, m1, k4, m1, k2 tog, k3, (m2, k2 tog) twice, k6, m2, k2 tog, k1.

Row 2: K3, p1, k8, p1, k2, p1, k23.

Row 3: Sl 1, k1, m1, k2 tog, k1, k2 tog, m1, k2 tog, m1, k3, (m1 k2 tog) twice, k2, m1, k2 tog, k19.

Row 4: K39.

Row 5: Sl 1, k1, m1, (k2 tog) twice, m1, k2 tog, m1, k5, (m1, k2 tog) twice, k1, m1, k2 tog, k3, (m2, k2 tog) twice, k7, (m2, k2 tog) twice, k1.

Row 6: K3, p1, k2, p1, k9, p1, k23.

Row 7: Sl 1, k1, m1, sl 1, k2 tog, psso, m1, k2 tog, m1, k7, (m1, k2 tog) 3 times, k23.

Row 8: K43.

Row 9: Sl 1, k1, m1, k2 tog, k1, (m1, k2 tog) twice, k3, k2 tog, m1, k2 tog, m1, k2, m1, k2 tog, k3, m1, k2 tog, m2, k2 tog, *m2, sl 1, k2 tog, psso. Repeat from * 5 times, k1.

Row 10: K3, p1, *k2, p1. Repeat from * 5 times, k25.

Row 11: Sl 1, k1, m1, k2 tog, k2, (m1, k2 tog) twice, k1, k2 tog, m1, k2 tog, m1, k3, m1, k2 tog, k24.

Row 12: Cast off 7 sts, k2 tog, k34.

Repeat rows 1–12 until length desired.

19. Designed for Giving

A display of articles designed for giving. Featured in this group:

Pot Plant Holder
Pomander Ball (see 1.)
Filigree Plate
Tea Cosy
Curtain Sample—WAGON WHEELS—made into Traycloth (see 16.)
Lavender Cornucopia (see 1.)
Tissue Box Cover
All the articles shown would make a welcome addition to a fete or a gift for someone special.

Pot Plant Holder

Cast on 85 sts. Knit one row.
Row 1: K1, *m1, sl 1, k1, psso, k1, k2 tog, m1, k2. Repeat from * to end of row.
Row 2: Purl.
Row 3: K2, *m1, sl 1, k2 tog, psso, m1, k4. Repeat from * to end of row, ending last repeat k3.
Row 4: Purl.
Repeat rows 1–4, 14 times.
Cast off. Sew side seam.

Top edging, using 2.50 crochet hook.

Row 1: 1 dc into join, work evenly 83 dc, 1 sl st into first dc.
Row 2: 1 dc into sl st, 1 dc in each of next 2 dc. *3 ch, 1 sl st into last dc, 1 dc into each of next 3 dc. Repeat from * omitting 3 dc at end of last repeat. 1 sl st into first dc. Fasten off.

Lower Edging

Row 1: As row 1 of top edging.
Row 2: 1 dc into same place as sl st, 1 dc into each dc, 1 sl st into first dc. Fasten off.

Filigree Plate

Cast on 8 sts; 3 sts on each of 2 needles, 2 sts on 3rd needle. Work with 4th.
Round 1: Knit.
Round 2: *M1, k1. Repeat from * to end of round (16 sts).
Knit 3 rounds.
Round 6: As round 2 (32 sts).
Knit 3 rounds.
Round 10: K1, *m1, k2. Repeat from * to last st, m1, k1 (48 sts).
Round 11: K1, *k1, p1 in m1 of previous round, k2. Repeat from * to last 2 sts, k1, p1 in m1 of previous round, k1 (64 sts).
Round 12: *K2 tog, m1, sl 1, k1, psso. Repeat from * to end of round (48 sts).
Repeat rounds 11 and 12 4 times.
Round 21: K1, *k1, p1, k1 into m1 of previous round, k2. Repeat from * to last 2 sts. K1, p1, k1 into m1 of previous round, k1 (80 sts).
Knit 3 rounds.
Round 25: *M1, k5. Repeat from * to end of round (96 sts).
Round 26 and alternate rounds: Knit.
Round 27: *Inc in next st, m1, sl 1, k1, psso, k1, k2 tog, m1. Repeat from * to end of round, knit 1st st of round onto end of last needle (thus moving end of round). This will now be referred to as (k 1st st) (112 sts).
Round 29: K2, *m1, sl 1, k2 tog, psso, m1, k4. Repeat from *ending last repeat with k2 instead of k4.
Round 31: *M1, k7. Repeat from * to end of round. (128 sts).
Round 33: *Inc in next st, m1, sl 1, k1, psso, k3, k2 tog, m1. Repeat from * to end (k 1st st) 144 sts.
Round 35: K2, *m1, sl 1, k1, psso, k1, k2 tog, m1, k4. Repeat from * ending last repeat with k2 instead of k4.
Round 37: *M1, k3, m1, sl 1, k2 tog, psso, m1, k3. Repeat from * to end of round (160 sts).
Round 39: *K1, m1, sl 1, k1, psso, k5, k2 tog, m1. Repeat from * to end of round.
Round 41: *M1, k2 tog, m1, sl 1, k1, psso, k3, k2 tog, m1, k1. Repeat from * to end of round.

Round 43: *Sl 1, k1, psso, m1, k1, m1, sl 1, k1, psso, k1, k2 tog, m1, sl 1, k1, psso, m1. Repeat from * to end of round.
Round 45: *(M1, k2 tog) twice, m1, sl 1, k2 tog, psso, m1, k1, m1, k2 tog. Repeat from * to end of round.
Round 47: *Sl 1, k1, psso, m1. Repeat from * to end of round.
Round 48: Knit.
Round 49: *M1, k2 tog. Repeat from * to end of round.
Round 50: Knit.
Insert needle into next st. Cast on 8 sts for **edging**.
Row 1: K8. turn.
Row 2: Sl 1, k2, m1, k2 tog, m2, k2 tog, k1.
Row 3: K3, p1, k2, m1, (k2 tog) twice (last k2 tog uses one st of edging and 1 st of centre), turn.
Row 4: Sl 1, k2, m1, k2 tog, k1, m2, k2 tog, k1.
Row 5: K3, p1, k3, m1, (k2 tog) twice, turn.
Row 6: Sl 1, k2, m1, k2 tog, k2, m2, k2 tog, k1.
Row 7: K3, p1, k4, m1, (k2 tog) twice, turn.
Row 8: Sl 1, k2, m1, k2 tog, k6.
Row 9: Cast off 3 sts, k5, m1, (k2 tog) twice, turn.
Repeat rows 2–9 until all centre sts have been worked. Cast off.

Tea Cosy

Cast on 159 sts.
Row 1: *P3, k10. Repeat from * ending with p3.
Row 2: K3, *p10, k3. Repeat from * to end of row.
Row 3: *P3, k2 tog, k6, k2 tog. Repeat from * ending with p3.
Row 4: K3, *p8, k3. Repeat from * to end of row.
Row 5: *P3, k2 tog, k4, k2 tog. Repeat from * ending with p3.
Row 6: K3, *p6, k3. Repeat from * to end of row.
Row 7: *P3, k2 tog, k2, k2 tog. Repeat from * ending with p3.
Row 8: K3, *p4, k3. Repeat from * to end of row.
Row 9: *P3, (k2 tog) twice. Repeat from * ending with p3.
Row 10: K3, *p2, k3. Repeat from * to end of row.
Row 11: *P3, k2 tog. Repeat from * ending with p3.
Row 12: K3, *p1, k3. Repeat from * to end of row.
Row 13: *P2, p2 tog. Repeat from * ending with p3.
Row 14: Knit.
These 14 rows make one row of the pattern.
In next row *k3, cast on 10 sts*. Repeat *—* to end of row (159 sts).
Repeat from 2nd to 14th row.
Continue in this manner until 5 rows of pattern are worked.
Cast off as follows: *Sl 1, k2 tog, psso*. Repeat to end of row.
Work another side. Neaten the ends. Sew sides together, allowing openings for spout and handle. Draw in top a little, to fit teapot. Trim with ribbon bow.

Lining:

Cast on 50 sts.
Knit until you have a length equivalent to 4 patterns. Shape top as follows:
Row 1: K2 tog, to end of row.
Row 2: Knit.
Row 3: K2 tog, to end of row.
Row 4: Knit.
Row 5: K2 tog to end of row.
Row 6: Knit.
Cast off.
Knit corresponding side. Slipstitch inside cosy. Cosy size can be adjusted by adding another row of pattern. Contrasting lining colour could also be used.

Tissue Box Cover

Cast on 60 sts.
Knit 5 rows. Inc 4 sts evenly across last row (64 sts).
Knit 2 rows.
Proceed in eyelet pattern, working 2 sts in garter st for border, in all rows.
Row 1: K2, *m1, p2 tog. Repeat from * until last 2 sts. K.
Row 2: Knit.
Row 3: Purl.
Row 4: Knit.
Row 5: K2, p1, *m1, p2 tog. Repeat from * until last 3 sts. P1, k2.
Row 6: Knit.
Row 7: Purl.
Row 8: Knit.
Repeat rows 1-8 twice.
Work 14 rows st st omitting garter st borders.

Row 1: Knit.
Row 2: P14, k36, p14.
Repeat last 2 rows once.
Divide for **opening** thus:
Row 1: K17, cast off 30 sts, k17. Continue on last 17 sts thus:
Row 2: P14, k3.
Row 3: Knit.
Row 4: P14, k3, break off cotton. Join to remaining sts. Work 3 rows st st, beginning with purl row, having 3 garter sts at opening edge.
Row 8: K17, cast on 30 sts. K to end. (64 sts).
Row 9: P14, k36, p14.
Row 10: Knit.
Row 11: P14, k36, p14.
Work 16 rows st st.
Proceed in eyelet pattern thus:
Row 1: (Keeping garter st border as before) k2, p1, *m1, p2 tog. Repeat from * to last 3 sts. P1, k2.
Row 2: Knit.
Row 3: Purl.
Row 4: Knit—keeping garter st border on all rows.
Row 5: K2, *m1, p2 tog. Repeat from * until last 2 sts, k2.
Row 6: Knit.
Row 7: Purl.
Row 8: Knit.
knit 2 rows st st and 5 rows garter st.
Cast off.
Work **side panels** thus: with right side facing knit 31 sts evenly along side edge between garter st borders.
Row 1: K2, purl to last 2 sts, k2.
Row 2: Knit.
Repeat rows 1 and 2, 14 times, then row 1 once.
Decrease 2 sts evenly across last row (29 sts).
Knit 5 rows.
Cast off.
Using flat seam, join corners. Press work. Trim with ribbon bows or thread ribbon through eyelets.

20. The Botham Bed

The Botham bed is made of brass. The canopy and hangings of delicate blue damask are original. The bed is possibly French.

Knitted lace enhancing this exquisite dolls' boudoir:

Materials

The *sheet edging*, and *pillows*, from the CARINYA set (see 13), were knitted on 1.25 mm needle and 60 cotton.
Circular Table Cloth: GENOWEFFA Design; approx. 59 cm (23") diameter.
2 mm needle and 20 cotton—2 balls 20 gm.
Dressing Gown Edging: 100 cotton, 1.25 needles.
ELEPHANT'S EYE pattern (see 16) used as floor covering.

Doll's Tablecloth: GENOWEFFA DESIGN

Cast on 8 sts; divide evenly on 4 needles. Knit with 5th needle.
Round 1: Knit.
Round 2: *M1, k1, Repeat from * to end of round (16 sts).
Round 3 *and following uneven rounds until after round 49:* Knit.
Round 4: *M1, k2. Repeat from * to end of round (24 sts).
Round 6: *M1, k3. Repeat from * to end of round (32 sts).
Round 8: *M1, k4. Repeat from * to end of round (40 sts).
Round 10: *M1, k5. Repeat from * to end of round (48 sts).
Round 12: *M1, k6. Repeat from * to end of round (56 sts).
Round 14: *M1, k7. Repeat from * to end of round (64 sts).
Round 16: *M1, k1, m1, sl 1, k1, psso, k5. Repeat from * to end of round (72 sts).
Round 18: *M1, k3, m1, sl 1, k1, psso, k4. Repeat from * to end of round (80 sts).
Round 20: *M1, k2, m1, sl 1, k1, psso, k1, m1, sl 1, k1, psso, k3. Repeat from * to end of round (88 sts).
Round 22: *M1, k2, (m1, sl 1, k1, psso) twice, k1, m1, sl 1, k1, psso, k2. Repeat from * to end of round (96 sts).
Round 24: *M1, k4, m1, sl 1, k1, psso, k3, m1, sl 1, k1, psso, k1. Repeat from * to end of round (104 sts).
Round 26: *M1, k11, m1, sl 1, k1, psso. Repeat from * to end of round (112 sts).
Round 28: Place last 2 sts of each needle on L.H. needle. *M1, k1, m1, sl 1, k1, psso, (k3, m1, sl 1, k1, psso) twice, k1. Repeat from * to end of round (120 sts).

Round 30: *M1, k1, (m1, sl 1, k1, psso) twice, k1, (m1, sl 1, k1, psso) twice, k1, (m1, sl 1, k1, psso) twice. Repeat from * to end of round (128 sts).
Round 32: *M1, k1, (m1, sl 1, k1, psso) 3 times, k1, m1, sl 1, k1, psso, k3, m1, sl 1, k1, psso, k1. Repeat from * to end of round (136 sts).
Round 34: *M1, k1, (m1, sl 1, k1, psso) 4 times, k3, m1, sl 1, k1, psso, k3. Repeat from * to end of round (144 sts).
Round 36: *M1, k1, (m1, sl 1, k1, psso) 5 times, k1, (m1, sl 1, k1, psso) twice, k2. Repeat from * to end of round (152 sts).
Round 38: Change to circular needle.
*M1, k1, (m1, sl 1, k1, psso) 6 times, k1, m1, sl 1, k1, psso, k3. Repeat from * to end of round (160 sts).
Round 40: *M1, k1, (m1, sl 1, k1, psso) 7 times, k5. Repeat from * to end of round (168 sts).
Round 42: *M1, k1, (m1, sl 1, k1, psso) 8 times, k4. Repeat from * to end of round (176 sts).
Round 44: *M1, k1, (m1, sl 1, k1, psso) 9 times, k3. Repeat from * to end of round (184 sts).
Round 46: *M1, k1, (m1, sl 1, k1, psso) 10 times, k2. Repeat from * to end of round (192 sts).
Round 48: *M1, k1, (m1, sl 1, k1, psso) 11 times, k1. Repeat from * to end of round (200 sts).
Round 50: *M1, k1, (m1, sl 1, k1, psso) 12 times. Repeat from * to end of round (208 sts).
Round 51, 52 and 53: Knit.
Round 54: *(P2 tog) twice, (m1, k1) 4 times, m1, (p2 tog) twice, p1. Repeat from * to end of round (224 sts).
Round 55, 56 and 57: Knit.
Round 58: Cut cotton. Place first 6 sts on R.H. needle. Rejoin cotton. *(K1, m1) 3 times, (p2 tog) twice, p1, (p2 tog) twice, (m1, k1) twice, m1. Repeat from * to end of round (256 sts).
Round 59, 60 and 61: Knit.
Round 62: *(K1, m1) 3 times, (p2 tog) twice, p3 tog, (p2 tog) twice, (m1, k1) twice, m1. Repeat from * to end of round (256 sts).
Round 63, 64 and 65: Knit.
Round 66: As round 62 (256 sts).
Round 67, 68 and 69: Knit.
Round 70: *(K1, m1) 4 times, (p2 tog) twice, p1, (p1 tog) twice, m1, (k1, m1) 3 times. Repeat from * to end of round (320 sts).
Round 71, 72 and 73: Knit.
Round 74: *(K1, m1) 4 times, (p2 tog) 3 times, p1, (p2 tog) 3 times, m1, (k1, m1) 3 times. Repeat from * to end of round (352 sts).

Round 76, 76 *and* 77: Knit.
Round 78: *(K1, m1) 4 times, (p2 tog) 3 times, p3 tog, (p2 tog) 3 times, m1, (k1, m1) 3 times. Repeat from * to end of round (352 sts).
Round 79, 80 *and* 81: Knit.
Round 82: *(K1, m1) 5 times, (p2 tog) 3 times, p1, (p2 tog) 3 times, (m1, k1) 4 times, m1. Repeat from * to end of round (416 sts).
Round 83, 84 *and* 85: Knit.
Round 86: *(K1, m1) 5 times, (p2 tog) 4 times, p1, (p2 tog) 4 times, (m1, k1) 4 times, m1. Repeat from * to end of round (448 sts).
Round 87, 88 *and* 89: Knit.
Round 90: *(K1, m1) 5 times, (2 tog) 4 times, p3 tog, (p2 tog) 4 times, (m1, k1) 4 times, m1. Repeat from * to end of round (448 sts).
Round 91, 92 *and* 93: Knit.
Round 94: As round 90 (448 sts).
Round 95, 96 *and* 97: Knit.
Round 98: *(K1, m1) 6 times, (p2 tog) 4 times, p1, (p2 tog) 4 times, (m1, k1) 5 times, m1. Repeat from * to end of round (512 sts).
Round 99, 100 *and* 101: Knit.
Round 102: *(K1, m1) 6 times, (p2 tog) 5 times, p1, (p2 tog) 5 times, (m1, k1) 5 times, m1. Repeat from * to end of round (544 sts).
Round 103, 104 *and* 105: Knit.
Round 106: *(K1, m1) 7 times, (p2 tog) 5 times, p1, (p2 tog) 5 times, (m1, k1) 6 times, m1. Repeat from * to end of round (608 sts).
Round 107: *K1, k1 into st under st on R.H. needle, k37. Repeat from * to end of round (624 sts).
Round 108 *and* 109: Knit.

Place 1st st of L.H. needle on R.H. needle. Use crochet hook, and cast off thus:
Round 1: *Insert hook into next 4 sts on L.H. needle. Make 1 dc above 4 sts, 5 ch 3 times (3 groups of 4 sts). Insert hook into next 5 sts on L.H. needle, make 1dc, 5ch, 3 times (3 groups of 5 sts). Insert hook into next 4 sts on L.H. needle, make 1 dc, 5 ch, 3 times (3 groups of 4 sts). Repeat from * to end of round, ending with 1 sl st into 1st dc.
Round 2: 3 dc, 3 ch, 3 dc into each loop ending with 1 sl st. Fasten off.

Doll's Gown Edging: ELLEN

Cast on 10 sts.
Row 1: K2, m1, p2 tog, k1, (m2, k2 tog) twice, k1.
Row 2: K2, (k1, p1 in m2 of previous row, k1) twice, m1, p2 tog, k2.
Row 3: K2, m1, p2 tog, k3, (m2, k2 tog) twice, k1.
Row 4: K2, k1, p1 in m2 of previous row, k1, k1, p1, in m2 of previous row, k3, m1, p2 tog, k2.
Row 5: K2, m1, p2 tog, k5, (m2, k2 tog) twice, k1.
Row 6: K2, k1, p1, in m2 of previous row, k1, k1, p1, in m2 previous row, k5, m1, p2 tog, k2.
Row 7: K2, m1, p2 tog, k7, (m2, k2 tog) twice, k1.
Row 8: K2, k1, p1 in m2 of previous row, k1, k1, p1 in m2 of previous row, k7, m1, p2 tog, k2.
Row 9: K2, m1, p2 tog, k14.
Row 10: Cast off 8 sts. K5, m1, p2 tog, k2.
Repeat rows 1–10 until length desired.

21. Dolls' Stand Cover

This knitted stand cover, ALICE, buttons and ties into place. The ideal solution to hide those unattractive, but necessary, dolls' stands. Make several for your collection. Any of the edgings illustrated would be suitable as an alternative trim. Why not match the lace on your doll's outfit? The stand cover can be varied in size by your choice of materials and size of needles.

Using **materials** for the stand illustrated: You will require one 50 gm ball of 4 ply cotton, a pair of 2.75 needles, 4 buttons.

Thread ribbon through inner edge of stand cover. Place cover on stand, button, then gently draw up ribbon to adjust opening. Tie ribbon into bow. The cover would be suitable as a skirt for a small Christmas tree.

Dolls' Stand Cover: ALICE

Centre

Cast on 67 sts.
Row 1: K6, *p1, k1. Repeat from * to last 5 sts, k5.
Row 2: K5, * p1, k1. Repeat from * to last 4 sts, k4.
Row 3: K2, m1, k2 tog (buttonhole), k2, *p1, k1. Repeat from * to last 5 sts, k5.
Repeat row 2 once, then rows 1 and 2 once, inc 10 sts evenly across row (77 sts on needle).
Row 7: Knit.
Row 8 and alternate rows: K5, p to last 5 sts, k5.
Row 9: K7, *m1, k4. Repeat from * to last 2 sts, k2 (94 sts).
Row 11: Knit.
Row 13: K7, *m1, k5. Repeat from * to last 2 sts, k2 (111 sts).
Row 15: K2, m1, k2 tog, knit to end of row.
Row 17: K8, *m1, k6. Repeat from * to last st, k1 (128 sts).
Row 19: Knit.
Row 21: K8, *m1, k7. Repeat from * to last st, k1 (145 sts).
Row 23: Knit.
Row 25: K9, *m1, k8. Repeat from * to end of row (162 sts).
Row 27: As row 15.
Row 29: K9, *m1, k9. Repeat from * to end of row (179 sts).
Row 31: Knit.
Row 33: K10, *m1, k10. Repeat from * to end of row, ending with k9 instead of k10 (196 sts).
Row 35: Knit.
Row 37: K10, *m1, k11. Repeat from * to end of row, ending with k10 instead of k11 (213 sts).

Row 39: As row 15.
Row 40: P4, *(p2 tog, p5) once, (p2 tog, p4) twice. Repeat from * to end of row (180 sts).
Cast on 7 sts for **edging**:
Row 1: K7, turn.
Row 2: Sl 1, k2, m1, k2 tog, m2, k2.
Row 3: K3, p1, k2, m1, (k2 tog) twice (last k2 tog uses 1 st of edging and 1 st of centre), turn.
Row 4: Sl 1, k2, m1, k2 tog, knit to end.
Row 5: K6, m1, (k2 tog) twice, turn.
Row 6: Sl 1, k2, m1, k2 tog, m2, k2 tog, m2, k2.
Row 7: K3, (p1, k2) twice, m1, (k2 tog) twice, turn.
Row 8: As row 4.
Row 9: K9, m1, (k2 tog) twice, turn.
Row 10: Sl 1, k2, m1, k2 tog, (m2, k2 tog) 3 times, k1.
Row 11: K3, (p1, k2) 3 times, m1, (k2 tog) twice, turn.
Row 12: As row 4.
Row 13: Cast of 8 sts, k3, m1, (k2 tog) twice, turn.
Repeat rows 2 to 13 incl until centre sts have been worked. Cast off.

22. Kirkwood Lace

A collection of cloths based on the KIRKWOOD pattern. This pattern can be used to make three sizes—*doily, table centre*, or a *circular cloth*.

The small antique doily appears to have been made using 100 cotton and approx. size 20 needles.

The table centre was knitted on bicycle spokes with an unfamiliar type of cotton made in the 1930s. The large cloth was knitted on 2.75 mm needles, and required 8 balls of 50 gm—No. 20 cotton.

For those of you who enjoy this beautiful type of work, the stitch count will be 1,680 at end of work. You will see the circular cloth in use in one of the coloured photographs.

KIRKWOOD *Lace*

Cast on 8 sts, 2 sts on each of 4 needles.
Round 1: K1, m1.
Knit next 5 rounds.
Round 7: (K1, m1) twice.
Knit next 3 rounds.
Round 11: K2 tog, m4, k2 tog.
Round 12: K1, k13 sts in m4 of previous round, k1, p1.
Knit next 8 rounds.
Round 21: K2 tog, k11, k2 tog, m1.
Round 22 and alternate rounds: Knit.
Round 23: K2 tog, k9, k2 tog, m1, k1, m1.
Round 25: K2 tog, k7, k2 tog, m1, k3, m1.
Round 27: K2 tog, k5, (k2 tog, m1) twice, k1, m1, k2 tog, m1.
Round 29: K2 tog, k3, (k2 tog, m1) twice, k3, m1, k2 tog, m1.
Round 31: K2 tog, k1, (k2 tog, m1) 3 times, k1, (m1, k2 tog) twice, m1.
Round 33: K3 tog, (m1, k2 tog) twice, m1, k3, (m1, k2 tog) twice, m1.
Round 35: Tw st, (m1, k2 tog) twice, m1, k2, m4, k2 tog, k1, (k2 tog, m1) twice.
Round 36: Knit, k19 sts out of m4 of previous round.
Round 37: Transfer 2sts from R.H. needle to L.H. needle, k2 tog, k1, (k2 tog, m1) twice, k25, m1, k2 tog, m1.
Round 39: K3 tog, m1, k2 tog, m1, k27, m1, k2 tog, m1.
Round 41: Tw st, m1, k2 tog, m1, k29, m1, k2 tog, m1.
Round 43: Transfer 2 sts from R.H. needle to L.H. needle, k2 tog, k1, k2 tog, m1, k31, m1.
Round 45: K3 tog, m1, k33, m1.
Round 47: Tw st, m1, k35, m1.
Round 49: Tw st, m1, k37, m1.
Round 51: K2, m1, k2 tog, k33, k2 tog, m1, k1.
Round 53: K1, (m1, k2 tog) twice, k31, (k2 tog, m1) twice.
Round 55: K2, (m1, k2 tog) twice, k29, (k2 tog, m1) twice, k1.
Round 57: K1, (m1, k2 tog) 3 times, k27, (k2 tog, m1) 3 times.
Round 59: K2, (m1, k2 tog) 3 times, k25, (k2 tog, m1) 3 times, k1.
Round 61: K1, (m1, k2 tog) 4 times, k23, (k2 tog, m1) 4 times.
Round 63: K2, (m1, k2 tog) 4 times, k21, (k2 tog, m1) 4 times, k1.
Round 65: M1, k1, *m1, k2 tog* repeat 5·times, k19, k2 tog, ** m1, k2 tog** repeat 4 times.
Round 67: M1, k3, *m1, k2 tog* repeat 5 times, k17, k2 tog, ** m1, k2 tog** repeat 4 times.

Round 69: M1, k2, m4, k2 tog, k1, *m1, k2 tog* repeat 5 times, k15, k2 tog, ** m1, k2 tog** repeat 4 times.
Round 70: P1, k19 sts out of m4 of previous round.
Round 71: M1, k25, *m1, k2 tog* repeat 5 times, k13, k2 tog, ** m1, k2 tog** repeat 4 times.
Round 73: M1, k27, *m1, k2 tog* repeat 5 times, k11, k2 tog, ** m1, k2 tog** repeat 4 times.
Round 75: M1, k29, *m1, k2 tog* repeat 5 times, k9, k2 tog, ** m1, k2 tog** repeat 4 times.
Round 77: M1, k31, *m1, k2 tog* repeat 5 times, k7, k2 tog, ** m1, k2 tog** repeat 4 times.
Round 79: M1, k33, *m1, k2 tog* repeat 5 times, k5, k2 tog, ** m1, k2 tog** repeat 4 times.
Round 81: M1, k35, *m1, k2 tog* repeat 5 times, k3, k2 tog, ** m1, k2 tog** repeat 4 times.
Round 83. M1, k37, *m1, k2 tog* repeat 5 times, k1, k2 tog, ** m1, k2 tog** repeat 4 times.
Round 85: M1 k39, *m1, k2 tog* repeat 4 times, m1, k3 tog, **m1, k2 tog** repeat 4 times.
Round 87: M1, k41, *m1, k2 tog* repeat 4 times, tw st, k2 tog, **m1, k2 tog** repeat 3 times.
Round 89: M1, k43, *m1, k2 tog* repeat 3 times, m1, k3 tog, **m1, k2 tog** repeat 3 times.
Round 91: M1, k45, *m1, k2 tog* repeat 3 times, tw st, k2 tog, (m1, k2 tog) twice.
Round 93: M1, k47, (m1, k2 tog) twice, m1, k3 tog, (m1, k2 tog) twice.
Round 95: M1, k49, (m1, k2 tog) twice, tw st, k2 tog, m1, k2 tog.
Round 97: M1, k51, m1, k2 tog, m1, k3 tog, m1, k2 tog.
Round 99: M1, k53, m1, k2 tog, tw st, k2 tog.
Round 101: M1, k55, m1, k3 tog.
Round 103: M1, k57, m1, tw st.
Round 105: (M1, k2 tog) twice, k51, (k2 tog, m1) twice, k1.
Round 107: K1, (m1, k2 tog) twice, k49, (k2 tog, m1) twice, k2.
Round 109: (M1, k2 tog) 3 times, k47, (k2 tog, m1) 3 times, k1.
Round 111: K1, (m1, k2 tog) 3 times, k45, (k2 tog, m1) 3 times, k2.
Round 113: *M1, k2 tog* repeat 4 times, k43, ** k2 tog, m1 ** repeat 4 times, k1.
Round 115: K1, *m1, k2 tog* repeat 4 times, k41, ** k2 tog, m1 ** repeat 4 times, k2.
Round 117: *M1, k2 tog* repeat 5 times, k39, ** k2 tog, m1 ** repeat 5 times, k1.
Round 119: K1, *m1, k2 tog* repeat 5 times, k37, ** k2 tog, m1 ** repeat 5 times, k2.
Round 121: *M1, k2 tog* repeat 6 times, k35, ** k2 tog, m1 ** repeat 6 times, k1.
Round 123: K1, *m1, k2 tog* repeat 6 times, k33, ** k2 tog, m1** repeat 6 times, k2.
Round 125: *K2 tog, m1 * repeat 6 times, k2 tog, k31, ** k2 tog, m1 ** repeat 7 times, k1, m1.
Round 127: *K2 tog, m1 * repeat 6 times, k2 tog, k29, ** k2 tog, m1 ** repeat 7 times, k3, m1.
Round 129: *K2 tog, m1 * repeat 6 times, k2 tog, k27, ** k2 tog, m1 ** repeat 7 times, k5, m1.
Round 131: *K2 tog, m1 * repeat 6 times, k2 tog, k12, m1,

k2 tog, k11, ** k2 tog, m1 ** repeat 7 times, k7, m1.
Round 133: *K2 tog, m1 * repeat 6 times, k2 tog, k9, k2 tog, m1, k1, m1, k2 tog, k9, ** k2 tog, m1 ** repeat 7 times, k9, m1.
Round 135: *K2 tog, m1 * 6 times, k2 tog, k7, k2 tog, m1, k3, m1, k2 tog, k7, ** k2 tog, m1 ** repeat 7 times, k5, m1, k2 tog, k4, m1.
Round 137: *K2 tog, m1 * repeat 6 times, k2 tog, k5, (k2 tog, m1) twice, k1, (m1, k2 tog) twice, k5 ** k2 tog, m1 **repeat 7 times, k6, m1, k1, m1, k6, m1.
Round 139: *K2 tog, m1 * repeat 6 times, k2 tog, k3, (k2 tog, m1) twice, k3, (m1, k2 tog) twice, k3, ** k2 tog, m1 **7 times, k5, k2 tog, m1, k3, m1, k2 tog, k5, m1.
Round 141: *K2 tog, m1 * repeat 6 times, k2 tog, k1 (k2 tog, m1) 3 times, k1, (m1, k2 tog) 3 times, k1, ** k2 tog, m1** repeat 7 times, k5, k2 tog, m1, k2 tog, k1, k2 tog, m1, k2 tog, k5, m1.
Round 143: *K2 tog, m1 * repeat 6 times, k3 tog, (m1, k2 tog) twice, m1, k3, (m1, k2 tog) twice, m1, k3 tog, ** m1, k2 tog ** repeat 6 times, m1, k5, k2 tog, m1, k1, m1, k3 tog, m1, k1, m1, k2 tog, k5, m1.
Round 145: *K2 tog, m1 * repeat 6 times, tw st, (m1, k2 tog) 3 times, m1, k1, (m1, k2 tog) 3 times, m1, tw st, **m1, k2 tog** repeat 6 times, m1, k5, k2 tog, m1, k3, m1, tw st, m1, k3, m1, k2 tog, k5, m1.
Round 147: *K2 tog, m1 * repeat 5 times, k2 tog, k1, (k2 tog, m1) 3 times, k3, (m1, k2 tog) 3 times, k1, ** k2 tog, m1** repeat 6 times, k5, k2 tog, m1, k2 tog, k1, k2 tog, m1, k1, m1, k2 tog, k1, k2 tog, m1, k2 tog, k5, m1.
Round 149: *K2 tog, m1 * repeat 5 times, k3 tog, (m1, k2 tog) 3 times, m1, k1, (m1, k2 tog) 3 times, m1, k3 tog, ** m1, k2 tog** repeat 5 times, m1, k5, k2 tog, m1, k1, m1, k3 tog, m1, k3, m1, k3 tog, m1, k1, m1, k2 tog, k5, m1.
Round 151: *K2 tog, m1 * repeat 4 times, k2 tog, k1, k2 tog, (m1, k2 tog) twice, m1, k3, (m1, k2 tog) 3 times, k1, **k2 tog, m1 ** repeat 5 times, k5, k2 tog, m1, k3, m1, tw st, m1, k5, m1, tw st, m1, k3, m1, k2 tog, k5, m1.
Round 153: *K2 tog, m1 * repeat 4 times, k3 tog, (m1, k2 tog) 3 times, m1, k1, (m1, k2 tog) 3 times, m1, k3 tog, **m1, k2 tog** repeat 4 times, m1, k5, k2 tog, m1, k2 tog, k1, k2 tog, m1, k9, m1, k2 tog, k1, k2 tog, m1, k2 tog, k5, m1.
Round 155: *K2 tog, m1 * repeat 3 times, k2 tog, k1, (k2 tog, m1) 3 times, k3, (m1, k2 tog) 3 times, k1 ** k2 tog, m1** repeat 4 times, k5, k2 tog, m1, k1, m1, k3 tog, m1, k11, m1, k3 tog, m1, k1, m1, k2 tog, k5, m1.
Round 157: *K2 tog, m1 * repeat 3 times, k3 tog, (m1, k2 tog) 3 times, m1, k1, m1, (k2 tog, m1) 3 times, k3 tog, (m1, k2 tog) 3 times, m1, k5, k2 tog, m1, k3, m1, tw st, m1, k6, m1, k2 tog, k5, m1, tw st, m1, k3, m1, k2 tog, k5, m1.
Round 159: (K2 tog, m1) twice, k2 tog, k1, k2 tog, (m1, k2 tog) twice, m1, k3, (m1, k2 tog) 3 times, k1, k2 tog, (m1, k2 tog) twice, m1, k5, k2 tog, m1, k2 tog, k1, k2 tog, m1, k2 tog, k4, k2 tog, m1, k1, m1, k2 tog, k4, k2 tog, m1, k2 tog, k1, k2 tog, m1, k2 tog, k5, m1.
Round 161: (K2 tog, m1) twice, k3 tog, (m1, k2 tog) twice, m1, k5, (m1, k2 tog) twice, m1, k3 tog, (m1, k2 tog) twice, m1, k5, k2 tog, m1, k1, m1, k3 tog, m1, k5, k2 tog, m1, k3, m1, k2 tog, k5, m1, k3 tog, m1, k1, m1, k2 tog, k5, m1.

Round 163: K2 tog, m1, k2 tog, k1, (k2 tog, m1) twice, k7, (m1, k2 tog) twice, k1, (k2 tog, m1) twice, k5, k2 tog, m1, k3, m1, tw st, m1, k5, k2 tog, m1, k2, m4, k2 tog, k1, m1, k2 tog, k5, m1, tw st, m1, k3, m1, k2 tog, k5, m1.

Round 164: Knit, k12 sts out of m4 of previous round.

Round 165: K2 tog, m1, k3 tog, m1, k2 tog, m1, k9, m1, k2 tog, m1, k3 tog, m1, k2 tog, m1, k5, k2 tog, m1, k2 tog, k1, k2 tog, m1, k2 tog, k4, k2 tog, m1, k18, m1, k2 tog, k4, k2 tog, m1, k2 tog, k1, k2 tog, m1, k2 tog, k5, m1.

Round 167: K2 tog, k1, k2 tog, m1, k11, m1, k2 tog, k1, k2 tog, m1, k5, k2 tog, m1, k1, m1, k3 tog, m1, k5, k2 tog, m1, k5, k2 tog, m1, k6, m1, k2 tog, k5, m1, k2 tog, k5, m1, k3 tog, m1, k1, m1, k2 tog, k5, m1.

Round 169: K3 tog, m1, k13, m1, k3 tog, m1, k5, k2 tog, m1, k3, m1, tw st, m1, k5, k2 tog, m1, k5, k2 tog, m1, k8, m1, K2 tog, k5, m1, k2 tog, k5, m1, tw st, m1, k3, m1, k2 tog, k5, m1.

Round 171: K22, k2 tog, m1, k2 tog, k1, k2 tog, m1, k2 tog, k4, k2 tog, m1, k5, k2 tog, (m1, k5) twice, m1, k2 tog, k5, m1, k2 tog, k4, k2 tog, m1, k2 tog, k1, k2 tog, m1, k2 tog, k5.

Round 173: K21, k2 tog, m1, k1, m1, k3 tog, (m1, k5, k2 tog) twice, m1, k6, m1, k1, m1, k6, (m1, k2 tog, k5) twice, m1, k3 tog, m1, k1, m1, k2 tog, k4.

Round 175: K20, k2 tog, m1, k3, m1, tw st, (m1, k5, k2 tog) 3 times, m1, k3, (m1, k2 tog, k5) 3 times, m1, tw st, m1, k3, m1, k2 tog, k3.

Round 177: K19, k2 tog, m1, k2 tog, k1, k2 tog, m1, k2 tog, k4, (k2 tog, m1, k5) 3 times, m1, k3 tog, (k5, m1, k2 tog) twice, k4, k2 tog, m1, k2 tog, k1, k2 tog, m1, k2 tog, k2.

Round 179: K18, k2 tog, m1, k1, m1, k3 tog, m1 * k5, k2 tog, m1 * repeat 3 times, k3, m1, k1, m1, k3, ** m1, k2 tog, k5 ** repeat 3 times, m1, k3 tog, m1, k1, m1, k2 tog, k1.

Round 181: K17, k2 tog, m1, k3, m1, tw st, * m1, k5, k2 tog * repeat 3 times, m1, k4, m1, k3, m1, k4, ** m1, k2 tog, k5 ** repeat 3 times, m1, tw st, m1, k3, m1, k2 tog.

Round 183: Transfer 1 st from R.H. needle to L.H. needle, k2 tog, k15, k2 tog, m1, k2 tog, k1, k2 tog, m1, k2 tog, k4, (k2 tog, m1, k5) 3 times, m1, k5, m1, k5, (m1, k2 tog, k5) twice, m1, k2 tog, k4, k2 tog, m1, k2 tog, k1, k2 tog, m1.

Round 185: K2 tog, k13, k2 tog, m1, k1, m1, k3 tog, * m1, k5, k2 tog* repeat 3 times, m1, k6, m1, k3, m1, k1, m1, k3, m1, k6 ** m1, k2 tog, k5 ** repeat 3 times, m1, k3 tog, m1, k1, m1.

Round 187: K2 tog, k11, k2 tog, m1, k3, m1, tw st, * m1, k5, k2 tog * repeat 4 times, m1, k4, m1, k3, m1, k4, ** m1, k2 tog, k5 ** repeat 4 times, m1, tw st, m1, k3, m1.

Round 189: K2 tog, k9, k2 tog, m1, k2 tog, k1, k2 tog, m1, k2 tog, k4, k2 tog, *m1, k5, k2 tog* repeat 3 times, (m1, k5) 3 times, ** m1, k2 tog, k5 ** repeat 3 times, m1, k2 tog, k4, k2 tog, m1, k2 tog, k1, k2 tog, m1.

Round 191: K2 tog, k7, k2 tog, m1, k1, m1, k3 tog, *m1, k5, k2 tog * repeat 4 times, m1, k6, m1, k3, m1, k1, m1, k3, m1, k6, ** m1, k2 tog, k5 ** repeat 4 times, m1, k3 tog, m1, k1, m1.

Round 193: K2 tog, k5, k2 tog, m1, k3, m1, tw st, *m1, k5, k2 tog * repeat 5 times, m1, k4, m1, k3, m1, k4, ** m1, k2 tog, k5 ** repeat 5 times, m1, tw st, m1, k3, m1.

Round 195: K2 tog, k3, k2 tog, m1, k2 tog, k1, k2 tog, m1, k2 tog, k4, k2 tog, *m1, k5, k2 tog* repeat 4 times, (m1, k5) 3 times, ** m1, k2 tog, k5** repeat 4 times, m1, k2 tog, k4, k2 tog, m1, k2 tog, k1, k2 tog, m1.

Round 197: K2 tog, k1, k2 tog, m1, k1, m1, k3 tog, *m1, k5, k2 tog* repeat 5 times, m1, k6, m1, k3, m1, k1, m1, k3, m1, k6, ** m1, k2 tog, k5** repeat 5 times, m1, k3 tog, m1, k1, m1.

Round 199: K3 tog, m1, k3, m1, tw st, * m1, k5, k2 tog, * repeat 6 times, m1, k4, m1, k3, m1, k4, ** m1, k2 tog, k5, ** repeat 6 times, m1, tw st, m1, k3, m1.

Round 201: M1, tw st, m1, k2 tog, k1, k2 tog, m1, k2 tog, k4, k2 tog, *m1, k5, k2 tog* repeat 5 times, (m1, k5) 3 times, ** m1, k2 tog, k5 ** repeat 5 times, m1, k2 tog, k4, k2 tog, m1, k2 tog, k1, k2 tog.

Round 203: M1, k3, m1, k3 tog, *m1, k5, k2 tog* repeat 6 times, m1, k6, m1, k3, m1, k1, m1, k3, m1, k6, ** m1, k2 tog, k5 ** repeat 6 times, m1, k3 tog.

Round 205: M1, k2 tog, k1, k2 tog, m1, tw st, * m1, k5, k2 tog* repeat 7 times, m1, k4, m1, k3, m1, k4, ** m1, k2 tog, k5 ** repeat 7 times, m1, tw st.

Round 207: K1, m1, k3 tog, m1, k1, k2 tog, k4, k2 tog, *m1, k5, k2 tog* repeat 6 times, (m1, k5) 3 times, ** m1, k2 tog, k5 ** repeat 6 times, m1, k2 tog, k4, k2 tog.

Round 209: K9, k2 tog, *m1, k5, k2 tog* repeat 6 times, m1, k6, m1, k3, m1, k1, m1, k3, m1, k6, ** m1, k2 tog, k5 ** repeat 6 times, m1, k2 tog, k4.

Round 211: K8, k2 tog, *m1, k5, k2 tog * repeat 7 times, m1, k4, m1, k3, m1, k4, ** m1, k2 tog, k5 ** repeat 7 times, m1, k2 tog, k3.

Round 213: K7, k2 tog, *m1, k5, k2 tog* repeat 7 times, (m1, k5) 3 times, ** m1, k2 tog, k5 ** repeat 7 times, m1, k2 tog, k2.

Round 215: K6, k2 tog, *m1, k5, k2 tog * repeat 7 times, m1, k6, m1, k3, m1, k1, m1, k3, m1, k6, ** m1, k2 tog, k5 ** repeat 7 times, m1, k2 tog, k1.

Round 217: *K5, k2 tog, m1 * repeat 9 times, k4, m1, k3, m1, k4 ** m1, k2 tog, k5** repeat 8 times, m1, k2 tog.

Round 219: Transfer 1 st from R.H. needle to L.H. needle, k2 tog, k3, k2 tog, * m1, k5, k2 tog* repeat 8 times, (m1, k5) 3 times, ** m1, k2 tog, k5 ** repeat 8 times, m1.

Round 221: K2 tog, k1, k2 tog, * m1, k5, k2 tog, * repeat 8 times, m1, k6, m1, k3, m1, k1, m1, k3, m1, k6, ** m1, k2 tog, k5 ** repeat 8 times, m1.

Round 222: Knit.

Crochet **edge** as follows:

Join sts tog, with 1 dc st in groups thus * 3, 7 sts, 9 times, 4, 3, 4, 7 sts, 9 times* repeat around cloth working 12 ch between each group of sts. Fasten off.

For small doily work to 50th row. Crochet edge as above.

For table centre work to 104th row. Crochet edge as above.

23. Pence Jug

This little jug was knitted from a Victorian pattern, published in 'The Complete Guide to the Work Table', *The Young Ladies Journal*, circa 1884.

Using one ball of 20 cotton, and a set of four needles size 1.25 mm, the jug measures 7 cm (2″). The pence jug appears to be a type of purse. Early examples date back to 1820. The jug has charm and is fun to knit. The construction of the tiny jug is ingenious—completely knitted in one piece, the only sewing required is to attach the handle. Why not knit one and use it for its original purpose, or hang it on a kitchen dresser. A unique gift for a jug collector.

Pence Jug

Cast on 9 sts; divide on 3 needles. Work with 4th.
Round 1: Knit.
Round 2 and following rounds: K in front and back of first and last sts on each needle, until there are 21 sts on each needle.
Knit two rounds.
Purl three rounds.
Knit three rounds.
Purl three rounds.
Knit three rounds.
Purl three rounds.
Knit three rounds.
Purl three rounds.
Knit two rounds.
Purl two rounds.

Raised Design

Round 1: M1, k1, m1, p8, repeat
Round 2: K3, p8, repeat.
Round 3: (K1, m1) twice, k1, p8, repeat.
Round 4: K5, p8, repeat.
Round 5: K2, m1, k1, m1, k2, p8, repeat.
Round 6: K7, p8, repeat.
Round 7: K3, m1, k1, m1, k3, p8, repeat.
Round 8: K9, p8, repeat.
Round 9: K2 tog tbl, k5, k2 tog, p8, repeat.
Round 10: K7, p8.
Round 11: K2 tog tbl, k3, k2 tog, p8, repeat.
Round 12: K5, p8, repeat.
Round 13: K2 tog tbl, k1, k2 tog, p8, repeat.
Round 14: K3, p8.
Round 15: Sl 1, k2 tog, psso, p8, repeat.
Round 16, 17 and 18: Purl.
Raised design completed, proceed as follows:
Knit two rounds.
Purl three rounds.
Work 21 rounds in k2, p2 rib.

Lip of jug

K seven rounds. Inc 1 st in each round.
Purl one round. Cast off all sts except 5 sts opposite the lip of the jug—these are knitted for the **handle** which is 2 inches (5 cm). Shape end of handle. K2 tog at end of each row, until 1 st remains. Cast off. Stitch handle to jug on the ridge above raised leaf design.

24. Tea Cloth

A Victorian *Afternoon Tea Cloth* superbly knitted in the popular TRELLIS Design.

Materials

The cloth was made from four large formal dinner napkins, joined with faggoting stitch. The damask has retained the delicate sheen of Irish Linen at its best.

The border has been worked with a fine thread and needles. The sample worked from the pattern for the TRELLIS Design, used 40 cotton, and 1.25 needles. This is a little finer than the original tea cloth but it is well worth working in fine thread for an heirloom of the future.

Tea Cloth: TRELLIS

Cast on 45 sts.

Row 1: Sl 1, k2, m1, k2 tog, k5, p20, k4, m1, k2 tog, k2, (m1, k2 tog) twice, m2, k2 tog, k1.

Row 2: K3, p1, k8, m1, (k2 tog) twice, (m1, k2 tog) twice, m1, k7, m1, k1, sl 1, k2 tog, psso, k1, (m1, k2 tog) twice, m1, k7, m1, k2 tog, k1.

Row 3: Sl 1, k2, m1, k2 tog, k5, p20, k4, m1, k2 tog, k3, (m1, k2 tog) twice, m2, k2 tog, k1.

Row 4: K3, p1, k9, m1, k2 tog, k2, (m1, sl 1, k1, psso) twice, m1, k1, sl 1, k1, psso, k5, k2 tog, k1, m1, k1, (m1, sl 1, k1, psso) 3 times, k5, m1, k2 tog, k1.

Row 5: Sl 1, k2, m1, k2 tog, k4, p20, k5, m1, k2 tog, k4, (m1, k2 tog) twice, m2, k2 tog, k1.

Row 6: K3, p1, k10, m1, k2 tog, k3, (m1, sl 1, k1, psso) twice, m1, k1, sl 1, k1, psso, k3, k2 tog, k1, m1, k3, (m1, sl 1, k1, psso) 3 times, k4, m1, k2 tog, k1.

Row 7: Sl 1, k2, m1, k2 tog, k3, p20, k6, m1, k2 tog, k5, (m1, k2 tog) twice, m2, k2 tog, k1.

Row 8: K3, p1, k11, m1, k2 tog, k4, (m1, sl 1, k1, psso) twice, m1, k1, sl 1, k1, psso, k1, k2 tog, k1, m1, k5, (m1, sl 1, k1, psso) 3 times, k3, m1, k2 tog, k1.

Row 9: Sl 1, k2, m1, k2 tog, k2, p20, k7, m1, k2 tog, k6, (m1, k2 tog) twice, m2, k2 tog, k1.

Row 10: K3, p1, k12, m1, k2 tog, k5, (m1, sl 1, k1, psso) twice, m1, k1, sl 1, k2 tog, psso, k1, m1, k7, (m1, sl 1, k1, psso) 3 times, k2, m1, k2 tog, k1.

Row 11: Sl 1, k2, m1, k2 tog, k2, p20, k7, m1, k2 tog, k7, (m1, k2 tog) twice, m2, k2 tog, k1.

Row 12: K3, p1, k13, m1, k2 tog, k3, k2 tog, (m1, k2 tog) twice, (m1, k1) twice, sl 1, k1, psso, k5, k2 tog, k1, (m1, k2 tog) twice, m1, k4, m1, k2 tog, k1.

Row 13: Sl 1, k2, m1, k2 tog, k3, p20, k6, m1, k2 tog, k8, (m1, k2 tog) twice, m2, k2 tog, k1.

Row 14: K3, p1, k14, m1, k2 tog, k2, k2 tog, (m1, k2 tog) twice, m1, k3, m1, k1, sl 1, k1, psso, k3, k2 tog, k1, (m1, k2 tog) twice, m1, k5, m1, k2 tog, k1.

Row 15: Sl 1, k2, m1, k2 tog, k4, p20, k5, m1, k2 tog, k16.

Row 16: Cast off 7 sts, k10, m1, k2 tog, k1, k2 tog, (m1, k2 tog) twice, m1, k5, m1, k1, sl 1, k1, psso, k1, k2 tog, k1, (m1, k2 tog) twice, m1, k6, m1, k2 tog, k1.

Repeat rows 1–16 until length desired.

25. Traycloth

Spiral edging used to border a Victorian tray cloth. This simple and effective lace has remained a favourite with knitters since the 19th century. You will see it in section 6 used as a shelf edging and as a bread cloth too (see 9). Instructions to knit spiral edging will be found in section 6.

Materials

Quantity of yarn required will depend on tray size. The sample knitted used No. 20 on 1.50 needles. These materials gave equivalent size and texture to that of the antique knitting.

Bibliography

DE DILLMONT, THERESE: *Encyclopedia of Needlework*, DMC Publication, Mulhouse, France, 1924.

GREIG, DENISE: *Potpourri and Perfumery From Australian Gardens*, Kangaroo Press, 1986

KLICKMAN, FLORA: *The Modern Knitting Book*, Published by Girls Own and Womans' Magazine, London, 1914

Mrs Leach's Fancy Work Basket, R.S. Cartwright, London, 1887

Needlecraft Practical Journals, W. Briggs Co. Ltd, 34 Cannon St, Manchester, c.1911–1930

RUTT, RICHARD: Bishop of Leicester: *A History of Hand Knitting*, B.T. Batsford Ltd, London, 1987

SIBBALD and SOUTER: *Dainty Work for Busy Fingers*, S.W. Partridge and Co. Ltd, London, 1915

THOMAS, MARY: *Mary Thomas's Book of Knitting Patterns*, Hodder & Stoughton Ltd, London, 1945

—— *Mary Thomas's Knitting Book*, Hodder and Stoughton Ltd, London, 1985

WALKER, BARBARA G.A.: *Treasury of Knitting Patterns*, Charles Scribner's Sons, New York, 1968

—— *Second Treasury of Knitting Patterns*, Charles Scribner's Sons, New York, 1970

Weldon's Practical Knitter, Series published by Weldon Ltd, The Strand, London, c.1890–1911

WRIGHT, MARY: *Cornish Guernseys and Knit Frocks*, Alison Hodges, Cornwall, 1979

—— *Granny's Lace Knitting*, Published by Mary Wright, 1986

—— *Great Granny's Lace Knitting*, Published by Mary Wright (undated)

ZIMMERMAN, ELIZABETH: *Knitters Almanac*, Dover, New York, 1981

—— *Knitting Around*, Schoolhouse Press, Pittsville, Wisconsin, 1989

List of Suppliers and Guilds

D.M.C. Needlecraft Pty Ltd
51–55 Carrington Road
Marrickville NSW 2204

Amies Tricote
Shop Nine
Style Arcade
Manuka ACT 2603

Queanbeyan Cottage Crafts
Millhouse Gallery
49 Collett Street
Queanbeyan NSW 2620

Buttons and Bows
6 Thetis Court
Manuka ACT 2603

The Sewing Spot
Shop Seven
Crawford Centre
Crawford Street
Queanbeyan NSW 2620

Suppliers of Antique Linen, Lace and Needles

Bramber Cottage Antiques
Hume Highway
Berrima NSW 2577

Palmerston Lane Antiques
Manuka ACT 2603

Second-Hand Rose
Shop Nineteen
Thetis Court
Manuka ACT 2603

Fyshwick Antique Centre
77 Wollongong Street
Fyshwick ACT 2609

Guilds

The Knitters Guild of New South Wales Inc. can help you pursue your craft. For details contact:

Honorary Secretary
Knitters' Guild of New South Wales Inc.
72 Bellington Road
Dundas NSW 2117

The British Knitting and Crochet Guild welcomes new members. The Guild promotes both crafts and publishes an informative booklet, *Slipknot*.

For membership details contact:

Elizabeth Gillett,
Membership Secretary
5 Roman Mount
Roundhay
Leeds LS8 2DP, England

Index